HUNT LIKE A TIGER
230 SQUADRON AT WAR
1939-1945

Woodfield Publishing Ltd
Bognor Regis ~ West Sussex ~ England ~ PO21 5EL
tel 01243 821234 ~ **e/m** info@woodfieldpublishing.co.uk

Interesting and informative books on a variety of subjects

For full details of all our published titles, visit our website at
www.woodfieldpublishing.co.uk

HUNT LIKE A TIGER

230 Squadron at War 1939-45

Portrait of a Royal Air Force Flying Boat Squadron

Tom Docherty

Woodfield

Second edition,
published in 2013 by
WOODFIELD PUBLISHING
Bognor Regis, West Sussex PO21 5EL
United Kingdom
www.woodfieldpublishing.co.uk

Copyright © Tom Docherty, 2003, 2013

All rights reserved.
No part of this publication may be reproduced
or transmitted in any form or by any means,
electronic or mechanical, nor may it be stored
in any information storage and retrieval system,
without prior permission from the publisher.

The right of Tom Docherty
to be identified as author of this work
has been asserted in accordance with
the Copyright, Designs and Patents Act 1988

ISBN 1-903953-37-5

CONTENTS

LIST OF ILLUSTRATIONS iii
PREFACE vii
ACKNOWLEDGEMENTS viii
INTRODUCTION ix

1. Early Days xi
2. The Squadron Goes to War *September 1939 – December 1940* 1
3. Backs to the Wall *January to December 1941* 27
4. Mediterranean Missions *January 1942 – December 1942* 61
5. African Adventures *January 1943 – December 1943* 83
6. Koggala, Ceylon *January – December 1944* 101
7. Fight to the finish *January 1945 – October 1945* 137
8. Post war postscript 189

Appendix A: Squadron Commanders 1939-1945 191
Appendix B: Squadron Awards & Honours 1939–45 193
Appendix C: Aircraft Allocated to No 230 Squadron 1939–45 195
Appendix D: The Short Sunderland 197
REFERENCES 198

LIST OF ILLUSTRATIONS

A 230 Sqn Sunderland over Singapore. xiv
Sunderlands at Seletar in 1939. Note the marking on the tail. xiv
Sports Day at RAF Seletar in 1939. xv
Squadron personnel in 1939. xv
The SS Dumana was used as accommodation by 230 Sqn. 3
Dundas Bednall at the controls of a Sunderland. 7
'Pass of Balmaha' used to refuel 230 Squadron Sunderlands at Suda Bay. 25
Sunderland Mk I T9050:NM-Y lands at Suda Bay with Dundas Bednall at the controls, April 1941. (DK Bednall). 28
Marshal Tito (saluting) and King Peter arrive to board a 230 Sqn Sunderland for evacuation 36
The officers of 230 Sqn at Aboukir after the evacuation of Greece. 37
Sunderland W3987:NM-X at anchor on the south coast of Crete during the evacuation of British and Commonwealth troops. 37
Sunderland in silhouette. W/Cdr Francis taking off during the evacuation of Greece 38
A Squadron Sunderland moored at Kalamata. 39
Shipping in Suda Bay under Stuka attack 41
Looking forward into the cockpit of a Squadron Sunderland. 49
Squadron maintenance staff pose for a picture, Egypt, 1941. 49
Squadron Store's staff at Aboukir in 1941. 50
Signalling to shore with the Aldis lamp, the crew hopes for rescue. 53
The crippled Sunderland flops in the Mediterranean, its load of twenty men at the mercy of the wind, but it is happily blowing landwards. 54
The crew of the crippled Sunderland sitting on the wing as the aircraft drifts. 54
The wounded air gunner is put in one of the two dinghies left serviceable to be pushed ashore. The other dinghy is used for emergency rations, water and food. 55
Having made it ashore they were followed soon afterwards by the drifting Sunderland, which began to break up. 55
The Italians arrived and the intrepid photographer continued to record the event. 56
The Sunderland finally broke its back on the rocks. (W Squires). 56
Sunderland T9071 beached and breaking up near Appolonia. 57
The first party of Italians arrives and a stretcher is improvised for the wounded air gunner. 57
Two officers drink from a pool of rainwater. 58
On the third day of their march the Italians left and the British party set out for British lines. 58
The Italians threw away their weapons and marched to captivity with the British party. 59
The group in the village of El Hania with their guide and some local Arabs. 59
Christmas Dinner menu, Aboukir 1941. 60
Yugoslav Dornier. 62
The Squadron song composed by LAC Campbell. 66
Another 'ditty' composed by LAC Campbell. 67
HRH The Duke of Gloucester visited the Squadron at Aboukir Bay in April 1942 to present decorations for the evacuations of Greece and Crete. 69

The Squadron on parade for the visit...70
The Squadron rugby XV during the 1941/2 season at Aboukir...70
A notice on the flammable fuel store on the former Imperial Airways slipway at Alexandria..............76
230 Squadron officers, Aboukir...79
230 Squadron aircrew with Sunderland..80
Dar es Salaam seen from the wing of a Squadron Sunderland...86
A Sunderland moored at the Advanced Flying Boat Base of Diego Garcia..89
The view from the office. The Sunderland cockpit was known as the 'Bridge' to the crew...................90
The figure on the tailplane gives scale to the huge fin and rudder of the Sunderland..........................91
F/Lt Watson (on right) with two American airmen he rescued from the Mediterranean.....................93
The above signal referred to the rescue of the Marauder crew on 17/18 July 1943..............................95
The 'Splendid Hotel' in Dar es Salaam. One of the Squadron's 'watering holes'...................................97
The crew enjoying the rescued beer..99
Haberaduwa village was on the Galle road just outside Koggala..106
The Silver Slipper was a popular 'watering hole' in Haberaduwa with 230 crews................................107
Koggala beach in 1944 was popular for surfing...107
Sunderland DP180:O offloading Chindit casualties on the Brahmaputra River...................................114
Instructions for the use of an improvised mooring buoy..125
W/Cdr Bednall's black painted Sunderland Mk III, JM673:P..126
A 230 Sqn Sunderland in flight over Pamanzi in the Grand Comores...127
Two crew members slip the moorings as the captain watches. The flaps have been lowered
fully to help the wind to drift the aircraft astern to clear the buoy..128
Sunderland EJ143:S pulled out of the water at Koggala...128
Black Sunderland MK III, JM673:P leads Mk IIIs, ML865:J and ML868 H in a flypast to bid
farewell to Koggala in October 1944..129
Sunderland ML865:J over the Gulf of Siam..130
Sunderland Mk III, W6078:N with a full array of ASV aerials flies near Dar es Salaam....................132
Sunderland JM711:M landing at Dar es Salaam...133
Sunderland Mk III, EJ141:R in flight over Dar es Salaam..135
A Sunderland Mk V 'on the step' taking off from Koggala Lake, 1945...135
Sunderland Mk V's moored at Koggala, Spring 1945...138
W/Cdr Bednall and S/Ldr Middleton with the Sqn HQ staff at Koggala...138
A graveyard of Mk IIIs at Koggala..139
Ernest Briggs and crew at Fanara, Egypt, 7 January 1945..140
A safety-briefing card provided to passengers flying in 230 Sqn aircraft...142
The SS Manela at Singapore in 1945..154
230 Sqn Sunderland near Mombasa in March 1945...155
The same Sunderland over Mombasa..156
Sunderland 259:M from which the photo above was taken..157
Warrant Officer CE Wykes and his crew on passing out of OTU..158
Artwork by a squadron artist on the Intelligence Officers office wall..159
Singora harbour and a Japanese ship found in Singora harbour..164
Sunderlands over the southern section of Lake Koggala, July 1945...165
A Sunderland flies over Koggala against a spectacular cloudscape. July 1945....................................166
One of the sampans attacked by F/Lt Nicholson on 22 July 1945..168
On the bomb run at 150 feet (left). After the attack the schooner is low in the water (right)............168

~ iv ~

Leaflets dropped by Squadron Sunderlands to encourage the Japanese to surrender. 169
An autographed menu from the Victory Dinner at Redhills Lake in 1945. 170
Ernest Briggs and crew in Madras, 30 August 1945. 171
Sunderland PP145:D photographed during the VJ Day flypast at Madras. 171
CE Wykes and crew at Redhills Lake. 174
Sunderland Mk V, DP200:B at Seletar. 175
The Squadron at Seletar in 1945.. 175
Sunderlands moored at Seletar in 1945. 176
Japanese seaplanes abandoned at Seletar in 1945. 176
A Japanese 'Ohka' Kamikaze aircraft abandoned at Seletar in 1945. 176
David Rees and Frank Murphy, groundcrew with the Squadron, model the latest in hats! 177
Dutch internees being loaded on board Sunderland Mk V. 177
Sunderland ML797:Q in North Borneo, 21 January 1946. 178
Ernest Briggs and crew at Killadeas, whilst training at No 131 OTU.. 179
Sunderland PP157:S on the VP slip at Seletar, January 1946. 179
Sqn personnel of No 2 Inspection Party with PP157:S in the background. 180
Servicing a Sunderland in the hangar at Seletar. 180
Sunderland PP154:Y at its mooring, Seletar 1945. 181
Refuelling a Sunderland at Seletar. 181
The Squadron barracks at Seletar. 182
The cockpit of a Sunderland Mk V. Note the flare racks on right 182
Squadron groundcrew make their way out to an aircraft by motor launch 183
Another offering from the Squadron Intelligence Officer's wall. 183
Report on the supply drop requested by the Ghurkas. 184
The request for a supply drop received from the Ghurka Brigade. 185
The captain's copy of the waybill listing supplies flown in for the Ghurka Brigade. 186
A booklet from the first Squadron reunion on returning to Seletar. 187

~ v ~

PREFACE

Whilst serving on No 230 Squadron it occurred to me that the story of the flying boat squadrons of the RAF was very poorly recorded and that the history of those serving outside of Coastal Command and the Battle of the Atlantic was particularly badly served. I therefore decided to set down the history of No 230 Squadron in World War 2 and during my research I discovered that it was a squadron with an incredible pedigree.

The Squadron started the war in the Far East in Singapore and during its service saw action in North Africa, the Mediterranean, the Aegean, Greece, Crete, East Africa, Ceylon, Madagascar and Burma before completing the circle and returning to Singapore. During this period the Sunderlands and crews of the Squadron engaged in dogfights with Italian and German fighters, made the sighting which resulted in the Battle of Cape Matapan, sank Italian submarines in the Mediterranean, worked behind Japanese lines with the Chindits and attacked Japanese shipping along the coast of Burma using the Sunderland in the role more commonly expected of a fighter-bomber!

I am proud to have served on such a great Squadron and I commend its history to you.

Tom Docherty, 2003

ACKNOWLEDGEMENTS

I could not have written this book without the assistance of very many people. They provided me with documents, personal reminiscences, photographs, log book, advice and encouragement. I have tried to credit all of the photos in the book to the original owner wherever possible and in particular I would like to thank the following for their help:

Sgt Gareth Attridge (230 Sqn Historian), Dundas K Bednall, Ernest Briggs, K Burton, J Cantley, Alan W Deller, Roy S Diss, D Dunn, W Elliott, Lord Gainford, Hugh A Halliday, Yvonne Henderson, Arnold Hutchison, T Hulme, Bert Kossen, Flt Lt Simon Kovach (230 Sqn Association Liaison Officer), J Laydon, Alan Lywood, Frank Morgan, DW McNichol, Alan S Pedley, DJ Rees, W Squires, Joan Stembridge, Mr Watson, S 'Chalky' White, JA Wilson, GT Woods, Leo N Worth and CE Wykes,

If I have forgotten anyone I apologise. All of the assistance I was given was invaluable and I thank you all. Finally I wish to thank my wife Catherine for her great patience and understanding.

TD

INTRODUCTION

On 1 April 1918 the Royal Air Force was formed from the Royal Flying Corps (RFC) and the Royal Naval Air Service (RNAS). Many of the RNAS units were equipped with flying boats and floatplanes and were formed into flights at various coastal bases around the UK. Their purpose was to patrol the North Sea hunting German U-boats and surface vessels. The reorganisation of these RNAS units into RAF squadrons took some time and it was not till August 1918 that two of the flights, Nos 327 and 328 combined to form No 230 Sqn.

The squadron was based at Felixstowe, commanded by W/Cdr CE Risk DSO and equipped with Curtiss 'Large America' H.12 and Felixstowe F.2A flying boats. The H.12 was built by Curtiss USA and powered by 160hp Curtiss engines supplied by Rolls Royce. The squadron was not to remain a solely water based unit for long when a third flight, No 487, was incorporated. This flight operated Sopwith 2F1 Camels from an airstrip behind the main flying boat base and the Camels were towed into the North Sea on lighters with the intention of taking off from them to attack marauding Zeppelin airships. The pilots would then ditch the Camel alongside the towing destroyer and be recovered. On 10 August 1918, Lt SD Culley had some success using this method when he shot down Zeppelin L53 in Camel N6812. W/Cdr Risk was replaced as CO in December 1920 by W/Cdr IT Courtney.

No 230 Sqn was one of the few flying boat squadrons to escape the axe at the end of the war and continued to operate from Felixstowe. The squadron received Felixstowe F.5s and moved to Calshot, another famous flying boat base, in May 1922. Less than a year later, on 1 April 1923, the squadron was reduced to Flight status and numbered No 480 Flt.

No 230 Sqn was reformed at Pembroke Dock on 1 December 1934 equipped with the Short Singapore Mk III. The squadron had to wait till April 1935 to receive its aircraft and began working up to operational readiness. On 13 September 1935 the Squadron received orders to proceed to the Middle East due to the Abyssinian emergency and on the same day Singapore Mk II K4580 was flown off the lake at Hever Castle in Kent, having force landed there eleven days previously. The lake was so small that the aircraft tail was made fast to a tree and with the engines at full power the Singapore was released and successfully flown off by F/L Hill, with only a fitter on board, landing safely at Rochester for repairs.

When Italy attacked Abyssinia in 1935 the squadron moved to Alexandria, the first aircraft leaving on 20 September, and was tasked with shadowing the movements of Italian shipping in the Mediterranean flying from Aboukir and Alexandria from September 1935. On 28 June 1936 the prompt action of F/O JAK Pettit and Cpl Berryman in putting out a fire on the port wing of K4579, after a backfire during engine testing, saved the fire from spreading to the rest of the aircraft and probably saved not only the aircraft but the complete squadron. The squadron returned from Egypt between July and September 1936 for a short period at Pembroke Dock before leaving for the Far East in October. The squadron moved to Hong Kong and then Singapore taking part in combined operations and submarine exercises and in June 1938 re-equipped with the brand new Short Sunderland. No 230 Sqn becoming the first squadron operational on the type IV of the aircraft were paid for by the Sultans of the Four Federated Malay States and named after them; Perak, Negri-Sembilan and Selangor. Their donors blessed the four aircraft in impressive ceremonies.

The squadron was based at Seletar from October 1936. The squadron also began operating from Penang in October 1939, one month after the outbreak of war with Germany. From February to November 1938 the squadron was commanded by W/Cdr WH Dunn DSC and he was replaced by W/Cdr GM Bryer OBE AFC, who would be No 230 Squadron's first wartime commander. The squadron's Sunderlands carried out pioneering and survey work amongst the island bases of the Indian Ocean from Ceylon, based at China Bay with detachments at Kogalla and Galle, leaving only a 'caretaker' flight at Seletar. No 215 Sqn absorbed this flight in February 1940. The squadron had received its new aircraft just in time as political developments in Europe were drawing the RAF towards war. No 230 Sqn would play a full and varied part in the major conflict, which was looming.

1. Early Days

"The first sight of a Sunderland for me was on the apron outside of the hangar at Seletar in Singapore at the end of 1938. I had been posted from No 43 (Fighter) Squadron at Tangmere, which at that time flew Hawker Fury's, but was in the process of converting to Hurricanes when I left, so to stand beneath the Sunderland was breathtaking.

After a couple of months with the squadron I was detailed to 'crew' an aircraft. My basic trade was Armourer and it therefore gave me responsibility for all of the weapons on board from Verey pistols through guns, bombs and pyrotechnics, all of which in the wet and salt laden conditions made for a never ending occupation.

The crew allocated to each aircraft rarely changed, except for sickness or postings, so that a good team spirit could be built, as it was with ours, and it stayed strong to the day we lost the boat.

Gun positions were allocated as follows;

Tail turret	*Armourer*
Port Mid-upper	*First Rigger*
Starboard Mid-upper	*Second Rigger*
Bow turret	*Second Fitter*

Position relief's rotated among available crewmembers.

Peacetime routines were far from arduous, an early start at 6am, a breakfast break then lunch, the afternoon siesta then work again at 4pm. Flying training for the whole crew was obviously essential, the aircraft was all new to all crewmembers and in this we were extremely lucky.

Our Captain was F/L W Campbell, who from the start shaped our future. Once the routines of take off and landing, mooring and slipping mooring had been practised to perfection we started in on other essentials. Practice bombing onto dye markers and air to ground gunnery on to the same markers gave us all the feel of the equipment. When some proficiency had been achieved we graduated to the bombing and machine gunning of a target towed behind a launch – the cable was very long and the bombs 'Smoke, practice'!

As a navigational exercise we were despatched to a spot on the map on the north coast of Malaya. The navy had laid a buoy in the estuary of a river and our task was to navigate to this spot after a patrol, land, moor up and stay the night. We duly found the buoy, landed and taxied towards it. The buoy turned out to be different to those we were used to, which were soft with a large wire loop. This one was steel with a heavy ring in the centre of its flat top. At the first pass the rigger missed the ring completely, at the second he almost lost the boathook. After discussion with the Captain the second rigger volunteered to jump onto the top of the buoy and pass a mooring line through the ring and back to the rigger. A slow approach was made and our volunteer jumped, passed the line through the ring, gave the end to the rigger and at this point the buoy spun round and threw him into the water. It was then remembered he could not swim. The mooring was cast off and he was rescued. Eventually we moored.

By this time it was dark. Boat watches were organised on a rota and at dawn we were hailed by the local Shell agent who had come to refuel us with 2,000 gallons of petrol in four-gallon tins! Every one of which had to be manhandled up onto the wing and poured through funnels fitted with chamois leather filters to remove any possible water content.

After this and our routine daily inspections and a hasty meal we set off for base again, very tired but much wiser.

As the prospect of war grew closer some modifications were carried out, one of which was the fitting of a material to the fuel tanks to make them 'self sealing', and the painting of the boat in camouflage.

Bombing practice was now carried out with live 250lb AS bombs, with which we soon became quite accurate. It did not take the native fishermen long to take advantage of the floating fish as soon as we left the area.

When war was declared we were detailed for detachment. We were allowed to take only issued tropical kit and had to leave behind all cameras and personal items – none of these were we ever to see again."

Roy S Diss

'LUMBERING GREAT BRUTES'

Arnold Hutchison joined 230 Sqn as a fitter in 1938 and remained with the Squadron until 1940.

> *"I spent nearly all of my ten years in the RAF on 'Boats' starting on Singapore's in 230 Sqn in 1938. These were lumbering great brutes, but lovely things to fly in. We got our first Sunderland, L2159, in June '38, which I took over as fitter on its arrival. After Singapore's it was a real luxury.*
>
> *At first most of our work was simply training on all the new gadgets and flying high-ranking officials around Malaya. My first real test came on 2 November 1938 when we went to Kalang to pick up His Excellency the Governor and five other high ranking naval officers. Our pilot that day was F/L Cecil-Wright. We then flew on to Penang where we dropped off His Excellency. The Navy stayed on board for the flight back to Seletar. Shortly after take off we developed an oil leak on the starboard inner engine. As the Mk I Sunderland did not have feathering props, this was serious. The loss of oil could lead to an engine seizure.*
>
> *I informed the pilot who shut down the engine. I then crawled through the wing to the inner nacelle, plugged in my intercom and removed the engine bulkheads. The trouble was a pinhole in the main flexible feed pipe. I informed the pilot over the intercom and returned to the upper deck where I raided the first aid kit for a broad roll of plaster, then on to my own kit where I had several rolls of black insulating tape. With three of these and the plaster in my pocket I went back to the engine nacelle. The broad tape went on first; this stopped the fine spray, then the black tape as tight as I could get it, two rolls of it, but no leak. Back on with the bulkheads then out of there for some fresh air. The pilot decided to leave the engine idling and we completed the flight on three engines. The naval officers downstairs enjoyed their flight home."*

Arnold Hutchison

A 230 Sqn Sunderland over Singapore.

Sunderlands at Seletar in 1939. Note the marking on the tail.

Sports Day at RAF Seletar in 1939. W/Cdr Bryer, OC 230 Sqn, is the figure wearing the hat and smoking a pipe. F/Lt Campbell (who would sink two submarines during the war) is on the extreme right.

Squadron personnel in 1939.

2. The Squadron Goes to War
September 1939 – December 1940

At the outbreak of war in September 1939, No. 230 Squadron was based at Seletar and Penang but within a month was on the move to Ceylon, based at China Bay. Detachments operated from Koggala and Galle and the squadron was tasked with carrying out survey work around the many island bases in the Indian Ocean. This routine and mundane work was carried out diligently although the squadron was based far from the war in Europe. This was not to last, however, for in May 1940 the squadron received orders to move from Ceylon to Alexandria as soon as practicable.

HQ Far East wished the squadron to route via Cochin, Bombay, Karachi, Bahrein, and Habbaniya to Alexandria. After discussion with two of the squadron pilots who had visited Bombay recently and found it unsuitable for the Sunderland, the squadron decided to omit it from the route and fly direct from Cochin to Karachi.

The first four Sunderlands – S, T, U and Y – under the command of S/Ldr Francis, set off from Koggala on the morning of 2 May 1940. Each Sunderland was carrying 17 personnel. They arrived at Cochin two hours later. At 0120 hrs the following morning they set out once again and routed via Bombay for extra fuel. The problems previously highlighted were evident on arrival at Bombay. The mooring buoys were found to be too large with insufficient weight on the sinkers to hold the Sunderlands at anchor. As soon as they were refuelled the Sunderlands left in pairs for Karachi, arriving on the afternoon of 3rd May. The four Sunderlands left for Bahrein on 5th May to refuel and proceed to Habbaniya for the night. The following day the four Sunderlands arrived at Alexandria.

The three remaining aircraft, V, X and Z, flown by F/L Smith, Flt Lt Garside and W/Cdr Bryer respectively, left Galle early on 7th May and arrived at Cochin to find no petrol or boats ready to receive them. The petrol finally arrived after 3½ hours and to add to the delay Sunderland X had to be refuelled by decanting the fuel into small drums, owing to a defect in the auxiliary power unit. The airmen elected to sleep aboard the aircraft after it was found that the allocated accommodation was of a poor standard and mosquito infested.

The three aircraft left for Bombay the following morning and on arrival, once again, had difficulty refuelling due to the short hoses and projecting rudder of the fuel barge. One of the aircraft had to let go of its mooring due to the barge swinging dangerously with the tide against the wind. Things went from bad to worse when Sunderland V sustained damage to its port float and wing surface during the second attempt to refuel.

Leaving V behind, Z and X departed for Karachi but an exactor control failure forced W/Cdr Bryer in Z to land and F/L Garside followed her down breaking a float bracing wire in the lumpy sea in the process. Repairs were carried out and the three aircraft finally left for Karachi on 9 May.

On arrival V required a new W/T receiver and P/O Brand was hospitalised with jaundice. The crews stayed the night and left for Bahrein early the following morning. After refuelling Z departed independently for Basra followed later by V and X and from Basra they proceeded together to Habbaniya. On landing X broke another float wire and after replacement all three Sunderland took off arriving at Alexandria on 11 May.

With all seven Sunderland's now at Alexandria and with the arrival of the support vessel *HT Dumana*, the squadron began to settle in. The following day the groundcrew would experience something that would cause them problems throughout the squadrons stay at Alexandria.

A *Khamsin* wind blew all day reducing visibility to 150 yards or less and coated the aircraft with dust inside and out. Dust was to be a major problem for maintaining engines and equipment and engine wore out more quickly due to its abrasive qualities.

On 13 May W/Cdr Bryer became OC No 201 Group which was newly formed and S/Ldr Francis took over as OC No 230 Sqn and the support vessel *HT Dumana*. The following day the squadron received its first operation order in the Mediterranean. The task was to provide anti-submarine protection for the Allied Mediterranean Fleet on exercises on 15 May and reconnaissance reports on two dummy bombing attacks by aircraft of No 202 Gp.

On 15 May Flt Lt Alington carried out the squadrons first Mediterranean patrol taking off at 0440 hrs. Two hours later F/L Garside took off to provide additional cover followed by Flt Lt Campbell at 1100 hrs. During the exercise the squadron's Sunderlands had difficulty in maintaining the outer anti-submarine patrol due to large changes of course by the Fleet not being passed to the aircraft on patrol. Two days later S/Ldr Francis took Sunderland Z to Mersa Matruh to examine the area for use as an advanced base. The BOAC slipway at Alexandria was tested by slipping Sunderland X there on the 29th with a view to using the slipway for 180 hour inspections. The squadron carried out local flying and gun testing until the end of the month.

The SS Dumana was used as accommodation by 230 Sqn. (N Gilbert via DK Bednall).

ON THE MOVE

"On 16 October 1939 the squadron moved out of Seletar. With stops at Penang and Trincomalee we finally arrived at Koggala Lake at the south of what was then Ceylon. We stayed there until 2 May 1940 doing training searches over the Indian Ocean. During our stay there, as there was no accommodation at the lake, we were billeted in a hotel at Galle, which was the nearest town.

On 2 May we left Koggala and after stops at Cochin, Bombay, Karachi, Bahrain and Lake Habbaniya we landed at Alexandria on 6 May. On 11 June Italy entered the war, we were no longer 'training', we were in the real war. My skipper by this time was a big, happy go lucky character, a real gentleman. We were crewing L5804 and we'd been together as a team since Koggala, so we were well prepared for what was to come."

Arnold Hutchison

S/Ldr Francis temporarily took control of No 201 Gp when W/Cdr Bryer was admitted to hospital and F/L Garside took control of the squadron. On 7 June trials were carried out to establish the suitability of Alexandria harbour for night flying but with the Fleet at anchor and much interference from small craft the single Sunderland used in the trial took 2 ½ hours to make four landings. The following day W/Cdr Bryer and S/Ldr Francis were promoted to G/Capt and W/Cdr respectively. On 10 June two aircraft, L5804:S captained by F/L Campbell and L2164:Z captained by F/L Smith carried out an anti submarine sweep ahead of a British destroyer force of eight ships sweeping for submarines to the west of Alexandria. Sunderland Z war relieved by F/L McCall in L5803:T a few hours later because of a leak in an oil cooler. The patrols were operated from dawn to dusk, with the first pair of aircraft relieved at noon and returning to Alexandria. The second pair of Sunderlands, L2160:X and L2166:U captained by F/L Garside and F/L Alinton respectively landed at Mersa Matruh. No submarines or enemy surface vessels were sighted on these patrols. That evening the squadron received the news that Italy had declared war on Great Britain. Four days later the Germans were in Paris and the French surrendered on 22 June. The already desperate situation at home and in the Mediterranean suddenly took a turn for the worse.

GOING TO WAR WITH SUNDERLAND L5804:NM-S (Part 1)

"We took off and our landfall was at Trincomalee in Ceylon. We were billeted in Naval Quarters, which although stark were not uncomfortable. The patrols we carried out were without incident, we had plenty of free time, most of which was spent swimming.

We were detailed to travel by truck to a destination in the south west of Ceylon. On arrival we found the place to be called Galle. It was near the coast and the principal buildings were an old Dutch fort and a 'Hotel'. We were to be accommodated in the hotel and as it was Christmas Day 1939 we were seated to a sumptuous meal, the bulk of which was curried, but no one complained since there was an endless supply of bottles.

We were soon introduced to the reason for our journey. Native labour had been engaged to cut an access road to a lake called Koggala. The felled coconut palm trees were laid across the road to form a base. This was virgin forest when we started and the wildlife was beautiful, with birds and flora, but frightening with deadly snakes, leeches and crocodiles. When the road had been cut shallow draught boats with outboard motors scoured the lake for palm trunks, which were floating or submerged, and which would present a serious hazard to a Sunderland on take off and landing. Eventually all was prepared, the moorings were laid and the boats flew in.

The time spent at Koggala was still fairly tame. The boats never left without an armed guard, we never suffered a problem, except for the occasional native boat with a yellow robed Buddhist priest sitting in the stern inviting a visit to see Buddha – 'You bring present for Buddha, wrist watch, radio?' and sometimes offering the local firewater, Arrack, for sale."

Roy S Diss

On 11 June a two aircraft forward screen was provided for a British cruiser force steaming westward from Alexandria by F/L McCall in N9029:V and F/L Smith in L2164:Z. They were relieved late morning by F/L Campbell in L5804:S and F/L Woodward in L5803:T. No enemy forces were sighted and the second pair of Sunderlands landed in the Eastern Harbour at Alexandria. The two aircraft forward based at Mersa Matruh were refuelled during the day in a long and laborious process involving 2,000 gallons of fuel for each aircraft in 4-gallon tins supplied by No 33 Sqn. They were supplemented by L2161:Y flown in by F/L McCall for the following days operations.

ALEXANDRIA

"230 Squadron had arrived at Alexandria, Egypt, from the Far East in the spring of 1940. Its role was to be the 'eyes and ears' of Admiral Cunningham's Eastern Mediterranean naval forces based in Alexandria harbour.

The squadron itself was quartered aboard the SS Dumana, an ex-troopship, berthed between the battleship Warspite and the submarine depot ship Medway. Engineering and slipway facilities were located ashore on the south side of the harbour. In charge of engineering was F/O Meech.

The squadron had recently been taken over by W/Cdr Francis from G/Capt GM Bryer, who went to 201 Group Headquarters, Alexandria, and our controlling Group. Squadron equipment was Sunderland Mk I flying boats powered by four Bristol Pegasus XXII engines developing 1010hp each.

Shortly before my arrival at the squadron in June 1940, F/L WW Campbell had sunk two Italian submarines and had brought back prisoners to confirm the incidents! Of life in the Dumana little is to be said as we were so infrequently there. Detachments were the order of the day. Bombing of the harbour was frequent but usually ineffective – the nuisance was worse than the damage caused. Nevertheless, there were occasional misgivings about being located at the centre of the prime British Mediterranean target.

Happily the Dumana remained afloat; the only hits scored on here were numerous lumps of shrapnel from our own AA guns. I went to 230 as a pilot and as Squadron Navigation Officer – surprising really, as I was a Blenheim pilot! I was indeed lucky to be introduced so readily to the 'Flying Boat Union'.

The navigation job was to ensure adequate navigation standards and supplies. The general standard was excellent. I personally used astro-navigation extensively. Patrols often meant hours out of sight of land and radio aids did not exist. Mk VIII and Mk IX bubble sextants were used together with several types of navigational tables – perhaps Hughes and Burton's were most popular. I preferred Hughes. Much use was made of 'flying up an astronomical position line' to locate specific spots and targets.

I was astounded to discover that the only means of taking drift in a Mk I Sunderland was either by telling the navigator to set up the bombsight in the mooring compartment – a lengthy and tiresome business; or by dropping a smoke float and asking the rear gunner to take a bearing using his turret – this was also unsatisfactory as the navigator was depending on someone else for vital information and the gunner had his difficulties as the aircraft tended to have a corkscrew motion making readings tricky.

I set out to put this right by getting our Instrument Section to make a drift sight consisting of a pair of parallel wires mounted outside one of the portholes near the navigators table and actuated from inside by a rod. Some time later, a standard optical drift sight was issued but, until then, my instrument (it was fitted to all our aircraft) afforded the only reasonably accurate way of measuring drift."

DK Bednall

Dundas Bednall at the controls of a Sunderland. (A Lywood via DK Bednall).

Operation on the 12th commenced with the departure of tow Sunderlands, L2160:X, F/L Garside and L2166:U, F/L Alington from Mersa Matruh in the dark. This pair returned to Alexandria at the end of an uneventful patrol. A second pair, L2164:Z, F/L Smith from Alexandria and L2161:Y from Mersa Matruh took over from the first, also landing at Alexandria after an uneventful patrol. McCall had only just landed when he was scrambled to search for a submarine after a report from a destroyer. With only a few minutes left of daylight he carried out a search landing at 2040 hrs. All of the Sunderlands were now back at Alexandria.

The squadron's introduction to operations in the Mediterranean theatre had thus far been relatively uneventful but events were to take a more exciting turn very soon. Just after midday on 14 June the Sunderlands were dispersed by taxying in the harbour with all guns fully manned in expectation of an air raid. The raid did not materialise but it did bring the war that much closer to the air and ground crews. In addition to the BOAC slipway the Imperial Airways slipway was brought into use for slipping aircraft from 15 June even though it was found to be in poor condition.

GOING TO WAR WITH SUNDERLAND L5804:NM-S (Part 2)

"Then the war started for us, we were ordered to Alexandria. After landing in the harbour and mooring we were informed that our temporary base was the naval supply ship Medway. Patrols were routine searches in areas generally parallel to the North African coast to Tripoli and beyond. They were, in the main, uneventful from the 'action' point of view. Take off in the harbour at Alexandria was in a path between moored ships and in the direction of the harbour entrance.

On one occasion an aircraft taking off had reached flying speed and was 'on the step' when an Arab felucca sailed from between two ships straight into her path. There was no chance of avoiding a collision. The hull of the felucca destroyed the port float and the mast and sail smashed into the wing. Only prompt action by the crew who raced onto the starboard wing saved her from turning over and sinking. The Arabs called the next day to ask for their sail back!

Returning from a long and tiring patrol late one evening we were astonished to be fired on by very close AA guns. We smartly turned away firing the recognition 'colours of the day'. It appeared we were some miles off course and as our navigator was one of the best we were puzzled. The answer was soon found – ½ inch armour plating had recently been fitted to the back of the pilots seats and re-setting of the compass had been overlooked."

Roy S Diss

On the 18th three aircraft searched for enemy forces in the vicinity of Rhodes and Cyprus without success. Two days later W/Cdr Francis left Alexandria in darkness for a recce of Tobruk in Sunderland L2160:X. Near Tobruk he sighted three submarines, but having been warned of British submarines in the area, he did not attack. Several enemy vessels including two cruisers were observed in and around Tobruk harbour and the enemy soon took an interest in the activities of Francis and his crew. Four Fiat CR32 or CR42 biplane fighters of the Italian Air Force attacked L 2160. The Sunderland is a prickly beast though and Francis' gunners shot down one Fiat into the sea. The remaining fighters broke off the engagement after about fifteen minutes and W/Cdr Francis turned L2160 for home. She had been damaged by explosive bullets and smaller calibre fire and had suffered a 6in by 8in hole in the hull and extensive holing if the fuel tanks. The ever-inventive crew stopped the holes with plasticene. Six hours after taking off W/Cdr Francis landed at Alexandria and L2160 was immediately put on the Imperial Airways slipway for repairs. The following day Alexandria harbour and the surrounding area was bombed but the squadron suffered no damage or casualties.

The pace of operations was increasing for the squadron and on 28th June L5803:T captained by S/Ldr Ryley left for Malta carrying out a recce patrol en route. At 1640 hrs he sighted three Italian destroyers. Ryley's sighting report enabled a British cruiser force to intercept the destroyers and one was sunk. Whilst Ryley was making his way to Malta, F/L Campbell in L5804:S, which had flown to Malta the previous day, sighted an Italian submarine to the west of Zante Island and attacked an sank it. The 600-ton *Argonauta* had been in transit from Tobruk to Taranto and was attacked whilst submerged.

L5803 and L5804 remained at Malta and the following day patrolled off the southern approaches to the Straits of Messina and the Gulf of Taranto respectively. F/L Campbell, flying L5804:S, was to double his score this day when he attacked another Italian submarine, the 590-ton *Rubino* forty five miles south east of Cape St Maria Di Leuca in the Ionian Sea at 1400 hrs. The *Rubino* had been returning from a patrol in the Alexandria area. Having successfully sunk the submarine, captained by Ten Vasc Liugi Trebbi, Campbell landed alongside and picked up four survivors. For good measure his gunners machine-gunned another submarine on the return journey to Malta.

On 30th June the Malta detachment continued its patrols and, though few would assess the Sunderland as a suitable dive-bomber, S/Ldr Ryley seemed to think L5803:T was. After investigating reported warships in Augusta harbour he attacked two destroyers outside the harbour by dive bombing them, unsuccessfully, damaging the elevator fabric in the process.

GOING TO WAR WITH SUNDERLAND L5804:NM-S (Part 3)

"We were detailed to fly to Malta to deliver torpedoes for use by the Swordfish based there. The torpedoes were in three sections. The warheads were loaded into the bow compartment, the centre sections into the central bomb compartment and the tail sections into the aft compartment. Take off was timed to give us a night landing in Malta and the return take off was before dawn. We only had to make these trips twice.

Next in April 1940 we were detailed to operate reconnaissance and anti-submarine patrols from our base at Malta. Most of our non-flying time was spent on board the boat at moorings in Kalafrana. We had from our arrival at Alexandria had a kitty from which we supplemented our issued rations with anything edible. I soon became the 'elected' cook. Some really substantial meals came from those small burners in that tiny galley."

Roy S Diss

July 1940 opened with three aircraft from Alexandria and L5803:T, captained by F/L Woodward, returning from Malta, providing protective patrols for a convoy routing from the Bosphurus to Alexandria. Woodward sighted and attacked an Italian destroyer off Tobruk. Dropping a stick of four bombs from 5,000 feet, one of which struck close to the stern of the destroyer, he left it dead in the water. The following day the second aircraft of the Malta detachment returned to Alexandria. On 4 July the Italian Air Force attacked Alexandria harbour but caused no losses to the squadron.

'ARGONAUTA'

"Our first taste of action came on 28 June. We were on patrol from Malta when we sighted a submarine on the surface, at last, our first real target. We hung back well behind her, wound out our bombs, manned all the gun positions, then dived in to attack. Our bombs straddled the sub. When we circled back all we could see was a large patch of oil and air bubbles. It was later confirmed by the Italian Navy that she was the 'Argonauta'. This was the first time a submarine had been sunk by a flying boat on its own."
Arnold Hutchison

'RUBINO'

"We took off from Malta again on another patrol and spotted a sub on the surface. F/L Campbell followed the same procedure as before and dropped his bombs smack on the sub. This time she broke in half and we saw her sink. We circled around and saw some survivors in the water. F/L Campbell decided to land and pick them up. There were four of them who we took on board. They were put into the wardroom between the front door and the kitchen, one in each corner. An armed guard was put in the kitchen to keep an eye on them. One of them was the Captain of the submarine. As we were working from base, all of us had spare clothing on board so we dug around and gave them some dry clothes to wear, then made them a pot of tea to warm them up on the journey back to Malta. On our way back to Malta another sub was sighted but as we had no bombs on board the skipper just dived towards him making him crash dive and hide for a while.

On arrival at Malta there was a military escort waiting to take them ashore. Before going ashore the Captain of the sub thanked us for saving their lives. Two days later our spare uniforms were delivered back to us all nicely laundered."
Arnold Hutchison

GOING TO WAR WITH SUNDERLAND L5804:NM-S (Part 4)

"The routine at that time was to take off at or just before dawn. The anti-submarine patrols covered considerable areas, some of which took us well within range of enemy air bases in Sicily and Pantelleria.

In the main this type of patrol is boring because of the monotonous vista of open sea and sky. The majority of alarms being birds or fish, until one day way off on the beam there was a submarine travelling at periscope depth. We turned away to wind out the bomb racks and prepare for the attack. In the early marks of boat the loading and winding out of the racks was manual and our previous practice now paid off. When all was ready we turned to come onto the submarine from astern. It had been under constant observation and was oblivious to our presence.

From the tail turret I could see nothing of the approach, but the running commentary from the Captain left nothing to the imagination. The attack was made with four 250lb AS bombs, which fell close enough to damage and disable it. The second attack with the remaining four bombs finished it off. The debris and oil were proof positive to us, but to our disbelief the claim for sinking was not confirmed 'as there was no knowledge of a submarine in that area'. This was later changed and we were credited with the squadron's first success. The date was 28 June 1940.

The next day brought our second success. The second submarine was spotted on the surface and our preparation time before attack was now much shorter. The attack was again made from astern. The bow turret was instructed to pour concentrated fire into the conning tower. No one could be seen on watch on the submarine. The first four bombs dropped, two on either side of the submarine, which promptly broke in half forward of the conning tower. The second four almost lifted the stern section out of the water. We stood off and wound in the bomb racks and as we circled survivors were seen in the water. Bill Campbell calmly advised us over the intercom that he was landing to 'Pick Up Our Proof From The Sea'. Against normal practice, I was to remain in the tail turret in case we were attacked. It was early in the morning and we were near to Sicily. How he managed to land and take off again in that swell I shall never know. I was looking up at wave crests above the tail fin.

The three Italian survivors were pulled on board and into the wardroom. Our message to Malta to lay on a POW escort caused confusion. How could a Sunderland 'collect' POWs? We were met by what seemed to be most of the 'Brass' on Malta. Bill Campbell's DFC was his reward. Sadly Bill has passed on, but I have often wondered what happened to those three very lucky Italian seamen. After those tow actions in both of which we had expended all of our offensive capability very early in our patrol, I suggested we carried a 'reload'. We tried out reloading the racks and found it possible. We never put it into use."

Roy S Diss

On 8 July Naval Intelligence reported two Italian battleships and four destroyers at sea and 230 Sqn were ordered to search for and to shadow this force. F/L Woodward was airborne in L5803:T at 1045 hrs and sighted the force at 1500hrs. He continued to shadow the force, which was now known to be two battleships and six cruisers until 1830 hrs when he made for Malta. The C in C requested that the force be shadowed throughout the night but this was impracticable due to the weather and sea conditions at Malta. Aboukir had been brought into use by the squadron for night take off and landings to avoid the busy Alexandria harbour traffic and three aircraft took off from there to carry out sweeps in search of the Italian force in the early hours of 9 July. A No 228 Sqn Sunderland was the first to sight the force between Sicily and Corfu. F/L Woodward took off from Malta in L5803:T at 0800 hrs and sighted the six cruisers just after midday. Thirty minutes later he sighted an enemy submarine and bombed it scoring a direct hit abaft the conning tower. There were no survivors. Keeping contact with the enemy force, the British battle fleet, including *HMS Warspite*, was sighted and the position of the Italians was passed. At 1530 hrs the British Fleet sighted and engaged the enemy. Woodward meanwhile had returned to Malta with unserviceable engines and a gun turret. At home the Battle of Britain was in its early stages and invasion looked imminent.

The groundcrew at Alexandria were not having a quiet time of it as the Italians raided the base just after midday on 15 July dropping two bombs near the W/T station on the mole. The following night the Italians were back dropping bombs at irregular intervals.

On the morning of 19 July F/L Woodward took off in L5803:T to shadow two enemy cruisers sighted in the Anti-Kithera channel by the Australian warship *HMAS Sydney*. S/Ldr Ryley in L2164:Z was also diverted to search for the surviving cruiser, *HMAS Sydney* having sunk the other, but he had no success. Ryley and his crew almost came to grief on this patrol when the starboard inner engine developed a problem, which resulted in the propeller falling off taking the starboard outer propeller with it and damaging the starboard float. Ryley force landed the crippled Sunderland at Aboukir. The following day F/O King took off from Aboukir on L5804:S to search for a missing Swordfish which had force landed in the sea east of Tobruk. No trace of the aircraft was found.

On the morning of 23 July F/O Lywood took N9029:V on patrol from Malta. Finding an enemy convoy of six merchant vessels, including three tankers, and a destroyer near Cape Spartivento, he set about attacking it. Dropping bombs and machine gunning the ships he estimated damage to two of the merchant vessels. The following day S/Ldr Ryley was on patrol in Sunderland L5804:S when he was attacked by a Macchi fighter. Ryley's gunners managed to drive it off and no damage was sustained.

> THE TIMES MONDAY JULY 8 1940
> ## Italian Submarines Destroyed: RAF Save Survivors
> FROM OUR CORRESPONDENT. CAIRO, July 7
>
> The successful co-operation of the RAF in action against enemy submarines in the Mediterranean is strikingly shown by the exploits of a flying boat attached to the Middle Eastern Command, which accounted for two submarines recently.
>
> While patrolling, the aircraft sighted the periscope of an enemy submarine, whereupon it immediately delivered a dive-bombing attack and released some special bombs, two of which burst abaft the conning tower. The force of the explosion almost blew the submarine out of the water. Her nose rose sharply to the surface and then the boat appeared to slide vertically downwards. Huge air bubbles were seen at once, while smaller ones continued to rise for some time and oil also appeared on the surface of the sea. Returning two hours later, the pilot saw a huge patch of oil, 300 by 500 yards in extent.
>
> The next day the same flying boat, with the same crew, again sighted an Italian submarine on the surface. Again a dive-bombing attack with special bombs sank the submarine. Some of the crew of the submarine were blown into the sea by the force of the explosion. The pilot brought his aeroplane down to the water and picked up three lieutenants and one petty officer, all unwounded but suffering from shock. A search for more survivors had to be abandoned as a local storm was blowing up.
>
> While returning to its base the aircraft spotted yet another Italian submarine. All its bombs having been used the aeroplane swooped down and raked the conning tower and bridge of the submarine with all its available machine guns. The operation was repeated a second time before the submarine crash-dived.
>
> One of the two submarines thus destroyed was included in the four, which were claimed to have been sunk in the naval communiqué of July 2.

Alexandria came under attack again in the early hours of 25 July when floating flares were dropped in the harbour to illuminate it followed by high explosive and incendiary bombs. Further heavy bombs were dropped in the harbour and on the Ras el Tin palace area. Two days later the Italians raided Alexandria again but did not press home their attack and dropped the bombs out to sea. With the regular bombing of Alexandria the squadron had need of alternate bases and F/L Woodward flew G/Capt Bryer to Port Said, Lake Timsah and Suez to inspect possible flying boat bases.

MALTA

"I was allocated as second pilot/navigator to F/O Alan Lywood in Sunderland N9029:NM-V. Our partnership started in earnest on 19 July 1940 with a long patrol of the Ionian Sea, landing at Kalafrana, Malta. Incidentally, the Sunderlands of 230 squadron together with those of a small detachment of 228 Squadron were the only RAF aircraft, apart from the famous Sea Gladiators, operating from Malta at this time. Later the odd Maryland was used from the island, notably for reconnaissance before the famous attack on Taranto. Our chief quarry was, of course, enemy submarines and the Italian Fleet.

We were quite an aggressive crew in N9029:V and happily it was not long before we went into action. On 23 July 1940 we made what was, I believe, the first attack of the war on Italian shipping in bombing five smallish Italian merchant vessels escorted by a destroyer within a mile or so of the enemy coast of Calabria, Southern Italy. The destroyer escort rapidly made smoke and sped off towards nearby Taranto leaving its charges to be attacked as we wished! Unfortunately, our bomb release mechanism ('Mickey Mouse') in the cockpit was faulty and only three anti-submarine 250lb bombs could be released, much to Lywood's fury. However, I saw one burst under the starboard bow of one of the ships, which then spewed large quantities of black smoke from her funnel. We also liberally sprayed the vessels with MG fire, which was returned sporadically by the Italians. One character loaded and fired a small gun on the stern of the leading ship, but as he retired to pull the firing lanyard the ship turned to starboard and his shot went very wide! We sustained one or two machine gun hits.

There was an extraordinary sequel to this action when we landed back at Kalafrana. The crew were sent for by the Operations Officer and we were severely told off for being thoroughly irresponsible in attacking enemy shipping – this would be likely to provoke bombing attacks on Malta as reprisals – and Malta could not defend itself. So, instead of congratulations, which we expected, (in other theatres of war recommendations for medals would most likely have followed such an action!) we were thoroughly 'carpeted'! What a way to fight a war! Fortunately for all of us this attitude changed rapidly and we could revert to the job of seeking out and trying to destroy the enemy."

DK Bednall

On 28 July Alexandria was again bombed. That afternoon F/L Garside took off from Malta in Sunderland L2160:X. It was to be an eventful sortie. Off Cape Spartivento Garside spotted an enemy submarine and bombed it. The attack was unsuccessful. Less than an hour later the Sunderland was attacked by three Macchi 200 fighters in a combat lasting fifteen minutes. During the first attack

Garside's gunners scored hits on one of the Macchi's and it broke off with smoke pouring from the engine. The gunners were successful again during the fighters third attack when one of the Macchis broke up in mid-air and crashed into the sea. The third fighter, seeing the fate of his companions, withdrew.

The fighters had had great difficulty in defeating the evasive action of Garside's Sunderland at low level and there were no casualties among the crew. F/O Lywood who was on patrol in N9029:V was also attacked. His crew fought off two Fiat CR42 fighters for twenty minutes and possibly scored hits on one of the fighters. As if this was not enough action for one day S/Ldr Ryley in L5804:S also came under attack. On a reconnaissance of Syracuse he was attacked by four Macchi 200s. One enemy aircraft was shot down in flames and the remainder were driven off, one of which was believed badly damaged.

The engagement lasted 57 minutes during which time three of the gunners received wounds in the legs. The Sunderland was extensively damaged by heavy calibre explosive and incendiary bullets. The gunners remained at their posts returning fire throughout the engagement despite their wounds and the 2nd Fitter, LAC DA Campbell worked in the wing of the aircraft plugging bullet holes in the fuel tanks until he was overcome by fumes. He was revived by being struck by bullet splinters!

A *Daily Mail* correspondent, Mr Alexander Clifford, was on board the Sunderland for this sortie and he rendered valuable assistance to the crew throughout the fight. (See page 17). On landing the Sunderland began to sink and S/Ldr Ryley had to beach her.

GOING TO WAR WITH SUNDERLAND L5804:NM-S (Part 5)

"I well remember our first practice trip with four 450lb Naval depth charges on the racks. The DCs had been modified from the normal dustbin shape with a dome shaped nose and a conical tail cone, both of which were crudely bolted on. The DCs were dropped as instructed. When I saw the impact mark I then saw the tail cone fly past my turret- we never dropped those DCs again."

Roy S Diss

FIGHTERS

"Another curious thing was that during our standard Ionian Sea patrols, which occurred almost daily, we were expected by the naval authorities to find out what shipping was in the well defended Augusta harbour, Sicily. To expect a large Sunder-

land to do this in broad daylight and not get punished was really moon-madness, but to crown it all it had to be done at 1000hrs each time! Small wonder that we were often attacked and precious Sunderlands and crews were lost – they could be ill spared. For example, on 25 July we were attacked by two Fiat CR42s; we flew very low above the sea, flat out and, although hit by the fighters, managed to reach Malta safely. One CR42 was seen to break off the fight trailing fuel vapour; our rear gunner saw him go into the sea and claimed hits on another CR42. Besides CR42s we also had to run the gauntlet of the much faster, cannon armed Macchi 200 monoplane fighters."
DK Bednall

August 1940 began with the usual routine of anti-submarine patrols and little excitement until F/L Woodward in L5803:T spotted three Italian cruisers and five destroyers leaving Benghazi. Hitler and Mussolini met in Rome on 5 August to discuss the future strategy following the defeat of France. The expansion of the conflict into other areas looked inevitable. The pilots of the squadron were given a talk by ACM Sir Arthur Longmore, the AOC in C Middle East on 13 August. Alexandria was raided by the Italian Air Force again on the 15th, dropping bombs in the harbour. One bomb exploded close to the *HT Dumana* causing damage to two of the lifeboats and the Photographic Section. On 16 August W/Cdr Francis, who had flown to England earlier, began the return journey from Mount Batten to Alexandria carrying General Wavell, the GOC Middle East, and his staff. They arrived at Alexandria on the 17th and W/Cdr Francis took back control of the squadron from S/Ldr Ryley. Ryley left the squadron on 19 August to take command of No 33 Sqn at Helwan.

Italy had been making threats against Greece for some time and on 22 August Britain promised help by sea and air forces to the Greeks in case of attack. The Italians were nothing if not persistent in their attacks on Alexandria and attacked again at dawn on the 22nd. A stick of six 150lb bombs was dropped near No 201 Gp HQ doing considerable damage to the neighbouring boat clubs but no damage to the HQ other than a few broken windows. They were back again in the early hours of the 23rd dropping bomb in the harbour. On 26 August F/L Campbell took off on patrol but had to make a forced landing due to engine failures in neutral Greek territory at St Nikolo Bay, Kithera.

He and his crew were interned but later released when Italy invaded Greece. The next day F/L Alington, operating from Malta took of on a search for a missing Blenheim. Despite a further sortie and flying as far as 80 miles west of Malta no trace was found of the missing aircraft. Following this Alington patrolled the route from Malta to Gibraltar at dawn and sighted four enemy destroyers and one merchant vessel south-west of Sicily steaming for the island. On the last day of the month F/L Garside in L2160:X sighted and reported a large force of enemy warships about 100 miles south of Taranto. The force comprised two or three battleships, twelve cruisers, eleven destroyers and other small vessels. Unfortunately the British Fleet was too far away to establish contact. F/O Lywood in N9029:V was diverted to locate this force and found it shortly before dark. The patrols continued into September but little was seen.

On 6 September the squadron found itself ferrying important passengers once again when ACM Longmore was flown to Malta by F/L Woodward in L5803:T. Two days later the Italians were back over the harbour making several raids that evening. On the 13th the Italians invaded Egypt from Libya and the war in North Africa stepped up a gear. Two weeks later Germany, Italy and Japan signed the Tripartite Pact recognising a 'new order in Europe and the Far East'. Britain and the Commonwealth now had its back to the wall. The air raids continued throughout September and the ground crews worked and sweated to keep the aircraft serviceable despite them. On the last day of the Month F/L Alington left Alexandria on patrol at 0530 hrs, in L2166:U, and found an Italian submarine, which he promptly attacked. The *Gondar*, captained by Ten Vasc Francesco Brunetti, was approaching Alexandria carrying human torpedoes when she was found. The submarine was subsequently sunk by the Australian destroyer *HMAS Stuart*. Attacks by the Sunderlands of the squadron may have been few and far between but they were certainly successful.

FRONT GUNNER

"On 28 July 1940 we left Malta for a recce to Augusta in Sicily and were caught on the way back by a pack of Breda fighters. An interesting point was that we had on board a war correspondent by the name of Mr A Clifford, so he had a front stalls seat as we dived down to as low as we dared. On this trip I was on L8504 with skipper S/Ldr Ryley. At the time of the attack I was doing my stint as front gunner, it wasn't nice sitting a few feet off the water, being shot at by some evil minded Italian and thinking, "if the pilot gets hit I'm going to be the first in the drink". We got back with some damage but they left us as we got nearer to Malta."

Arnold Hutchison

October saw a continuation of the patrols by the Sunderlands from Alexandria, Aboukir and Malta and the nuisance of the Italian air raids. Several bombs were dropped on the evening of 16 October but no damage was caused. Two days later newly promoted S/Ldr KV Garside took over command of the squadron from W/Cdr Francis who was posted to become OC No 201 Gp. More Italian bombs fell on Alexandria on the 20th an 21st but no damage was caused. Two days later they were back again dropping bombs in the early hours of the morning. The bombing was almost a daily routine throughout the month and caused much frustration to the groundcrew, who had to take cover every time the air raid warning sounded. Tired and overworked they laboured in the heat of the day and the cold of the night to keep the Sunderlands in the air. On 28 October Italy declared war on Greece and one of the squadron's Sunderlands was immediately despatched on a reconnaissance of the north coast of Crete, Macarin bay and the Southern Aegean. British troops landed in Crete the following day. Preparations were started to establish a temporary advanced base in Suda Bay, Crete for Sunderland operations. The Navy also planned to use Suda Bay as a naval refuelling base. F/O Leatherbarrow was sent from the squadron to organise shore facilities and to erect a W/T station. The following day a Sunderland left for Suda bay with Naval, Air Force and military personnel to start setting up base. Stores for the advanced base left for Crete in *HMS Chakkla* and *HMS Fiona* including a spare Sunderland engine.

FLEET SHADOWERS

"On September 1st we sighted the Italian Fleet in the Ionian Sea but they were making high speed on a course of 320 degrees for their base at Taranto and nothing could be done to attack them as they were far out of range of our strike aircraft and ships."

DK Bednall

THE WAR ILLUSTRATED – AUGUST 23rd 1940
I was there! My day over the Mediterranean

The thrills and dangers of a British air patrol in the Mediterranean – a typical day's work for the men who keep the sea clear for the convoys – are vividly depicted in the following story by Alexander Clifford "Daily Mail' special correspondent, who accompanied the crew of an RAF flying-boat on patrol.

"We made an early take off. The sun was rising as we began to scour miles of the motionless Mediterranean for enemy submarines and shipping. As we approached Sicily, with Etna looming in the background, we spotted something. The pilot swung the machine towards it, and the something took shape as an escorted water-carrying vessel of the sort Mussolini uses for supplying his troops in Libya. Our crew was at action stations. I was holding my breath. The flying-boat went into a steep dive. Three bombs went screaming down. The sea swirled up in foam as they dropped immediately behind the vessels stern. The smaller escorting ships went scurrying away.

It was only a few minutes after this that we were first attacked. I knew nothing until a noise like violent typewriters suddenly broke out all over the fuselage of our plane. Tumblers leapt from their rack and burst about my ears. Something ripped through the seat of my shorts. Whether it was a bullet or a splinter of glass I did not look to see. Bullets pinged around me. I tore open the communicating door and looked aft. The Italian fighter which had attacked us was hurtling towards the blue sea in flames. But the rear gunner who had shot it down was slumped across his gun. Both our midships gunners had blood trickling down their legs.

Smoke was pouring up from where incendiary bullets had struck. I felt a spray of petrol in my face. For a minute it seemed that we were hopelessly afire. "Get ready in case we have to bale out" said the navigator to me as we passed each other carrying extinguishers and tins of water. We damped and we doused and we managed to control the main outbursts. For some time after this we kept our eyes skinned for smoking rags and cushions. We moved the wounded forward and bound up their injuries. Fortunately they had only flesh wounds in the legs. There was urgent work to be done everywhere. And we were still flying along the coast of Sicily, where Mussolini's fighter squadrons are based.

The fitter, who had now manned the rear gun turret, waved to me. Our rudder mechanism was damaged. I clambered up to tell the pilot, but he already knew. He was using his engines to steer. Then I took down a message for transmission to headquarters. But we could not send it. Our radio was soused with petrol, and we dared not risk a short circuit. There were holes everywhere, but the machine kept flying on as if nothing had happened. The crew moved about their emergency duties completely calm.

Then came the next attack. I watched our gunners pumping bullets at Breda monoplanes as they swooped above us, soaring dizzily into the deep blue sky and diving down along our length with guns blazing. I was too busy to count the number of attacks on our plane, but one enemy machine dived out of sight, apparently out of control. The gunner who shot him believes that he must have crashed. When Malta came into sight the Italians were still attacking. But with all guns firing we made them keep their distance. No further damage was done. A bullet struck one of our gunner's goggles, but the glass did not break.

As the enemy planes finally sheered off back towards their bases we set to work stopping holes in the hold preparatory to alighting on the sea. We knew that our petrol and oil could not last much longer. With our hearts in our mouths we flew low over Malta's minefields and alighted safely. The coolness of our pilot, the magnificent teamwork of our crew had saved our lives for all of us, and a costly flying-boat for Britain."

> **LONDON GAZETTE – 13 SEPTEMBER 1940**
>
> CAMPBELL, F/L William Weir (37835)
> Distinguished Flying Cross – No 230 Squadron
>
> "While commanding a flying boat in the Eastern Mediterranean, Acting Flight Lieutenant Campbell showed skill and initiative in surprising and attacking enemy submarines, sinking two with bombs and machine-gunning personnel in the conning tower of a third submarine. The bomb explosions on one of these submersions resulted in wreckage and a number of the crew coming to the surface. Although in the open sea and in the face of an approaching storm, Acting Flight Lieutenant Campbell alighted and taxied the flying boat about the wreckage from which he recovered four survivors. Owing to shock and injuries, the state of the sea and lack of a suitable boat, the manoeuvring of the flying boat and the recovering of the survivors demanded the greatest skill and patience. After the survivors were safely on board Acting Flight Lieutenant Campbell made a further search and then resumed patrol, handing over his prisoners at the end of the day."

GOING TO WAR WITH SUNDERLAND L5804:NM-S (Part 6)

"On a later detachment to Malta we were detailed for a photo recce of the harbour of Port Augusta in Sicily. We were flying with a new 'Skipper' and after making the photographic run he decided to attack some small coasters. Bombs were dropped and the ships sailed on, but the explosions awakened those ashore. We made off but soon saw aircraft making for us. On this trip we had a passenger, a Special War Correspondent, Alexander Clifford of the Daily Mail. His account in the War Illustrated of August 23rd 1940 is fairly accurate; bearing in mind it was wartime reporting. We soon counted nine Breda monoplanes, which tore into the attack. We maintained too much height and did none of the ducking and weaving we had practised with Bill Campbell. One of the Breda's was very persistent and came within 100 yards of my turret, despite nearly 5,000 rounds a minute on a no deflection shot pouring into his radial engine. Eventually he pulled straight up then dived in flames into the sea. Of the nine, three were shot down and two were heavily damaged.

Because of our failure to get down on the deck and take evasive action we had suffered. Both mid-upper gunners and myself were wounded. Alexander Clifford had the seat of his shorts torn, by either a piece of glass from broken bottles in the wardroom or a bullet. The 500,000 candlepower flares in launching chutes on the port side were set on fire in the chutes. When I looked forward from the rear turret all I could see was smoke and fire. Expecting to have to bail out, I opened the turret door and felt for my parachute. It was a ragged mess, full of bullet holes. I made my way down the catwalk and just beyond the rear door the floor collapsed under me and I fell, breaking my left ankle. The same leg with the bullet holes in it. The flares were chopped away and the fires extinguished and eventually we reached Malta. Soon after landing the boat sank near to our beaching apron. We three wounded were on stretchers on the quayside. Someone stuck a cigarette in my mouth and was about to light it but I was able to stop them – I was soaked in petrol. We were taken to hospital and had a grandstand view of an air raid that followed.

When we were mobile again we were taken to see the boat, which was under repair. Below the hull was like a pepper pot. The hull was punctured from stern to bow. There wasn't a window left in the turret. There were bullet holes in the turret door, which was behind me when sitting in the turret. The hydraulics were severed, but most frightening of all were Italian bullets lodged in the breeches of the Brownings, which had been in line with my stomach. Our 'Skipper' of that day was posted shortly after the incident, but at least he got us back to base. I felt very lucky to be alive. I received a MID for the action. After repairs were completed we returned to Alexandria."

Roy S Diss

ITALIAN RESCUE

"On October 13th we hit the headlines when we sighted an Italian Hospital Ship in the Ionian Sea and led it to some survivors from an Italian destroyer who had escaped on their Carley float. This 'mercy mission' was featured in the UK press at the time. Later that month Italy declared war on Greece and Suda Bay, Crete and Scaramanga near Athens were to become our operational bases. This latter was a Greek Torpedo Station on the eastern shore of Lake Eleusis below the slopes of Mount Daphni."

DK Bednall

GOING TO WAR WITH SUNDERLAND L5804:NM-S (Part 7)

"The next detachment was to Scaramanga in Greece, which was near to the Greek naval base and to Piraeus. Nothing of great note happened except the loss of our boat. During a storm it broke from its moorings and came ashore to break up on the beach. I feel sure this came about through weakening of the structure in its last action. This boat surely repaid its cost and the care the crew lavished upon it.

Things moved fairly rapidly during the war in Greece and having no aircraft we were sent to Suda Bay in Crete. We were subjected to fairly constant air raids, but living in tents in an olive grove, with plenty of slit trenches, life was tolerable. A small item which may be of interest is the then rate of exchange with the locals – one case of 'Bully Beef' for a carboy of four gallons of Retsina or one large turkey. The turkeys grew fat in the olive groves in time for Christmas.

Our departure from Crete was on the squadron petrol tanker; a coaster called the 'Pass of Balmaha'. Knowing we were evacuating, every machine gun and every box of *ammunition was taken on board. Mountings were improvised in every part of the ship. We sailed for Alexandria and arrived without being attacked. The ship was not allowed to enter harbour and anchored outside. All except the ships crew went ashore. That night the ship was torpedoed and lost with all hands.*

I never flew on operations in a Sunderland again. I was posted in April 1942 to No 203 Sqn, Bomber Command."

Roy S Diss

Roy Diss moved from No 203 Sqn to a transit camp in Suez, tour expired in December 1942. He was embarked on the *Mauretania* guarding 3,000 German POWs and sailed to America to disembark the POWs. Crossing the Atlantic his ship was rammed by another tanker and left alone to make the crossing. Sailing via Iceland he eventually reached Liverpool and ended the war teaching French pilots gunnery on a small airfield in Northamptonshire.

The squadron shifted its focus towards the Greek islands and on 30 October a Sunderland patrolled ahead of a double convoy heading for the Kaso Strait before flying into the south east Aegean and along the north coast of Crete searching for enemy forces. The following day one of the squadrons Sunderlands escorted *HMS Ajax* proceeding from Alexandria to Suda Bay loaded with troops.

On the first day of November declared itself neutral in the Graeco-Italian conflict and thus relieved the Allies from the threat of the Turks coming into the war on the Axis side. The squadron was kept busy resupplying the troops in Greece and Crete and on this day one of the Sunderlands carried a large number of anti tank rifles from Alexandria to Athens for the Greeks.

The squadron detachment at Suda bay was busy laying moorings but was experiencing difficulty due to a lack of suitable boats. Accommodation was in short supply and the work was being hampered by enemy bombing raids, which caused little damage but slowed progress. A decision was made to move the squadron personnel away from the target area and accommodate them in tents.

LETTER RECEIVED 5 NOVEMBER 1940

"I have read with much interest the report of the Captain of Sunderland Flying Boat L5806 on his reconnaissance carried out from Malta on 12th October 1940. It is requested that you will convey to Wing Commander G Francis, Royal Air Force, my appreciation of the invaluable work he and his crew carried out for the Fleet that day."

(Signed) AB Cunningham. Admiral.

> **SIGNAL HQ RAF MIDDLE EAST 3 DECEMBER 1940**
>
> "On recommendation of HM the King is graciously pleased to award the Distinguished Flying Cross to Wing Commander Francis for Determination, Leadership and Devotion to Duty."

The squadron's Sunderlands were now operating far and wide over the Mediterranean carrying out anti-submarine patrols, transporting supplies and troops to Greece and Crete and escorting convoys. A further reinforcement of the ground party at Suda Bay was carried out on the 7th. Sunderlands searched the coast of Crete and the Anti-Kithera channel on the 9th and 10th with no success and the Sunderland which had been interned in Athens since August returned to the squadron strength that day. While the squadron was busily patrolling the eastern Mediterranean the Fleet Air Arm had attacked the Italian Fleet at Taranto on the night of 11/12 November claiming three battleships, two cruisers and two auxiliaries sunk or damaged. This victory gave the allies a great morale boost during difficult period. On 13 November a squadron Sunderland flew General Sir Archibald Wavell and his staff to Suda Bay. The following day a bomb, which had been dropped on the 12th, was discovered unexploded close to the squadron moorings placing some of them out of use for some days in case the bomb was of the delayed action variety. The same day General Wavell was returned to Alexandria by the squadron.

Over the next days the squadron was kept busy providing escort to troop convoys and on 18 November a Sunderland acted as escort to the Gladiators of No 80 Sqn en route from Sidi Haneish to Heraklion, Crete. The following day a further group of Gladiators of No 80 Sqn were escorted over the same route. Patrols and escorts continued through the following days and on the 27th the fighter force at Heraklion was to be reinforced by a group of Gladiators of No 112 Sqn escorted to Crete by a squadron Sunderland. Unfavourable weather over the next few days postponed this operation for several days. In the preceding week Hungary, Slovakia and Romania had joined forces with the Germans and Italians and the future began to look decidedly grim for the hard-pressed Greeks and their allies.

VIP

"We still visited Malta and on 5 November at Kalafrana we were attacked on the water by a CR42 fighter. Fortunately damage was slight with no casualties. But later, Sunderlands were lost through similar attacks from Me 109s. November was also memorable a 'George', the automatic pilot, was fitted and although inclined to be a bit temperamental, it relieved us of constantly flying manually through 10 or 12 hours of patrol. It enabled the pilot to devote more time to watching the seas.

It was inevitable that we should be called upon to transport VIPs from time to time. The squadron can count kings, queens, princes and princesses among its passengers. 'V' had its share of royalty. We also carried generals – Gambier-Perry, Wavell, and also Anthony Eden. During the latter's journey from Crete to Egypt at night we were shadowed by an aircraft some distance from the south of Crete. Fortunately for the well being of our distinguished passenger, no attack developed."
DK Bednall

Investigation began on 29 November into the advanced basing of half of the squadron at Scaramanga Naval Shipyard, ten miles west of Athens. The plan was to provide moorings at the Naval Dockyard on Salamis Island and at the Torpedo School in Scaramanga Bay and also at Mrgalo Pefco, fifteen miles west of Eleusis airfield thus extending the patrol area in the Ionian and Aegean Seas. Suda bay was proving to be a poor base owing to bad weather, land and naval obstructions and communications difficulties.

The Gladiators of No 112 Sqn were eventually escorted to Heraklion along with a Bombay transport on 1 December. The Sunderland landing at Keraton Bay to offload supplies. And spares. F/L Leatherbarrow, who was instrumental in setting up the squadron detachment at Suda Bay, was replaced by F/L Stidolph as the Senior Air Force Officer (SAFO) Crete that same day. The Greek army, which had advanced into Albania the previous month, continued to push back the Italians and in response to this the Italians requested German intervention in the war with Greece a week later. A further eight Gladiators of 112 Sqn were escorted to Heraklion on the 4th. The following days of December were filled with anti-submarine patrols in the south-east Ionian Sea, convoy escorts and searches for missing and overdue shipping. On 9 December British forces launched 'Operation Compass' attacking Italian troops in the Western Desert. By the 17th 20,000 Italians had surrendered and the situation for the Italian forces in North Africa was becoming critical. Squadron morale was much boosted by this success. On 10 December the squadron was reinforced by the allocation of a new Sunderland,

T9050, to the strength. By the 21st it had been decided to set up an advanced base at Scaramanga and the squadrons equipment would be moved by road through to the *Pass of Balmaha* and thence by sea. S/Ldr Garside flew in the first aircraft into Scaramanga on the 27th. The squadrons first full year of war ended with a patrol searching for enemy vessels on the 30th with no success.

GREECE

"We were lucky to be one of the first operational Sunderlands to arrive in Greece after Churchill's declaration to assist the Greeks in their war against the Italians. Early 1941 was devoted to daily patrols of the Ionian Sea and in ferrying important passengers and stores to and from Egypt and Malta via Greece and Crete.

Some measure of the level of effort is shown in my log book for March 1941 – no less than 157 operational hours were recorded by me!"

DK Bednall

'Pass of Balmaha' was used to refuel 230 Squadron Sunderlands at Suda Bay . (D Dunn via DK Bednall).

3. Backs to the Wall
January to December 1941

The first week of 1941 was taken up in patrols to cover convoys passing through the Ionian Sea to Greece and Crete and anti-submarine and surface vessel sweeps. In retaliation for the comprehensive defeat of their forces in Libya the Italians launched a strong counter-offensive in Albania and, with Luftwaffe assistance, began to gain ground. On 5 January, while the Italians surrendered at Bardia, one of the squadron Sunderlands picked up a formation of Gladiators off Sidi Barrani and escorted them to Eleusis in Greece via Crete. On the morning of 8 January a Sunderland carrying out a search for enemy vessels evacuating Tobruk in the southern Mediterranean sighted a possible submarine and attacked it with a depth charge and two bombs. No results were observed.

The squadron's Sunderlands were being kept very busy during this period, not only escorting convoys, but shadowing and searching for the shipping evacuating the beleaguered Italians from Tobruk. On the morning of 12 January one Sunderland, operating from Scaramanga, had an encounter with a Cant 506B which resulted in the Sunderland cutting short its patrol. During the fight the Sunderlands gunners damaged their own tailplane forcing an early return.

By 14 January Suda Bay had closed as an operational base and would henceforth be used as an emergency-landing base. The refuelling vessel *'Pass of Balmaha'* which serviced the squadrons Sunderlands accordingly moved from Suda bay to Scaramanga and the squadron detachment had fully moved there by the 20th. The following day British and Australian troops began a strong attack on Tobruk accelerating the Italian evacuation. Two days earlier the Italians had been attacked by British troops advancing from the Sudan into Eritrea and by the end of the month troops from Kenya were advancing into Italian Somaliland. Things were not going well for the Italians in Africa at the beginning of 1941.

On the afternoon of 23 January one of the Sunderlands force landed at Patras running out of fuel on returning from patrol. It returned to Scaramanga the next day. The following days were taken up with repeated searches for enemy forces which might interfere with the naval operations off Tobruk and convoy movements in the Aegean. By 27 January it had been decided to abandon the laying of moorings at Patras and the petrol and oil destined for that location were diverted to increase facilities at Argostoli in Cephalonia.

Sunderland Mk I, T9050:NM-Y lands at Suda Bay with Dundas Bednall at the controls in April 1941. (DK Bednall).

On the last day of the month the Royal Navy reported a torpedoed tanker and requested air cover for it. A Sunderland was diverted to establish an anti-submarine patrol ahead of and around the ship but had to break off and land at Suda bay with an unserviceable turret mechanism. Another aircraft was despatched from Scaramanga but found the tanker had been abandoned and returned to base.

The squadron continued to patrol both the Aegean and Ionian Seas throughout February and on the 4th Sunderland N9029:V was tasked with searching for the crew of a Blenheim which was last seen east of Naxos Island en-route to Egypt. The Sunderland searched for three hours but with no success. Allied progress against the Italians on the North African mainland was going well and the Australians captured Benghazi, and six generals, two days later. The balance was about to change though as the first German forces left Italy for North Africa on 8 February followed by Lt Gen Erwin Rommel four days later.

On 8 February Sunderland L2166:U carried out a patrol from Alexandria to Scaramanga encountering three Cant 506B tri-motor floatplanes but evading any engagement with the Italians. The following day the same aircraft was involved in a search for a missing Anson off Phalconera with no success. On the 12th L2166:U again encountered a Cant 506B but once again there was no engagement. Also on the 12th Sunderland L5804:S escorted a formation of Gladiators from El Adem to Heraklion and after refuelling onward to Eleusis in Greece before landing at Scaramanga. On 18 February Sunderland L2161:Y carried out a five hour search for the crew of a Wellington which had force landed in the sea returning to Egypt form a raid on Rhodes. The search was unsuccessful.

With his troops established in North Africa, Rommel began his campaign with an attack on El Agheila on 22 February and began the see-saw battles with the British and Commonwealth forces which was to last for many months to come. The previous day Sunderland L2161:Y left Alexandria for the former Italian seaplane base at Bomba in Cyrenaica to examine the facilities available and the practicability of using it as an advanced base for the squadron. The following day the Sunderland took off for Tobruk with the same intention but was forced to return to Alexandria due to a sandstorm. On 25 February a very severe gale struck Scaramanga and Sunderland L5804:S broke free of its moorings and was completely written off. The following day the squadron began to salvage what spares it could from the wreck.

The gloomy situation for the Allies became worse on 1 March when Bulgaria joined the Axis and German troops marched into Bulgaria the following day. The fighting in Greece was draining Allied resources in the theatre and was in need of reinforcement. To that end the squadron became involved in a naval operation codenamed 'Operation Lustre' on 5 March. The operation was intended to transport a large military and air force to Greece from Egypt and the squadron was tasked with air reconnaissance to ensure freedom from surprise by enemy surface forces. N9029:V carried out the first of these patrols and the squadron detachment at Scaramanga was reinforced for the operation. The squadron flew many patrols in support of the shipping convoy, which had sailed on the 4th, over the next days. On 9 March Sunderland T9050:P reinforced the Scaramanga detachment and the patrols continued. The increase in patrols brought an increasing strain to both the aircrew and the groundcrews, who were stretched to the limit to keep the aircraft serviceable, both at Alexandria and Scaramanga.

L2164:Z was at its moorings in St Pauls Bay, Malta on 10 March when it was set on fire and sunk in an air raid. On 13 March N9029:V patrolled the western Aegean area and was shadowed for some time by a Cant 506B. Scaramanga signalled the Sunderland that a submarine had been sighted and S/Ldr Alington searched the area for it with no success. The following day Sunderland's L2160:X and L2161:Y were involved in a taxiing accident at Scaramanga reducing the effective aircraft for the detachment to Sunderland T9050:P.

On 18 March Sunderland L2166:U, captained by S/Ldr Alington, was returning from a routine patrol when it was diverted to assist a destroyer in an anti-submarine hunt. Ansons of the Greek Air Force were also involved in the search. The destroyer dropped about 15 DCs and the Ansons dropped two bombs. Alington dropped two bombs and two DCs but the attacks did not result in a confirmed sinking. Two days later the Germans began to make demands of the Yugoslavs and four Yugoslav ministers resigned rather than accept the German terms. Five days later the Yugoslavs signed the Tripartite Pact but a revolution on the 27th saw King Peter take control and a new Cabinet formed. Meanwhile in North Africa British Somaliland was cleared of Italian troops on the 24th and three days later the British were victorious in the second phase of the Battle of Keren in Eritrea. The victories were not all on the Allied side however and on 30 March the Axis forces began a counter offensive in Cyrenaica with the German 5th Light Division under Rommel's command and the Italians sank two British cruisers, *HMS York* and *HMS Bonaventure* in the last week of the month.

During this period the squadron was kept busy patrolling the sea-lanes and was instrumental in the safe recovery to port of a Brazilian ship, the *Taubate* on 22 March. S/Ldr Alington was returning from Athens to Alexandria in L2166:U when he was diverted to investigate the SOS and escorted the vessel safely to port.

On 27 March Sunderland T9050:P left Scaramanga for a dawn to dusk search patrol. The crew sighted three Italian cruisers and a destroyer. The sighting served as a partial confirmation that the Italians intended a large naval action against the Allied convoys in the Aegean and south of Crete. The following day the Italian Fleet was engaged at the battle of Cape Matapan losing the cruisers 'Fiume', 'Pola' and 'Zara'. The British force lost only two aircraft. Prior to the engagement the squadron was instrumental in providing accurate intelligence on the strength and position of the Italian forces and Sunderland N9029:V, piloted by F/L Lywood was kept busy throughout the day. At 0620 hrs they sighted three unidentified ships and an hour later were instructed to search to the west of this force. Twenty minutes later Lywood was ordered to shadow the three ships and some time later he sighted a further two battleships in the area. This force was then reported as five cruisers and three destroyers. The first force sighted had now been assessed as three cruisers and three destroyers. At 1245 hrs Lywood was requested to confirm the presence of a second force and at 1500 hrs it was confirmed that two strong

Italian naval forces were in the area. Following the naval engagement Sunderland L2160:X, flown by F/L Woodward was ordered into the area on the 29th to search for crippled ships. At 0630 hrs Woodward reported that he had landed amidst a huge patch of oil and wreckage around which about 25 rafts were afloat carrying around 600 survivors from the *'Zara'*, *'Pola'* and *'Fiume'* which had been sunk by *HMS Warspite* in the previous night's action. Woodward attempted to identify which ship the survivors came from but their only response was a request for water. At 1325 hrs, whilst at the limit of its patrol area L2160 was attacked by a Me 110. The fighter carried out four quarter attacks and scored hits on the elevators and tailplane of the Sunderland. The damage was slight and Woodward landed at Suda Bay to make repairs to one of the engines before returning to Scaramanga. Later that day Sunderland T9050:P reported sighting an aircraft dinghy with four survivors, probably the crew of an Italian spotting aircraft which had been shot down by the Royal Navy.

Three days later Sunderland T9050:P was returning from Scaramanga to Alexandria for a major overhaul when the crew sighted an overturned lifeboat. The lifeboat was most probably from *HMS Bonaventure*, which had been sunk with two torpedoes from a submarine on 31 March. On 2 April Sunderland N9029:V, captained by F/L Lywood, sighted the Italian hospital ship *'Gradeca'* still engaged in picking up survivors from the naval action off Cape Matapan.

On 3 April the Germans and Italians began an advance eastwards from El Agheila while the British withdrew. On 5 April S/Ldr Alington carried out a search from Alexandria for a missing Blenheim crew in Sunderland L2166:U. The Blenheim crew had been sighted in their dinghy late in the afternoon of the 4th but despite searching for three hours in the vicinity of the sighting they were not found. The following day Germany invaded Greece. Over the following days the Yugoslavian withdrawal in the south exposed the Greek flank and the Germans broke towards Salonika. By the 9th German armoured columns had entered Thessaloniki. On the North African front Rommel had captured Bardia and on 10 April the Germans entered Zagreb and Hungary invaded Yugoslavia.

The squadron detachment at Scaramanga was reinforced by Sunderland L2166:U flown in by S/Ldr Alington. Departing Alexandria on the 7th with passengers, priority freight and mail for Crete and Greece, the Sunderland landing at Suda bay after carrying out a patrol of the western Aegean.

THE BATTLE OF CAPE MATAPAN

"On March 27th F/O Bohm, flying with F/L IM McCall in Sunderland 'P' sighted the Italian Fleet 100 miles off Sicily, steering a south easterly course. Although we did not know it at the time, the Navy mounted a supreme effort and actually engaged some of the enemy south of Crete and claimed to have damaged the battleship 'Vittorio Veneto' with torpedoes from aircraft from the 'Formidable'.

Early on March 28th Woodward, as duty aircraft, was ordered to search south west of Crete, but he became unserviceable and we in N9029 were hastily summoned in the middle of the night to replace him. We took off at 0410hrs.

On the way to the search area given to us by Operations I thought I saw ships to starboard, to the south west, somewhat concealed by the dawn mist. There were doubts among us whether they were, indeed, ships but Alan Lywood set course immediately and we discovered they were a squadron of 8" Italian cruisers heading for Taranto at high speed. We identified them positively as the 'Fiume', 'Zara' and 'Pola'. This was some distance to the west of the proposed search area so luck was really with us that day, as we so easily could have missed them.

We shadowed them, on our own all day, except for a diversion for more ships to the south. We discovered a further force of 6" cruisers and what we thought were two battleships (the 'Cavour' class of battleships and the 'Garibaldi' cruisers were notoriously difficult to tell apart, even for naval observers). Later their speed revealed that they must be, in fact, 'Garibaldi 6" cruisers.

Late afternoon our fuel was running low and we debated whether to land at sea to keep the Italians in view, but we decided that we would be too vulnerable and could be more useful by staying in the air as long as we could so we could transmit the latest accurate position to Operations.

We were fired on by the Italians – their shells burst about 400 yards astern but were accurate for height. We left when our fuel was dangerously low, after sending a final position report. A short time later that evening Admiral Cunningham's forces found themselves amidst this 8" cruiser squadron and effectively destroyed them. So, therefore, we could claim, with some justification, that our sighting that morning enabled the historic Battle of Matapan to take place. No other shadowing aircraft was engaged on the enemy cruisers that day. Alan Lywood was awarded the DFC and Waterland, our flight engineer, the DFM for this mission of 13 hours.

After Matapan patrol work went on as usual. Prince Philip of Greece was then a lieutenant in 'Warspite' and became a familiar figure with the squadron and was our passenger in 'V' on one occasion."

DK Bednall

Alington arrived in Scaramanga the following day. Patrols were frequent from both Alexandria and Scaramanga over the period and with the constant need to improve the aircraft defences and striking power Sunderland L2160:X was flown on a local flight test on 10 April by S/Ldr Woodward to test an improved midships gun mounting. The following day Sunderland T9050:P, whilst on a flight test after its major overhaul, was tasked to search for two enemy submarines which had been reported the previous day. Neither was sighted. Returning to Alexandria the aircraft was ordered to search for a Cant Z1007 that had been shot down near Ras el Tin during an attempt to reconnoitre Alexandria. The Cant was not seen.

By now the situation for the British and Greek troops was becoming precarious and by the 12th the Allies had fallen back to the Mount Olympus Line. That same day Rommel's troops encircled Tobruk and the squadron detachment at Scaramanga reported that German mine laying and bombing attacks had made the base highly dangerous for use by Sunderlands. Arrangements were made to move to Suda Bay but the move was made difficult by the need to maintain the Aegean patrols, evacuate personnel from Yugoslavia and keeping aircraft on immediate notice to move for the AOC Greece.

The squadron was also required to meet naval reconnaissance requirements of the C in C Mediterranean. The *'Pass of Balmaha'* was used to move much of the equipment and the Sunderlands moved the rest between the other commitments. The pace of operations was stepped up that same day and Sunderlands N9029:V, T9050:P and L5804:S flew patrols in support of a naval operation which resulted in the sighting of two Me 110s and one unidentified aircraft. None of these aircraft were engaged. Later the same day Sunderland T9050:P carried out an offensive patrol from Alexandria between Benghazi and Tobruk searching in conjunction with naval forces for enemy shipping which might be attempting to use parts of the Libyan coast to supply their troops advancing from Benghazi.

RETREAT

April was another momentous month for the squadron as, together with a detachment of 228 Squadron, we played a leading role in the evacuation from Greece and later Crete. In fact, it was becoming boring always being on the retreat! During the evacuation Imperial Airways unarmed civil aircraft were also pressed into service, but always had a Sunderland as escort (though the prospect of defending the civilian against a determined fighter attack conjures up an intriguing operation!). At no time were we ever escorted by fighters – they were too busy at the front.

I had now been given my own aircraft, T9050:Y. Day after day Sunderlands were overloaded to bring out personnel and stores from ports and beaches. Woodward took 83 passengers and we in T9050:Y took 63 passengers and 4,600lbs of ammunition (chiefly for Hurricane cannon) and stores. I believe this was the heaviest load of the campaign. Although a fair breeze was blowing with a nice 'popply' sea it took about five miles to get off the water from Suda Bay. Maximum height for the journey back to Alexandria was about 800 ft. This was on April 23rd and I see from my logbook that we made it in the comparatively good time of 3 hours 50 minutes.

The strain of take off eventually must have told as on a subsequent journey we blew a cylinder on the port inner engine. We had no facilities for extensive repairs so the propeller was lashed (there was no feathering mechanism on the Mk Is) to prevent further damage and I took off on three engines. Unfortunately, south of Crete, the lashing became loose and the propeller started to revolve. We could either risk a seized engine with it possibly breaking loose from the aircraft or the propeller flying off, or risk a landing and take off at sea. I chose the latter. The prop was re-lashed and once again the gallant 'Y' managed to get airborne on three engines and Alexandria was made without further ado.

During the evacuation I made one infamous journey. During a particularly busy day ferrying troops back from Greece and Crete I was sent back for yet another load. On arrival the usual gathering of troops or stores waiting to be ferried was missing. Eventually a marine tender arrived with the AOCs wife and her pet parrot. In spite of my protests I was instructed to 'carry on'. The only occasion during the evacuation when a Sunderland was so lightly laden!

The number of flying hours put in was prodigious – thanks to the devotion and skills of our riggers, fitters, electricians and armourers. We must no forget the loyal, unstinting efforts of the marine craft crews on whom we depended for refuelling, servicing and ferrying to and from the aircraft.

Serviceability of the aircraft was incredibly high, especially in view of the extensive emergency conditions. At that time each crew had its own aircraft and, although the general benefits of the later maintenance system of pooled aircraft were undeniable, the rich rewards of having one's own aircraft to fly looked after by its own crew paid off for 230 Squadron in 1940-41. This period is an important one in the Squadron history, not only for Greece, Crete and Matapan, but also for operating from Malta at a time when it was thought to be impossible to use.

As far as I was concerned, having completed nearly 900 hours of operational flying in one operational tour, my eyes eventually packed up through constant staring at the glistening Mediterranean and I developed an acute form of conjunctivitis and was told that it was the end of my flying days. Happily on being posted to Kenya (No 70 Blenheim OTU) I gradually recovered and returned to full flying duties.

DK Bednall

On 13 April Sunderland L2166:U, piloted by F/O Brand carried out the first patrol from the squadrons detached base at Suda Bay. Two Ju 88s were sighted but they did not approach the Sunderland. By the 14th the detachment was fully established at Suda Bay but two aircraft remained at Scaramanga under instructions for a special operation. The nature of the special operation became clear when L2160:X and L2166:U, flown by S/Ldr Woodward and F/O Brand respectively, flew to Kotor in Yugoslavia to evacuate important passengers from the country after the rapid German penetration. The passengers were delivered to Greece.

On 17 April the Yugoslavian army capitulated and the following day King Peter of Yugoslavia was flown out along with Gen Simonovitch and members of the Royal family and military staff by Sunderland N9029:V. Earlier that day the same aircraft had been used to begin the evacuation of British troops from Greece when the last remnants of the 230 Sqn detachment at Scaramanga were evacuated to Crete along with elements of HQ British Forces Greece. The Germans pressed home their attacks in Greece on the 19th and the squadron found itself increasingly being used to fly urgent equipment and stores in one direction and evacuees in the other. Over the following days the British forces withdrew further in Greece and by 21 April elements of the Greek army began to surrender and the British were asked to withdraw. That day Sunderland N9029:V, captained by F/L Lywood flew from Alexandria to Scaramanga with a party of Naval personnel and stores, who were to form the shore party for the evacuation by sea of the British forces in Greece. The following day Sunderland T9050:P flew into Scaramanga to evacuate RAF personnel. Embarking 34 passengers, F/L McCall took off but an engine failure just after take off force the Sunderland to return and disembark the passengers. S/Ldr Woodward in L2160:X was also involved in the evacuation from Scaramanga and flew out 18 RAF passengers. The Sunderland also flew out the

Crown Princess of Greece, Princess Katharine of Greece, Princess Alexander of Greece and several other members of the Greek Royal Family. In the early hours of 23 April King George II of Greece along with Crown Prince Paul and the Prime Minister, Mr Paliaret, were flown out of Scaramanga by S/Ldr Woodward in L2160:X. Later the same day Woodward flew into Nauplia in L2160:X and anchored off the town embarking 37 RAF personnel during the night before returning to Suda Bay. Whilst the King of Greece was being evacuated from Scaramanga Sunderland T9050:P attempted to leave for Alexandria from Scaramanga on three engines, heavily laden with fuel. The attempts to take off were unsuccessful and F/L Bednall returned to the moorings. The Sunderland was attacked at the moorings by 7 Ju 87s returning from a dive bombing attack on Piraeus. The Sunderland caught fire and was totally destroyed, as was the refuelling lighter alongside. One of the Ju 87s was destroyed by return fire from the midships guns and the uninjured pilots and crew were able to swim ashore.

Marshal Tito (saluting) and King Peter arrive to board a 230 Sqn Sunderland for evacuation

The officers of 230 Sqn at Aboukir after the evacuation of Greece. Rear L to R: ?, Jillings, DK Bednall, Odhams, Addison, Kilpatrick, Deeds (Intelligence officer), Brand. Front L to R: ?, ?, ?, McCall, W/Cdr Francis (CO), Lywood, Alington, Bohm, Milligan, ?. (DK Bednall).

Sunderland W3987:NM-X at anchor on the south coast of Crete during the evacuation of British and Commonwealth troops.

Sunderland in silhouette. W/Cdr Francis taking off during the evacuation of Greece loaded with 84 troops and a crew of 10. The take off run was 5 miles and on arrival at Alexandria all four engines had to be changed

On 24 April the AOC Greece and Gen Blamey and his staff were evacuated from Greece in Sunderland L2166:U by F/O Brand. With the evacuation of Greece in full swing the squadron's Sunderlands worked alongside those of No 228 Sqn and flying boats of BOAC to evacuate personnel. Sunderland L2161:Y arrived at Alexandria on three engines. The aircraft had taken off from Suda bay with the port inner airscrew lashed and then had to land off the south coast of Crete to renew the lashing. The forced landing was reported to Suda bay by coast watchers and as a result a 228 Sqn Sunderland was despatched to investigate. Meanwhile L2161 had taken off again and the 228 Sqn aircraft was recalled. Evacuation of troops from Nauplia continued and Gen Mackay was evacuated on the 25th. RAF personnel at Kalamata were evacuated on the 25th by S/Ldr Woodward in L2160:X. 72 RAF personnel were crushed into the Sunderland. That day the sole remaining refuelling lighter used by the squadron at Scaramanga set sail for Suda bay with a scratch crew made up of S/Ldr Allarch (?), P/O Kirkpatrick, two W/T operators and a Greek. Also on board was two Territorial Army Nursing Association sisters as passengers. The pack W/T station from Scaramanga had been installed and the launch armed with Vickers machine guns salvaged from the destruction of 33 Air Stores Park equipment. The remainder of the most valuable stores from Scaramanga were transported to Suda Bay on the launch. Two Pegasus engines, which could not be carried, were machine gunned before departure.

A Squadron Sunderland moored at Kalamata.

On 26 April Sunderland L2161:Y escorted two BOAC aircraft to Suda Bay carrying four tons of Hurricane ammunition and stores and personnel for the squadron detachment. The same day F/O Brand in L2166:U patrolled the western Aegean and was diverted to search for a crashed Sunderland at Kalamata. No trace of it was seen but the town had been recently bombed. On 27 April as German troops entered Athens S/Ldr Woodward flew to Myli in the Gulf of Nauplia and embarked 65 army personnel including Generals Wilson and Rankin, the Greek Prime Minister and a Prince of the Greek Royal Family. On the same day Axis forces crossed the Egyptian border. On 28 April L2166:U carried out a dawn to dusk patrol of the Aegean and was ordered to drop a message at St Nikola Bay, Kithera instructing RAF personnel there to stand by to embark on destroyers at 2000 hrs that night. The message was successfully passed. The month of April ended with British troops regrouping on Crete and fighting a desperate rearguard action on the border of Egypt.

With the impending invasion of Crete the squadron was ordered to reduce the Suda Bay detachment to a care and maintenance basis leaving behind only W/T and marine craft. Accordingly N9029:V arrived at Aboukir from Suda Bay on 1 May bringing the main body of the detachment. On 3 May S/Ldr Woodward was flying the AOC in C to Malta in L2160:X when an enemy submarine was sighted on the surface. Unfortunately the Sunderland had no bombs and the opportunity to attack was lost. After a pro-Axis coup in Iraq at the beginning of April the Iraqis had attacked British troops at Habbaniya on 2 May.

The following day newly promoted F/L Brand was despatched to Cairo in L2166:U to be briefed for a special flight in connection with the fighting in Iraq. The Sunderland then flew on to Habbaniya to rescue Imperial Airways staff reported to be on board a powerboat on the lake. The aircraft arrived at Habbaniya in the early hours of the 4th but reported no trace of the powerboat. The lake was surrounded by Iraqis and Brand proceeded to Basrah. On the 4th a Sunderland was despatched to intercept enemy shipping attempting to pass supplies from the Dodecanese to Syria where German aircraft had been reported to be operating. On return the aircraft landed at Famagusta to investigate the possibility of operating Sunderlands from that base.

During the period the evacuations from Crete continued and on the 6th six members of the Greek Royal Family were evacuated to Alexandria from Suda Bay. On 7 May, L2159 was damaged beyond repair in an air raid at Greenock whilst on a return flight to the UK. By 8th May the squadron had begun to disperse its aircraft to Ismalia and Aboukir from Alexandria to minimise losses from air attack. By the middle of the month the dispersed aircraft had returned to Alexandria and patrols continued unabated. The Germans invaded Crete on 20 May in the first ever large-scale airborne invasion. In the following days heavy air attacks sank the cruisers *HMS Fiji* and *Gloucester* and the destroyer *HMS Greyhound*. The battleships *HMS Warspite* and *Valiant* were damaged and the RAF was forced to withdraw its fighters from the island by the 23rd.

The Royal Navy managed to break up a second German supply convoy and further seaborne attacks on Crete were repulsed but two more British destroyers, *HMS Kashmir* and *Kelly* were sunk. The following day the Germans continued with heavy bombing of targets on the island. Towards the end of the month the squadron's Sunderlands were involved in several searches. The first on the 24th was for the crew of a Wellington force landed in the sea. The search was unsuccessful. On 28 May F/L Brand in L2166:U searched for two liferafts containing survivors from the sinking of HMS Gloucester. Once again the search was unsuccessful. The pilot of a ditched Tomahawk was luckier when he was found by W/Cdr Francis fifty miles off Ras el Tin whilst he was air testing L2160:X. W/Cdr Francis landed on the sea and picked up the pilot returning him to Alexandria.

Shipping in Suda Bay under Stuka attack

By 27 May the Germans had captured Canae on Crete and the British had decided to withdraw from the island. On the North African front Rommel had retaken the Halfaya Pass. The following day the Allies pulled out of Heraklion and the evacuation was in full swing. On 29 May the cruiser *HMS Orion*, taking part in the evacuation, was sunk with the loss of 200 men and two other destroyers were sunk. On 30 May Sunderland L2166:U working with two No 228 Sqn Sunderlands evacuated 70 RAF and Army officers from Sphakia on the south coast of Crete. The aircraft landed there after dusk, embarked the passengers and returned to Aboukir without incident. A second flight to Kavi Morus by F/L Lywood on N9029:V was carried out the following day to evacuate further personnel.

By 1 June 17,000 Allied troops had been safely evacuated from Crete and the squadron was keeping a Sunderland on standby for further evacuations. F/L Lywood took Sunderland N9029:V out on patrol early on 3 June but force landed at Temassel due to a broken turret hydraulic pipe. The crew was able to make repairs and continue the patrol before returning to Aboukir in the afternoon. By June a flight of Yugoslav Dornier flying boats had been attached to the squadron and one of these carried out flying practice on the 3rd. Later that day two of the Dorniers carried out their first patrol with the squadron but had nothing to report.

On 4 June there was a large enemy raid on Alexandria and 100 people were killed. F/L Lywood was despatched in N9029:V to search for a Wellington crew on 6 June but returned early U/S. A second aircraft L2160:X flown by F/O Powell took over the search. The Wellington had ditched 85 miles north of Mersa Matruh and Powell's crew sighted the dinghy at 1100 hrs. The sea conditions prevented a landing and the Sunderland dropped supplies. One of the Dorniers, which were based at Aboukir, collided with and sank a dinghy on take off on 7 June and had to return to its moorings.

That same day W/Cdr Francis resumed command of No 230 Sqn from S/Ldr Woodward. On the night of 9/10 June L2160:X was despatched to Eremopoli to investigate a report from a 201 Gp Maryland that about 1,000 British troops were still at large in this vicinity. The Sunderland landed to the east of Paxmadra Island and taxied to Eremopoli. A machine gun opened fire on the Sunderland from the shore and it was forced to take off and return to base without having confirmed the sighting. A bullet found later in the aircraft proved to be German. Over the next few days both the Sunderlands and the Dorniers patrolled regularly but many of the patrols were curtailed by unserviceabilities.

During June Allied and Free French forces had invaded Syria and Lebanon and on 15 June Operation Battleaxe commenced in an attempt to relieve the pressure on Australian-held Tobruk. On that day one of the squadron's Sunderlands was sent to intercept a French destroyer. The destroyer was found and its course, speed and position were passed. The Sunderland finally lost sight of the destroyer in the darkness. The destroyer was firing at some unseen target. Later swordfish of No 815 Sqn attacked the destroyer scoring one confirmed and two possible hits. A later search revealed six lifeboats and a number of Carley floats, wreckage and oil in the position of the attack. This was a highly successful example of the co-operation between the squadron and the Royal Navy.

By 17 June Operation battleaxe had failed with the loss of 1,000 British casualties and 100 tanks. Rommel had beaten back the British attack at Sollum. The following day Sunderland T9050:P, flown by F/L McCall carried out a search for a Wellington crew but had no luck.

By 12 June No 230 Sqn had moved from Alexandria to Aboukir completely in order to move out of the Alexandria target area and minimise the risks of collision in the busy harbour area. The Yugoslav No 2 Sqn which had been co-located with No 230 Sqn officially came under the administration of the squadron although the Yugoslavs were almost self-supporting. Under the command of Commander LV Petrovitch the eight Dornier 22s and a single Rogosarski Sim floatplane operated from Aboukir. The personnel lived in hotels under RAF arrangements and were assisted by a small number of RAF personnel manning two workshop lorries. On 20 June S/Ldr Woodward once again took command of the squadron. That same day a signal was received from HQ RAF ME to the effect that F/L AMG Lywood had been awarded the DFC and Sgt G Baxter the DFM.

On 22 June one of Hitler's most momentous mistakes commenced with the invasion of Russia. This would prove to be a turning point in the war. This would not affect the situation in the Middle East and the Mediterranean at this point, however, and the squadron and the Yugoslavs continued to patrol. On 25 June on of the Dorniers was sent out to search for a dinghy reported to hold four men but had no luck in locating them. The following day the Yugoslav Dorniers carried out eight sorties searching for another dinghy containing four to six -personnel before it was sighted at 1600hrs. The Dornier set course for a trawler, which had joined the search. The trawler was nine miles from the dinghy and the Dornier signalled the position before returning to base. On 27 June the Dorniers were once again out in search of the dinghy first sighted on the 25th. Two of them located the dinghy and whilst one circled it the other directed a destroyer to the survivors, which it successfully picked up.

At the beginning of July a British column advanced from Iraq into Syria and by the 9th the Allies were nearing Beirut. Gen Dentz, the Vichy commander, sued for peace in the Middle East. Two days later the Vichy Government in France rejected the Syrian armistice but Gen Dentz defied his government and accepted. The Syrian armistice was signed in Acre on 14 July and British troops entered Beirut the following day. While all this was occurring the crews of Sunderlands and Dorniers continued their patrols with little to report. The first days of the month were mainly taken up in patrols to search for Vichy shipping. On 7 July Sunderland N9029:V, piloted by F/L Lywood was tasked with a search for Vichy destroyers. The Sunderland was fired on by one of the enemy vessels but was not hit.

On 8 July the squadron was signalled with the information that it had received more awards. W/Cdr G Francis was awarded the DSO and S/Ldr PH Alington the DFC. The Yugoslav Dorniers were occasionally subject to misidentification errors by friendly forces due to their German origin. On 9 July one of them was carrying out a radar calibration test when it was fired on by the AA batteries. Luckily no hits were scored.

F/L McCall took L2166:U out to search for an enemy submarine of 11 July. Blenheims had attacked the submarine earlier but McCall failed to find any trace of it. The following day W/Cdr Francis carried out trials of the MV1 Dropping Apparatus, used for rescue work, from L2166:U over Aboukir aerodrome in order to test their serviceability. The tests were continued on the 13th by F/L McCall in L5806:Q and again on the 15th by W/Cdr Francis in L2166:U. By 21 July the Yugoslav Dorniers were being used on a daily basis to calibrate the radar stations in the area. The Sunderlands were mainly concentrating on searches for enemy shipping and the reinforcement of Malta with men, equipment and stores. On 25 July the squadron was notified of the award of the DFC to S/Ldr PR Woodward and the DFM to Sgt J Smith

A search for a rubber dinghy reported by a reconnaissance aircraft was carried out by F/L McCall in L2160:X on the 27^{th,} but without success. The testing of the MV1 Dropping Apparatus continued on the 30th when L2166:U flown by F/L Brand, dropped it on Aboukir aerodrome.

ORDERLY ROOM CLERK

Leo Norman Worth served on a Balloon Squadron for a year before being posted overseas to the Squadron:

"I was posted abroad on 20 June 1941 and arrived after a long convoyed sea journey at Alexandria. I was delivered to 230 Sqn HQ and met by an airman named Brian Hughes, who gave me a warm welcome. My trade was Clerk General and I worked in the Orderly Room. It was a job where you handled all administration for every airman, officers and other ranks. Typical things were pay, promotion and postings. You knew everybody.

Aboukir was a good spot for a 230 Sqn airman. The Aboukir Sea bordered the village and the Sunderlands lazed peacefully on the water, being serviced or flying on anti-submarine patrols in the Med.

We lived six to a bungalow, working in the morning and evening, resting in the afternoon or going down to the beach to swim. We had some good CO's and Adjutants. I worked with an adjutant named P/O Bentley and he was very capable.

I found it very interesting to get to know the officers and other ranks and how they felt due to separation from home. There we would be, drinking and talking about home, wives, girlfriends, peacetime jobs and so on. As I worked with the men on personal matters they seemed to trust me and tell me all their private worries. They liked me to listen.

Flies were a problem in Egypt. They followed you and the food (especially sweet cakes) all the time. Alexandria was a colourful place, populated by several nationalities living in their own groups. To go out there in the evening required the companionship of another man. Theft was done very quickly. Drinking bars were all too prevalent and fights broke out frequently, sometimes with Australians rather than the enemy!

Interesting things happened to airmen. One man got friendly with a Greek girl. After a while the father hired a boat and they sailed out to sea. Then the father said, "Offer to marry my daughter. If you don't you can swim back and I know it is too far for you"!

The following year the big desert war against Rommel was alive. In Alexandria we began to hear the guns. Our Squadron was put on stand by to move the Staff if required. Squadron preparations for a quick move were made. I was on one trip and we started the take off in troubled waters. I looked out and saw the starboard float dropping. The captain, W/Cdr Taylor, called us all to climb on the plane's wing and lie down on the port side whilst we motored back. That stopped the plane toppling. We were very cold but got a second breakfast!

LN Worth

The squadron suffered its first loss since T9050:P had been destroyed at its moorings at Scaramanga in April when L2166:U was lost on 1 August. F/L Brand and his crew had been carrying out an anti-submarine search off the Gulf of Sollum in conjunction with four destroyers when it went missing. No signals were received from the aircraft and aircraft carried out a number of fruitless searches. News was finally received from a German broadcast on 5 September, which revealed that the Sunderland had been shot down by an Italian submarine and the crew taken prisoner. The *Delfino*, captained by CC d'Cerrioni was damaged by F/L Brand's attack.

PART TIME FLIGHT ENGINEER

J Cantley trained as a Flight Mechanic and, after serving in Bomber Command, was posted to 230 Sqn at Aboukir.

"I caught up with them at Aboukir Bay (one of Nelson's victories) and sometimes helped out as Flt Eng (2/6d a day and one had to wear stripes in case one was shot down). It was at Aboukir that I had my first bit of bad luck. The engines had to be serviced daily and parts had to be taken ashore for repair or rebuild. The Sunderlands were fitted with Hercules III's and had extra booster controls which required a little extra care. On one occasion I had to remove these controls to replace some and repair. I had removed all eight and wrote so in the Form 700. I had fixed two engines and was fixing the rest ashore when I heard the sound of engines running. Lo and behold, some clot was attempting to take off (nuff said). Years later I met this clot at a RAFA Club where he was relating his 'wizard prang'!

J Cantley

The squadron was able to take some measure of revenge for the loss of F/L Brand and his crew on 9 August. Sunderland L2161:Y, flown by F/L Milligan, was on an unsuccessful search for a Wellington dinghy when he sighted and engaged a Dornier 24 which was patrolling the area. After two engagements, each lasting five minute, the Dornier withdrew to the north. Milligan assessed the Dornier to have been seriously damaged and that it may not have reached its base.

By 12 August the situation at Tobruk was beginning to improve with a partial relief operation by sea assisting the besieged Australians. On 16 August the Yugoslav Dorniers, which had been mainly involved in coastal patrols and radar calibration flew three sorties searching for a missing Swordfish, with no success. The search continued the next day but was called off when it was reported that the Swordfish had landed in the desert. Two days later Sunderland N9029:V took off from Aboukir, piloted by F/L Hughes to search for an aircraft reported to have crashed in the sea off Baltin. Once again the search was fruitless. A Yugoslav Dornier also carried out a search for the missing aircraft but also had no success. 25 August saw the Yugoslavs out again searching for a missing aircraft. This time it was a Beaufighter. The search continued into the next day. They also searched for a German aircraft reported shot down in the sea. Later the same day Dornier 311, piloted by Vod Korosa force landed on the sea at 1700 hrs. Sunderland L2160:X was airborne fifty minutes later to search for the missing Dornier but had no success. A destroyer picked up the Dornier crew at 2150 hrs that night. The following day the Yugoslavs continued to search for the missing Dornier, which was thought to be still afloat but had no success.

On the second anniversary of the outbreak of war the Yugoslavs were out searching for a Wellington crew in a dinghy but, once again, they had no success. On 10 September they searched unsuccessfully for another ditched Wellington. There were several searches for reported enemy submarines throughout the month but none were found. The Sunderlands were still heavily involved in the resupply of Malta during the month and on 24 September a new threat entered the arena when the first German U-boat entered the Mediterranean. On the last day of September T9050:Y crashed on landing at Aboukir.

October saw a change of command for the squadron when Sunderland 3987:W arrived from the UK with the new CO W/Cdr Collins on board. On the 11th Dorniers 308 and 312 were carrying out a search for a Blenheim when 312 had to force land in the sea 18 miles west of Dekheila. Dornier 307 was sent out and circled the position of 312 whilst the crew of a destroyer picked up 312" crew. By this time the Dornier was sinking. Meanwhile Dorniers 308 and 309 continued the search for the Blenheim, but it was not found.

On 12 October the Sunderlands of the squadron began a shadowing operation, keeping track of a group of enemy warships. N9029:V was the first aircraft to detect the warships using ASV. They were identified as two cruisers and two destroyers steaming south-east at 16 knots. A further destroyer was also located heading in the same direction at a similar speed. On the 13th F/L Hughes took N9029:V out again on a repeat of the previous day's shadowing and sighted two destroyers followed shortly after by a further two destroyers and then two cruisers and three destroyers. This large force was steaming east south-east at 15 knots. These sightings were followed by a further sighting of another force of four ships but due to the darkness it was unclear as to whether they were destroyers or cruisers. The course speed and position of all of these vessels was reported.

On 14 October the Dorniers were out in force when 306, 307 and 309 made a parallel search along the Egyptian coast from Ras el Kanais to Ras el Rum for a missing Blenheim. The bomber was not found. Three days later the Sunderlands began a search for an enemy submarine. First off was T9071:M at 0445 hrs. N9029:V took over the search mid-morning and was relieved by T9071:M again just after 1044hrs. Two hours later N9029:V was back on station but the 23 hour search found nothing.

The monotony of hours of anti-submarine patrol day after day with nothing to report was finally broken on 22 October when Sunderland W3987:X (previously coded W) located a submarine at 1557 hrs. It was first sighted breaking the surface two miles on the port bow. The Sunderland delivered a quarter attack dropping two bombs from 300 feet and firing guns simultaneously. Flame floats were dropped to mark the position but turning for a second attack the crew found the submarine had submerged. More flares were dropped and a further attack was carried out but no results were observed.

November 1941 was a bad month for the Royal Navy with *HMS Ark Royal* torpedoed off Gibraltar by U-81 on the 13th, sinking the next day. The Sunderlands and Dorniers were kept busy searching for reported enemy shipping and submarines and on 18 November, the day the British launched Operation Crusader, the offensive in Libya, Sunderland W3987:X was carrying out a patrol between Alexandria and Ishmalia Rocks, ten miles off the coast. The radar operator picked up an ASV plot at a range of six miles on the port bow and the Sunderland turned to investigate. At 2132 hrs a flare was dropped over the target and it revealed a submarine on the surface, proceeding on a northerly course. As a second flare ignited the submarine was observed crash-diving. The Sunderland was not able to manoeuvre into a favourable attack position before the submarine disappeared. An effort was made to relocate the submarine, which the crew thought might have re-surfaced, by firing machine gun bursts at an estimated position, but this proved to be unproductive.

On 25 November Rommel broke out in Libya and attacked the 8th Army in the rear. The following day the squadron was tasked with locating enemy surface vessels trying to transport fuel to Derna for Rommel. F/L Milligan searched in T9071:M without success. The Sunderlands and Dorniers were kept busy for the rest of the month with surface vessel and anti-submarine patrols. The last action of the month came on the 29th when F/L Bohm took T9050:Y out to search for two Italian destroyers. The destroyers were found just after midday and later over Navarin harbour Bohm encountered heavy anti-aircraft fire and machine gun fire sustaining one bullet hole to the Sunderland.

Looking forward into the cockpit of a Squadron Sunderland.

Squadron maintenance staff pose for a picture, Egypt, 1941. (W Squires)

> LONDON GAZETTE – 4 NOVEMBER 1941
>
> SCARTH, William Gillyard, Sergeant (519821)
> No 230 Squadron - Distinguished Flying Medal
>
> This airman displayed exceptional keenness and devotion to duty during an evacuation flight from Yugoslavia to Greece, in adverse conditions, and during several evacuation flights from Greece. Sergeant Scarth was also a member of the crew of an aircraft which carried out a reconnaissance for the Fleet. This flight was of great assistance as three destroyers and three cruisers of the Italian Navy were located.

December opened with more action for F/L Bohm on the 1st. Flying T9050:Y he encountered two destroyers and a number of other vessels on an anti-submarine patrol between Ras el Tin and Ras Assaz. The ships opened fire on the Sunderland but scored no hits. December was to be another turning point in the war, which was to become truly global. On the 2nd the Germans were only five miles from the Kremlin and it appeared the Russian campaign was all but over.

Squadron Store's staff at Aboukir in 1941. (Watson via JA Wilson).

Five days later on 7 December Japan attacked Pearl Harbour, Malaya, Shanghai, Hong Kong and Thailand. On 10 December the siege of Tobruk finally came to an end but further bad news was received when the Japanese sank the battleships *HMS Prince of Wales* and *Repulse*. The following day Italy and Germany declared war on the USA and the USA declared war in return. By the 17th Rommel was again on the retreat from the Gazala area of Libya in the seesaw North African campaign. Two days later the British recaptured Derna.

On 22 December the Yugoslavs sent out a Dornier, 307, flown by F/S Pishpok on an anti-submarine patrol from Alexandria harbour to Damietta. Fifteen miles north of Rosetta a ship was sighted and on closing with it the ship opened fire with small calibre cannon. One shell burst under the gunner's cockpit, injuring the gunner's legs and Pishpok was forced to return to base.

On the same day F/L Hughes left Aboukir for Malta in Sunderland T9071:M loaded with passengers and freight. En route he was attacked by enemy fighters and force landed five mile north west of Ras Aamr. F/O BEL Odhams, one of the air gunners, would die two days later of wounds received during the engagement.

The following appeared in 'Parade', a service newsletter available in North Africa during the war.

SHOT DOWN!

A remarkable series of events followed an attack by two Messerschmitts on a Sunderland flying-boat of the Royal Air Force over the Mediterranean on December 22nd.

The encounter with the enemy was brief. One of the Messerschmitts was shot down and the other was damaged and made off. During the battle, however, the starboard engines of the flying-boat were hit and ceased to function. One of the passengers in the aircraft was killed and one of the gunners badly wounded.

Land was in sight but the Sunderland lost height rapidly. A forced landing in the rough seas was made. The aircraft ricocheted twice, bounced from the water to a height of fifty feet for the first time, and then finally came to rest. The ailerons were damaged and one of the floats broke off.

Yet the Sunderland remained afloat for two and a half hours, and fortunately, was blown towards land by a strong north-west wind. Morphia was administered to the badly wounded man. Finally it was decided to leave the rapidly breaking up flying-boat and to attempt to swim the remaining distance to shore. In all there were twenty on board. The wounded man was put in the only serviceable dinghy and, two at a time; the other slid down the wing into the sea. The second pilot was nearly drowned as a strong undertow carried him away, but the captain, a strong swimmer, dragged him to safety. Eventually all got ashore.

It was midday. They discovered themselves on a rocky beach and estimated their position to be just west of Apollonia. Suddenly from behind a wall of rocks there appeared about twenty armed Italian soldiers. The captain of the aircraft went forward to surrender as his party was without arms. To his astonishment the nearest Italian raised his rifle above his head and threw it away. He advanced with outstretched hands.

It was an unusual situation and the British party had not quite recovered from seeing the Italians behave as friends when another group of Italians arrived. This time there were about eighty. These were more aggressive and formally declared the British party to be their prisoners.

A stretcher was made of oars from the dinghy for the wounded man and in a long procession the mixed band started off along the coast. Three of the airmen had lost their boots. It was raining and vivid streaks of lightning lit up a leaden sky. Night came and with it small comfort. There were no blankets and the provisions had been stolen. The wounded man suffered in silence. No fires were allowed because the Italians feared Arab sharpshooters.

With the dawn, another start was made. Suddenly twenty Italian officers ran forward from a cluster of bushes. The Germans, they said, had taken their vehicles and had told them to go to safety as best they could. So disturbed were they that they actually proposed to the leader of the British party that an agreement should be reached whereby, in exchange for their help, they should receive favoured treatment in the event of their capture by the English.

Once again the party was increased in number. This time by an Italian major, with about fifty men. He was a strange fellow, middle-aged, with a face as lined and sun tanned as an old boot. He carried a cat o' nine tails at his belt, presumably as a fly whisk, but he used it for its original purpose later when one of the British party indignantly announced that an Italian soldier had stolen the wounded man's flying boots. The thief was flogged in front of his comrades.

Later that day the wounded man died and the major conducted a military burial and sobbed as the body was lowered into the grave.

In due course the band arrived at the Arab village of El Hamia. There they were given macaroni and a lot of coffee. Three eggs were bartered for a two-shilling piece and a wristwatch, and it required an Egyptian pound to purchase a bag of dates. One of the Royal Air Force officers whispered to an Arab that if he could get a note delivered to the British forces not more than fifteen miles away a reward would be forthcoming. The Arab agreed and slid off into the darkness.

The morning brought another unusual situation. The strange major sent for the RAF leader and said he proposed to leave for Benghazi. The question arose as to who actually held the town and they had a bet on it. Finally, the major decided that he would leave with his men allowing the British to remain with the Arabs. He even offered to leave rifles as protection.

The end of this remarkable story is the most astonishing thing of all. After having travelled for an hour the party overtook some of the Italian major's men. One of them ran over to the group, drew his bayonet, propped it on a rock and started to jump on it till it snapped. There were some two dozen Italians. Each one threw away his rifle or handed it over and then joyfully joined in the procession. Similar incidents happened on four occasions and after three hours the company was more than a hundred strong.

In due course the British lines were reached and the young New Zealand flight lieutenant who had led his men through so many trials handed over his prisoners.

Signalling to shore with the Aldis lamp, the crew hopes for rescue. (W Squires).

The crippled Sunderland flops in the Mediterranean, its load of twenty men at the mercy of the wind, but it is happily blowing landwards. (W Squires).

The crew of the crippled Sunderland sitting on the wing as the aircraft drifts. (W Squires).

The wounded air gunner is put in one of the two dinghies left serviceable to be pushed ashore. The other dinghy is used for emergency rations, water and food. (W Squires).

Having made it ashore they were followed soon afterwards by the drifting Sunderland, which began to break up. The officer holding his head was injured whilst negotiating the rocks coming ashore. (W Squires).

The Italians arrived and the intrepid photographer continued to record the event. (W Squires).

The Sunderland finally broke its back on the rocks. (W Squires).

Sunderland T9071 beached and breaking up near Appolonia. (W Squires).

The first party of Italians arrives and a stretcher is improvised for the wounded air gunner. (W Squires).

Two officers drink from a pool of rainwater. The dog accompanied them throughout the adventure. (W Squires).

On the third day of their march the Italians left and the British party set out for British lines. They were soon joined by Italian stragglers. (W Squires).

The Italians threw away their weapons and marched to captivity with the British party. (W Squires).

The group in the village of El Hania with their guide and some local Arabs. (W Squires).

Christmas Day 1941 saw the fall of Hong Kong, but not all of the news was bad as British troops retook Benghazi the same day. On 28 December F/L Milligan, flying Sunderland N9029:V left Aboukir to sweep ahead of a convoy and its escorts for submarines. At 1005 hrs, having escorted the convoy of just over an hour, Milligan observed anti aircraft fire from the convoy and two twin engined aircraft, possibly Ju 88s. Three hours later aircraft again attacked the convoy and *HMS Ajax* was seen to drop astern. *Ajax* later regained its original position. Milligan remained with the convoy for several hours before returning to Aboukir. F/L Bohm in T9050:Y carried out the last anti-submarine patrol of the year on 31 December between Bardia and Alexandria. He landed at Aboukir at 1040 hrs with nothing to report.

Christmas Dinner menu, Aboukir 1941.

4. Mediterranean Missions
January 1942 – December 1942

The first week of 1942 was a routine one for the squadron with a succession of anti-submarine patrols, convoy escorts and coastal patrols by the Yugoslav Dorniers being carried out. The first action of the year occurred when S/Ldr Garside took off from Aboukir on 9 January in W3987:X for an anti submarine patrol. The ASV operator reported a plot at six miles on the port beam and Garside turned towards it. He spotted a submarine two miles ahead with its conning tower just visible. It was only a fleeting glimpse as the submarine quickly submerged. Garside dropped three DCs, which straddled the spot. Flame floats were then dropped to mark the position. A second attack was made, this time dropping four 250lb anti-submarine bombs. A huge bubble appeared on the surface and on a fourth run over the area a huge patch of oil and bubbles was seen. The submarine, type VIIC U577, captained by Kptn Lt Herbert Schanenberg was sunk north west of Mersa Matruh. At the time it was thought the submarine might have some sort of early warning device as the visibility was poor and the camouflaged Sunderland had approached from upwind.

The following day Sunderland W3987:X was on patrol again but had no success in the extremely poor visibility caused by a sandstorm. The crew were pleased to observe though that the ASV equipment was working well and two aircraft, a Blenheim and a Yugoslav Dornier were picked up on it.

On 12 January Sunderland W3987:X, captained by S/Ldr Garside was tasked with carrying out an anti-submarine patrol around *HMS Kimberley*. The Sunderland arrived over *HMS Kimberley* at 0717 hrs and observed that she was steaming, down at the stern with the after deck awash, escorted by four destroyers. Garside set up a patrol of 20 miles radius and on the final leg of his search sighted a suspicious oil streak 18 miles south-east of *HMS Kimberley*. He dropped two DCs on the streak and passed the position to one of the destroyers. The Sunderland then carried out another full sweep for 20 miles around the ship with no result. Returning to the Kimberley, Garside saw she was now under tow with the escort and had air cover in the form of four Martlets. The rough seas and many white caps had made it extremely difficult to spot a submarine periscope.

The following day F/L Milligan took over the escort duty in N9029:V but other than a few oil streaks sighted no enemy activity.

On 17 January the last German garrison in Cyrenaica, Halfaya, fell to the Allies but four days later Rommel launched his second counter attack in North Africa. By the 29th he had recaptured Benghazi. Whilst these events were occurring the squadron sent S/Ldr Williams out on anti submarine patrol in T9050:Y on the 22nd. During the patrol an enemy aircraft with white markings between the cockpit and tail was sighted but it did not see the Sunderland which was positioned up sun from it. Shortly afterwards a submarine was spotted, which dived giving off yellow smoke. The submarine surfaced twelve minutes later and was found to be friendly. Two days later F/L Milligan in N9029:V sighted an oil streak, one and a half-mile long, on the surface. A flame float was dropped and this was followed by a 250-lb AS bomb. No results were observed from this attack.

Yugoslav Dornier.

On 25 January S/Ldr Williams was carrying out an anti-submarine patrol ahead of Force 'B' when he spotted a semi-submerged lifeboat. Reporting this to the convoy leader he continued on his patrol. Shortly afterwards a long streak of oil was seen followed by a liferaft containing one man. This was reported to the convoy and a destroyer was detached to pick up the survivor. The following day the Yugoslavs sent out the Rogozarski Sim XIV on a rare patrol, but no enemy were sighted by this floatplane. Two days later S/Ldr Garside was provided with an example of naval aircraft recognition when he took W3987:X out to escort a convoy. On approaching the convoy from down sun and firing the appropriate signal colour the convoy opened fire with its AA guns. Garside contacted the convoy by W/t and R/t and the firing ceased. He then continued with his patrol. Returning from this patrol at 1725 hrs the crew sighted a submarine on the surface two miles on the starboard bow. Garside made a diving attack along the track of the submarine and dropped one AS bomb, which fell 15 yards short. The submarine remained on the surface and turned hard to port before crash-diving. Judging the submarines position from the first bomb burst and allowing for the bombing error, Garside made a low-level attack dropping three DCs. A third attack was made dropping a further three DCs and shortly afterward oil appeared in the depth charge swirls. Unfortunately the results could not be confirmed due to the poor night visibility. The submarine was assessed as damaged.

On 29 January F/L Milligan in N9029:V was on the receiving end of more poor aircraft recognition when on an anti submarine patrol. Just after 100 hrs the tail gunner fired a short burst at a fighter aircraft, which had dived at the Sunderland. After breaking away the fighter flew at right angles to the Sunderland and was identified as a Royal Navy Fulmar. On the same day S/Ldr Garside was on patrol in Sunderland W3987:X when the ASV operator picked up a plot at a range of six miles. At 2.5 miles visual contact was obtained and the contact was identified as a submarine on the surface. Garside positioned his aircraft to attack and dropped eight 250lb bombs from a dive. The submarine did not attempt to dive and it is probable that, with a strong wind and the moon obscured and running in heavy seas, it neither heard nor saw the Sunderland until it was too late. Part of the stick of bombs straddled the conning tower and after the spray had subsided the submarine had momentarily disappeared. A second or two later the stern was seen to rise vertically out of the water and then slide out of sight. An oil patch appeared and spread over the surface for about 400 yards. Garside circled the spot and fired Verey cartridges to attract the attention of a destroyer, which was in the area.

The attack and destruction of the submarine was reported back to base. Two days later S/Ldr Garside had more luck. Again in W3987:X on an anti-submarine patrol the ASV picked up a plot at 2.5 miles range. Turning south the aircraft homed on the target and visual contact was made at two miles. It was a submarine on the surface proceeding west. Garside used his previously successful dive bombing attack to drop eight 250lb bombs in a stick. Unfortunately four of them failed to release. The remaining four overshot the target by 15-20 yards. As Garside circled the diving submarine the gunners opened fire on it and Garside made a second attack in an attempt to get the bombs to come off the racks. The gunners were pouring accurate fire at the submarine and many hits were observed. After the bombs had dropped the submarine returned fire with its cannons then crash-dived and was not seen again. The submarine scored no hits on Garside's Sunderland. A few minutes later another ASV plot was obtained six miles due south and the Sunderland homed to it. A head on collision with a Swordfish was narrowly avoided. The Swordfish had been simultaneously homing on the Sunderland! Garside signalled details of the attack to the Swordfish, which then made its way to the position and carried out a depth charge attack on the flame floats left by the Sunderland.

The month of February brought tragedy to the Yugoslavs when Rogazarski Sim XIV, 157, went out on an anti-submarine patrol on the 2nd. The aircraft was patrolling off Ras el Tin when it reported to base that it was caught in a sand-storm. The aircraft crashed into the sea and the pilot and wireless operator were killed. The observer managed to swim ashore. The following day S/Ldr Williams took T9050:Y out on patrol and found the wreck of merchant vessel forty miles from the coast. Some time later he sighted the wreckage of a Wellington, coded 'P' on the beach at the waters edge with a rubber dinghy close by. On 6 February S/Ldr Garside, again in W3987:X, picked up an ASV plot on the starboard beam. Visual contact with the target was made at 2 miles and it was a submarine on the surface. Garside made a diving attack dropping eight 250lb AS bombs while his gunners opened fire on the submarine during and after the dive. The submarine did not return fire. The submarine had made no attempt to crash dive and the bombs straddled the centre section. After the spray from the bomb blast subsided the submarine was observed to have completely broken up. The disconnected sections were briefly observed showing above the surface but the wreckage quickly sank and oil began to spread over the surface. Garside was having a very successful run of luck.

The following day his crew sighted another submarine on the surface at a range of only 0.5 miles. Before Garside could position to attack the submarine crash-dived and due to the poor visibility he decided against an attack. Just over an hour later another ASV plot was obtained four miles on the port bow. The U-boat had resurfaced and visual contact was made at 1 mile. Garside dived the Sunderland to attack from the port bow to the starboard quarter releasing eight 250lb bombs. The last bomb of the stick landed just by the U-boats stern and it turned to port and crash-dived. A very distinct yellow streak was trailed behind it. At dawn Garside returned to the attack position but nothing was sighted. Yet another ASV plot was obtained and the target identified as a submarine on the surface. With all of his bombs expended Garside dived to attack and the gunners opened fire on the submarine. The tracer and armour piercing rounds were seen to ricochet off the submarine hull. The submarine made no attempt to dive until after the attack.

On 14 February a Yugoslav Dornier on an anti-submarine patrol between Alexandria Harbour and Damietta sighted a Sunderland, a Catalina and a dinghy all on the surface. This turned out to be a Russian Catalina, which had been allocated to No 230 Sqn. The Catalina was being escorted by S/Ldr Garside in Sunderland N9029:V when it had to force land with engine trouble. Garside laded alongside and made two unsuccessful attempts to tow the Catalina into Aboukir. He then took off and returned to base and a launch was despatched to find the Catalina and tow it into Aboukir.

The Sunderlands and Dorniers continued to patrol daily and on 22 February S/Ldr Williams had some poor luck. Flying T9050:Y he attacked some foam on the surface with four bombs. On investigation the foam turned out to be over some semi-submerged rocks. Later an enemy submarine was sighted but he was unable to attack. A short while later he returned to the submarines last known position and searched for 40 mins with no success.

During March 1942 the squadron continued to regularly fly personnel and supplies into and out of Malta during the battle for that beleaguered island. The lifeline provided by the squadron was important to the survival of the island, as were the efforts of the Royal Navy, who fought a three day running battle, beginning on 22 March, successfully beating off air and naval attacks on a crucial resupply convoy. By 25 March Malta had suffered 1,600 air raids. The squadron kept flying in. Often the Sunderlands had to turn back either due to the failure of the fighter escort to arrive or on instructions from Malta itself. F/L Brown attempted to get to Malta with passengers and freight on the 12th in T9050:Y but the Beaufighter escort was late and he returned to base. Two days later he tried again but was turned back on instructions from Malta. S/Ldr Williams had more success on the 20th, returning to base the next day.

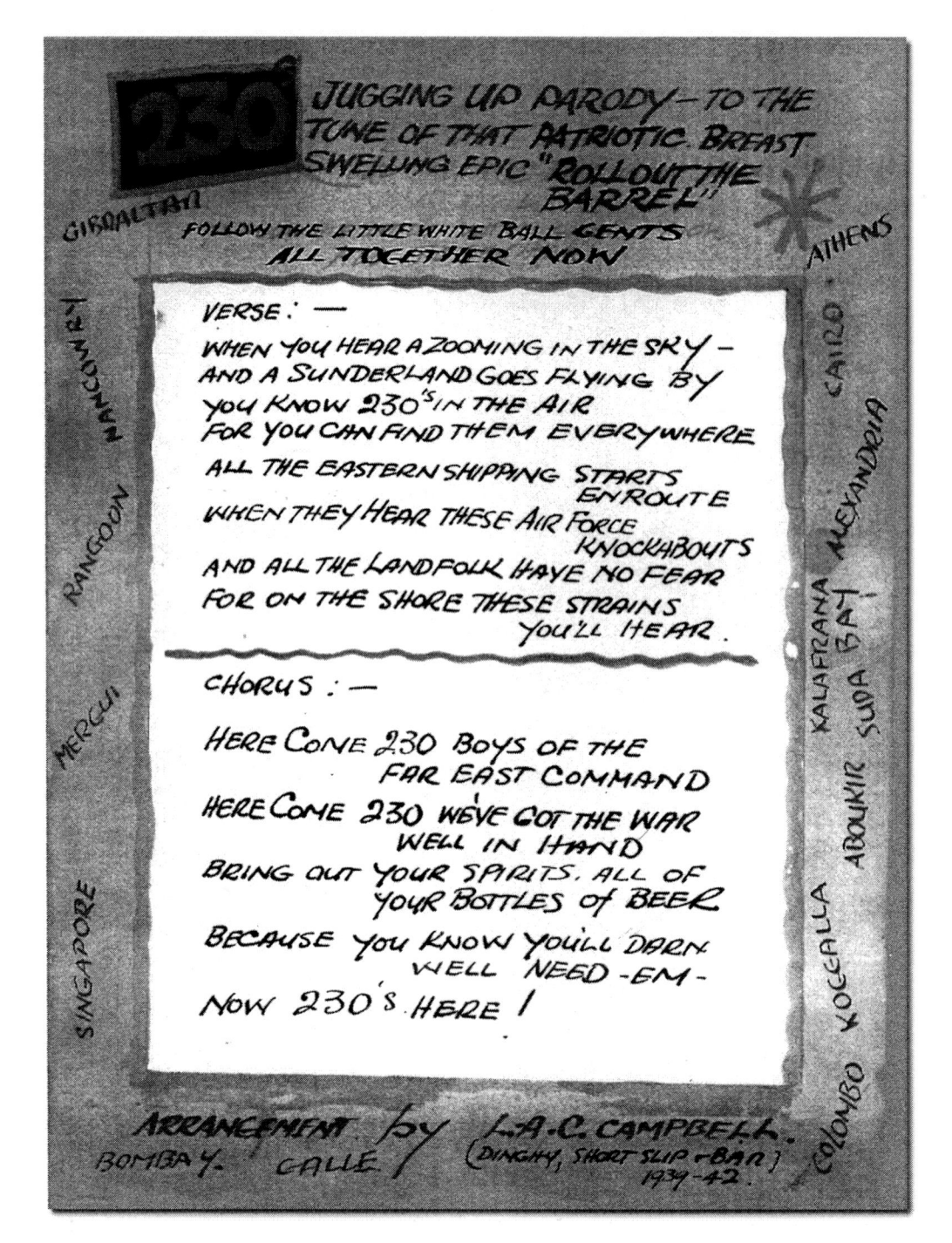

The Squadron song composed by LAC Campbell.

230 IN THE MED 1940-1942

1
OUR FRIEND MUSSO MADE ON MISTAKE HE THOUGHT 230 WERE ON KOGGALA LAKE NEVER DREAMED THEY WERE IN THE MED. FLYING WHERE ANGELS FEARED TO TREAD.

2
HE GOT CIANO ON THE PHONE, HOW BOUT MY ICE CREAM CONE, CIANO SAID "GET GUNS INSTEAD 230'S IN THE MED."

3
TWAS A SUNNY DAY FROM ICE CREAM SHORES. THAT "ITEY" PATROLS TOOK OFF IN FOURS, SHOOT TO KILL OLD MUSSO SAID. SO OFF THEY WENT TO CLEAR THE MED.

4
NOW ONE LONE KITE WAS IN THE SKY. "PIECE OF CAKE" THOUGHT THE ITEY. DOWN THEY SWOOPED TO MAKE THE KILL, BUT OVERLOOKED 230's SKILL.

5
THEY FOUND MUCH TO THEIR SURPRISE, NOT A CREW OF "ROOKS", BUT REAL "OLD SWEATS" ONE RAKE FROM TURRET BROWN, A GREASY "ITEY" WENT HURTLING DOWN THEN THREE JUST TURNED AND FLED, THEY KNEW 230 WERE IN THE MED.

6
AN "ITEY" SUB WAS ON PATROL, MIGHT WELL HAVE BEEN ON THE DOLE, A 230 KITE WAS FLYING BY, WAITING TO BLOW SUBS SKY HIGH.

7
TWO BOMBS WERE DROPPED, NOW WHO COULD GUESS, WHETHER THAT SUB WENT EAST OR WEST, TWAS BUT ANOTHER TO MAKE THE ITIES DREAD, THE DAY 230 HIT THE MED.

8
BOMBING RAIDS CAME AND WENT, BUT 230'S SKILL A FORCE UNSPENT NOT ONE HIT DID THE ITIES SCORE BUT MADE OUR BOATGUARDS RATHER A BORE.

9
THE C.O. WAS OF EASTERN FAME. GEOF FRANCIS WAS HIS NAME, HE JUST KNEW WHEN AND WHAT TO DO EVEN TO MUCKING IN ON THE BULLY STEW

10
NO TIGER BEER OR TIGER BALM, SOME SAID OUR TIGER WOULD TURN CALM. BUT, AS YOU SEE, HIS CLAWS WERE SHARP. JUST ASK THOSE "ITIES" WITH THE HARP.

Another 'ditty' composed by LAC Campbell.

On 22 March F/L Milligan set out from Aboukir on an anti-submarine patrol in Sunderland L5806: Q. During the patrol he sighted a Fiat BR20 fighter but it did not come to fight. At 1314 hrs a submarine was sighted on the surface which dived one minute later. The Sunderland reached the diving position just over three minutes later but the crew could see no sign of the submarine in the poor visibility. Two days later Milligan was escorting the Fleet towards Alexandria and was on station five miles ahead of it when enemy aircraft attacked. The crew observed a cruiser firing its guns and the escorting Beaufighters broke of to investigate the raid. The Fleet reached Alexandria harbour and Milligan returned to base.

F/L Milligan was on patrol again, in L5806:Q, on 27 March. At 0710 hrs an oil patch was sighted off the port bow, eight miles away. Milligan altered course toward it and when he was almost on top of the oil patch a periscope feather was sighted. Milligan quickly turned to port to come round into an attack position and made an attack at right angles to the submarine's track. In a diving attack Milligan dropped two 250lb AS bombs set to a depth of 60ft. He aimed slightly ahead of the position where the periscope had been seen to disappear. A second attack was carried out with two more 250lb AS bombs set for 100ft, again at right angle to the mean track of the submarine. The attacks produced considerable disturbance of the surface and oil was seen by the rear gunner spreading between the original oil patch and the explosion swirls.

On the same day S/Ldr Garside left Aboukir, mid-afternoon, to carry out an anti submarine patrol. At 1703 hrs both visual and ASV contacts were made simultaneously with a submarine on the surface with its decks awash. Garside made a steep diving attack as the submarine crash-dived. At the moment of attack the conning tower was still visible and Garside's bombs fell from 600 feet around the submarine. Six of the eight 250lb AS bombs appeared to be direct hits and a large patch of oil appeared on the surface after the bomb burst had subsided. The submarine was assessed to have been destroyed. Garside attempted to land on the attack position but the swell was considered too heavy and he returned to base. S/Ldr Garside was out on patrol again later that day in W3987:X when his ASV operator picked up a contact three miles off the starboard beam. Garside homed to the target and visual contact was made with a submarine at less than one mile on the port beam. Garside attempted a turning, diving attack but he was unable to gain an attack position due to the steep angle. Dropping flame floats to mark the position he turned away to reposition for another attack. The submarine commenced a crash-dive. Garside made a low-level attack at 400 feet from the starboard beam and dropped a stick of seven 250lb AS bombs which straddled the white foam of the diving area. This was the largest enemy submarine Garside had encountered and he assessed it as only slightly damaged by the attack.

HRH The Duke of Gloucester visited the Squadron at Aboukir Bay in April 1942 to present decorations for the evacuations of Greece and Crete. (Watson via JA Wilson).

F/L Milligan was on patrol again in the early hours of 28 March. A large raft like object was sighted and Milligan dropped a flame float and sea marker. Very close to this they sighted a submarine periscope but were not in a position to attack. Leaving the target Milligan continued his patrol before returning to Aboukir. Milligan had better luck the following night when he encountered a submarine 200 yards ahead. Passing overhead he dropped a flame float and turned to attack. He dive bombed the submarine at right angle to its course and dropped three 250lb DCs in a stick. The midships and turret gunners reported that the DCs had burst ten yards ahead of the swirl of the submerging periscope. The gunners also attacked the submarine with their machine guns. No results were observed from the last action of the month.

The first weeks of April were fairly routine for the squadron with a number of convoy escorts and anti-submarine patrols being carried out. On the day Malta received its George Cross from King George VI, 15 April, the squadron received a new aircraft, W4021, from the UK. This was followed by W4022 the next day. On 19 April F/L Squires, in Sunderland W3987:X, sighted a submarine to starboard at a range of five miles. The submarine crash-dived as the Sunderland attacked and Squires dropped eight 250lb DC". The submarine was assessed as damaged and the Sunderland itself received slight damage from splinters thrown up by the explosions.

The Squadron on parade for the visit.

The Squadron rugby XV during the 1941/2 season at Aboukir. (Watson via JA Wilson).

On 22 April F/L Milligan sighted two submarines but on both occasions was not in a position to attack. However, F/L Brown, in T9050:Y did sight a submarine on the surface and made an attack dropping three 250lb DCs which possibly damaged the submarine. The following day Milligan was on patrol again in W4022:Z. Locating a submarine with the ASV he made an attack and dropped a single DC. No results were observed. Three days later, on 26 April, Milligan was involved in a 'friendly fire' incident when he attacked a target ten miles off the Palestinian coast. The suspected U-boat turned out to be a friendly motor launch, which was not notified as being in the area on the intelligence summary.

F/L Frame took Sunderland T9050:Y out on patrol on 28 April and found an enemy submarine on the surface in the Gulf of Sollum. He attacked from the port quarter to the starboard bow with four 250lb DCs spaced at 40ft intervals. After the explosions had subsided a large circular oil patch appeared and began to spread. White patches on the surface, presumed to be air bubbles, were seen fifteen minutes later and the submarine was thought to be destroyed.

May 1942 began well for the squadron with an attack by P/O Howell on a submarine. Howell was the captain of L5806:Q carrying out a close patrol around convoy 'Master' when a medium sized submarine was sighted in the moon lane about 30 miles astern of the convoy. Howell carried out an attack from the starboard quarter to the port bow dropping two 250lb AS bombs which exploded five to ten yards off the submarines starboard bow. The submarine appeared to slow and come completely to the surface and Howell pressed home a second attack. This time he dropped two 250lb AS bombs and four 250lb DCs in a salvo which fell alongside the starboard side of the submarine. The submarine came to a halt and slowly sank. During both attacks the Sunderland's gunner's machine-gunned the submarine. As it sank thick oil came to the surface and gradually spread out. The submarine was assessed as probably destroyed.

On 11 May F/L Frame was providing anti-submarine protection for two destroyers when several ASV plots were picked up. These turned out to be ships approaching to assist the destroyers, which were disabled. Another ASV plot was soon obtained and a submarine was found on the surface by firing illuminating cartridges from the Sunderland. Frame commenced a steep turn to attack and dropped four 250lb AS bombs on the target in the turn. The midships gunner also opened fire in the turn before the submarine disappeared. The Sunderland circled the area for nearly half an hour but no results were observed. The squadrons Sunderlands could not hope to protect every ship in the Mediterranean though and on this day the Royal Navy lost three destroyers, *HMS Jackal, Kipling* and *Lively* to Luftwaffe attack south of Crete. On the 16th Frame was airborne in W4022:Z and after investigating several ASV plots managed to get a firm fix on one. Illuminating the area with a parachute flare and two illuminating cartridges the crew sighted a submarine. Frame turned to attack but the submarine had disappeared.

On 21 May the inhabitants of Malta were able to breathe a sigh of relief when Hitler postponed the invasion of the courageous island indefinitely.

On the day that the Battle of Gazala opened with Rommel's third counter offensive in North Africa the recently promoted W/Cdr Garside was on anti-submarine patrol in W3987:X on 26 May and obtained an ASV plot at 1927 hrs four miles on the starboard beam. This turned out to be a submarine on the surface which he attacked with four 250lb AS bombs, with flash bombs attached, and four 250lb DCs set at 50 ft depth. Sgt Adamson, the rear gunner, and Cpl Atkinson, positioned in the astrodome, both saw the bombs hit the conning tower and the DCs landing just ahead of it. After the smoke and spray had subsided no further trace of the submarine was sighted. The new flash bombs fitted to the AS bombs greatly assisted in observing the results and Garside stated that they lit up he whole area. The U-boat was considered destroyed. Almost immediately three airborne ASV plots were picked up. These were probably on a protective patrol for the submarine and circled the area dropping flares Garside remained in the area for another ten minutes evading the enemy aircraft before resuming his patrol.

On 28 May F/O Howell was patrolling in L5806:Q when an enemy submarine was sighted crash-diving on the port bow. Howell attacked with four 250lb AS bombs and four 250lb DCs and a large explosion was seen causing a large waterspout ahead of the wake of the U-boat. A large patch of oil and foam, 100 yards in diameter appeared and the submarine was assessed as possibly damaged. By 29 May Rommel had swept around the Allied lines and thrust towards Tobruk with 560 tanks. Only 25 miles from Tobruk the tank battle raged on in the desert as the squadron patrolled the seas. On the last day of the month Sunderland W4023:U, captained by F/L Squires was patrolling five miles off the coast when an ASV plot was picked up at 1920 hrs. Squires turned to port and the front gunner sighted an object at a range of 1.5 miles on the port bow. Flying closer it soon proved to be a U-boat in the act of diving. Squires circled the area but nothing further was seen.

On 1 June 1942, while German tanks were wiping out the 150th Brigade in Libya, the squadron received two signals notifying the award of the DFC to W/Cdr Garside and F/L Milligan. The next day F/O Pare, piloting W4022:Z picked up an ASV plot at 1930hrs. A few hours later a second plot was picked up and he turned to investigate. This turned out to be a submarine in the process of submerging. It was lost to sight soon afterward and though further plots were picked up later on the patrol nothing further was seen.

The middle weeks of June 1942 were very bad for the allied forces in the Mediterranean and North Africa. Between the 11th and 16th two convoys, 'Harpoon' and 'Vigorous' attempted to relieve Malta and failed with heavy losses. On the 13th British forces were caught in a disastrous ambush at El Adem and by the 17th Tobruk was once again under siege. Tobruk would fall on the 21st and by the 24th the Germans had advance into Egypt following the retreating British forces. On 26 June Rommel, now a Field Marshal, attacked Mersa Matruh and three days later took the town. Once again Alexandria came in range of the Axis bombers and was bombed on 29 June.

Whilst these disastrous events were occurring the squadron was busy hunting submarines and providing convoy escorts. In the early hours of 14 June P/O Finch, in Sunderland L5806:Q sighted a submarine at a range of six miles. No attack was made as the submarine had crash-dived before the aircraft could reach it. On 18 June S/Ldr Williams took W4021:W out on anti-ship patrol and at 1912 hrs sighted an enemy destroyer steaming north-east.

LONDON GAZETTE – 2 JUNE 1942

GARSIDE, W/C Kenneth Vernon (36107)
No 230 Squadron – Distinguished Flying Cross

This officer has served with the squadron for the past 2-½ years. He has completed a large number of sorties, including attacks on enemy submarines at night. It is probable that three were destroyed and the others damaged. In one of these attacks, his aircraft came under the enemy's machine gun fire whilst flying at low level. Squadron Leader Garside has performed much valuable work both operationally and in the training of new pilots.

He shadowed the destroyer for over an hour before making an attack with eight 250lb GP bombs which fell fifty to one hundred yards astern of the destroyer. Williams broke away and continued his patrol but had to return to base with engine trouble. The next day F/L Squires was carrying out a convoy escort in W4023:U when an ASV plot was picked up at 0222 hrs. The possible wake of a submarine was sighted on the port bow and one minute later Squires dropped flame floats on the position. Firing white Verey cartridges and signalling the escorting cruiser he remained over the position until two destroyers from the convoy arrived to investigate. He then set course for base due to shortage of fuel. On the last day of the month P/O Finch, in L5806:Q, was escorting a convoy between Alexandria and Haifa when he came across an area of sea strewn with wreckage and oil

---

LONDON GAZETTE - 2 JUNE 1942

MILLIGAN, F/L David Neville (40553)
No 230 Squadron – Distinguished Flying Cross

This officer is a most courageous and determined pilot. He has completed a large number of sorties, and on three occasions when his flying boat developed engine failure, his superb airmanship was responsible for the safe return of his aircraft and its passengers. On the first occasion, one of the engines shed its propeller and then caught fire. Although the aircraft was vibrating badly (making it impossible to read the instrument panel), and despite bad weather, Flight Lieutenant Milligan succeeded in flying his heavily laden aircraft to Kalafrana. Two days later, whilst flying to Malta, he experienced another engine failure but he succeeded in reaching Kalfrana where he made an emergency landing without the aid of a flare path. On 9th March 1942, whilst taking off from Malta during a heavy raid, a large bomb burst close to his aircraft. The explosion apparently affected the port engine cowling for, after about an hour in the air, the main cowling became partially adrift, causing the aircraft to lose height. Flight Lieutenant Milligan regained control and flew safely to Tobruk. On each of these occasions, this officer has magnificently overcome extremely severe tests.

One ships lifeboat was seen afloat and another submerged. After taking photos he returned to his convoy escort. F/L Brown had poor luck on this day when his ASV went partially u/s. Despite this he sighted a submarine but it submerged before an attack could be made. Further searches were fruitless and he returned to base.

While Rommel was trying to break through the British lines at El Alamein at the beginning of July the squadron was in the process of moving to Fanara, Kasfareet. By the 3rd the squadron move was complete, leaving only a detachment at Aboukir, and Rommel's attack was blunted. The British held on and Rommel ordered his troops to dig in after being reduced to only thirteen serviceable tanks in the final assaults on the British positions. By the 5th the Germans were on the defensive and began laying minefields along the El Alamein line.

On 6 July P/O Finch in L5806:Q sighted a submarine periscope, whilst on anti-submarine patrol. Unfortunately it submerged before he could get into a good attacking position. During the patrol he returned several times to the area and though suspicious oil streaks were sighted there was no sign of the submarine. At 1936hrs an aircraft was sighted about eight miles to the north. It was identified as a Ju 88 which, luckily, did not move south to engage the Sunderland. The next day Finch was on patrol again and after sighting large oil patches and wreckage he was ordered to investigate another area. Here he discovered another large oil patch and dropped three DCs. Nothing was seen and he returned to base.

Just after midnight on 9 July F/O Howell, flying W3987:X was patrolling an area up to 95 miles off Beirut when an ASV plot was picked up three miles on the starboard beam. The crew soon sighted a submarine on the surface but it submerged before an attack could be carried out. Shortly afterwards the Sunderlands starboard inner engine seized and Howell was forced to return to Fanara.

On 15 July the Allies attacked from the El Alamein line and three days of fierce fighting at 'Kidney Ridge' began. The New Zealanders captured over 2,00 prisoners and 115 guns. By 26 July the attack was blunted and the final Australian attack failed. The Allies went back on the defensive after taking over 7,000 prisoners. While the land battle was in progress the squadron sent Sunderland L5806:Q out on anti-submarine patrol under the command of F/O Finch. Just after 2200 hrs a single ASV plot was obtained and four minutes later was identified by its wash as a submarine. Finch dropped two flares and a flame float but was unable to reacquire the target. The following days were taken up with convoy escorts with the Sunderlands operating from Fanara and Aboukir.

On 25 July the squadron suffered its first loss for many months when Sunderland L5806:Q failed to return to base. F/L Brown and his twelve man crew had left Aboukir to carry out an anti-submarine patrol working between 10 and 30 miles off the coast. Nothing was heard from them and they were posted missing, presumed lost. Over the next two days several searches were made for the missing Sunderland between Alexandria and Cape Brulos but nothing was found.

By 28 July the squadron's sojourn at Fanara was over and the aircraft returned to Aboukir. The ground personnel started to return by road convoy and the move continued into the next day. On 30 July F/O Thornicroft was on anti-submarine patrol when two ASV plots were picked up. These were investigated with no success and shortly afterwards another plot was picked up. This turned out to be a destroyer, which was shining a bluish light on the water. When Thornicroft approached it the destroyer opened fire, even though the Sunderland was four miles away. Thornicroft decided to give the destroyer a wide berth and continued his patrol before returning to Aboukir. By 4 August all of the remaining personnel at Fanara had returned to Aboukir.

A notice on the Squadron flammable fuel store on the former Imperial Airways slipway at Alexandria. (Watson via JA Wilson).

During August a change of command in North Africa took place when General Auchinleck was replaced by General Gott. Unfortunately Gott was shot down en route to Cairo and General Montgomery was sent to replace him on the 7th. The arrival of this new commander was most opportune for the Allied forces in North Africa and heralded a new beginning, which would ultimately drive the Axis forces from the continent.

While Operation pedestal was being carried out between 11 and 15 August in an attempt to get a vital convoy through to Malta the Sunderlands were busy hunting a submarine in co-operation with two destroyers. Although the search went on for several days it was hampered by aircraft unserviceabilities, engine failures and ASV faults. The squadron had no success in finding the submarine and Operation Pedestal was only marginally successful, with only five of the convoy's merchant ships getting through to Malta.

The attempts to locate the enemy submarine continued into the 16th and F/O Holcombe in W3987:X, working in conjunction with four destroyers was patrolling an area north and east of Rosetta when a suspicious oil streak was sighted. Holcombe dropped a flame float, which revealed that the oil streak was spreading. He flew over the streak at 250 ft and dropped two DCs 150 yards from the end of the streak. Unfortunately, they failed to detonate. The remainder of August was taken up with convoy escorts and nothing was seen of the enemy. On land the Battle of Alam Halfa commenced on 30 August and Rommel sustained heavy losses in the first two days of fighting. By 3 September the new Zealanders were attacking the Axis supply lines and on the 7th Montgomery stabilised his lines on Alam Halfa and called a halt to the attacks on the retreating Germans. For the rest of the month Montgomery satisfied himself with desert raids on Benghazi, Barce and Tobruk.

> ### LONDON GAZETTE – 18 SEPTEMBER 1942
>
> **BARNETT, Flight Sergeant Dennis**
> **No 230 Squadron – Distinguished Flying Medal**
>
> As first wireless operator on Sunderland aircraft, this airman has seen service in Great Britain, Egypt, Malta, Gibraltar, Crete and Cyrenaica. On one occasion his rapid passing of messages enabled British naval forces to intercept and sink a French destroyer off the south coast of Turkey. He has taken part in two successful sea rescues, his wireless skill being an important factor in the result. On three occasions, when under enemy fire, his coolness in passing messages was outstanding. In the last engagement, his aircraft was shot down, but Flight Sergeant Barnett continued to transmit messages to base until the aircraft began to break up on the rugged coast near Appolonis. After being taken prisoner by the Italians, he ably assisted his captain to turn the table on their captors, won freedom, and finally helped to guard 150 Italians until the crew were able to hand them over to British forces.

F/L Thornicroft had a narrow escape in the early hours of 2 September when on anti-submarine patrol in Sunderland W4022:Z. Having completed tow sweeps of his area he was turning for another when the oil pressure on the starboard outer engine began to drop. He set course for base and shortly afterwards the propeller flew off. Thornicroft managed to fly back to Aboukir and landed safely. On 7 September, F/L Howell was not so lucky. Taking off with a crew of thirteen in W3987:X he headed for Alexandria, where the aircraft was due for an inspection, and crashed into the sea off Port Burg just after take off. The Sunderland was completely written off and there were eight fatal casualties. This was the squadron's second aircraft loss in less than three months. On 18 September the squadron Daily Routine orders carried notification of the award of the DFM to F/Sgt D Barnett, F/Sgt WG McGhee, Sgt KJ Cole and F/Sgt E Lewis for courage, determination and devotion to duty. The squadron's second loss of the month occurred in the early hours of 30 September. Sunderland T9050:Y, captained by F/O Murphy was returning from an anti-submarine patrol along the Egyptian coast when he crashed on landing. Three of the crew were killed and nine injured. September was not a happy month for the squadron.

> LONDON GAZETTE – 18 SEPTEMBER 1942
>
> **McGHEE, Flight Sergeant William Gilmour**
> **No 230 Squadron – Distinguished Flying Medal**
>
> A most capable wireless operator, this airman has also specialised in turret gunnery. His shooting has been of a high order while his observation has been so efficient that his pilots have always been warned in ample time to evade enemy aircraft. A total of 35 have been observed during his patrols. Sergeant McGhee has taken part in nine attacks on enemy submarines, his accurate shooting being of great assistance. He helped in the rescue of a Swordfish crew off Sicily and a Fulmar crew from the Ark Royal, who were afloat in the Western Mediterranean. On three occasions, whilst his aircraft was on the water, he stood by his guns to ward off enemy bombing attacks.

October 1942 was a frustrating month for the squadron. The sorties comprised, in the main, convoy and Fleet escorts and anti-submarine patrols with little to report until almost the end of the month when, on 29 October, F/L Thornicroft was carrying out an anti-submarine patrol in W4023:U off Port Said. In the early hours of the 30th an ASV plot was picked up five miles to starboard. The area was searched for the possible enemy submarine but no more plots were found. Naval forces subsequently searched the area and the submarine was located and sunk.

On land the pendulum was swinging in favour of the Allies and on 16 October the convoys for Operation Torch began to assemble. One week later on 23 October the second Battle of Alamein commenced with a 1,000-gun bombardment. The 8th Army quickly gained ground over a six-mile front and all of the Axis counter attacks were repulsed. Fierce fighting continued along the front until the 26th when Montgomery switched his main attack to the north. With his armies in disarray Rommel was forced to return from sick leave in Germany to take control.

On the 27th the Germans counter attacked but were repulsed with the loss of fifty tanks. By 3 November Rommel had issued order to retreat, defying Hitler's order to stand fast. With only twelve tanks left by 4 November Rommel had few options left open to him. By now the Germans had lost over 10,000 prisoners, including nine generals.

On 5 November Allied forces attacked Rommel's rearguard and had advanced over 100 miles from El Alamein. The back door was about to close on the Axis forces when Operation Torch began in North West Africa the following day. In an attempt to reinforce and to reverse the defeat the Germans landed troops in Vichy French Tunisia unopposed by the French on the 9th. That same day the British captured Sidi Barrani and on 11 November the French in North West Africa signed an armistice with the Allies.

By 12 November the British had entered Tobruk and the following day the last German troops were cleared from Cyrenaica. On the same day the Allied First Army entered Tunisia from Algeria. The Axis in North Africa was about to be squeezed in the closing vice.

November started well for the squadron also. On the first day of the month F/O Holcombe was on anti-submarine patrol in N9029:V when an oil streak was sighted. The streak was lengthening and bubbles were seen rising to the surface. Holcombe attacked dropping four DCs. Two were dropped 600 yards ahead of the streak whilst the other two were dropped a further hundred yards ahead. No results were observed from the attack.

230 Squadron officers, Aboukir.

On 3 November F/O Holcombe was involved in an ASR task which failed to find the downed aircrew, however, the following day F/L Squires continued the search in N9029:V. Sixty miles north of Sidi Barrani two dinghies were located with a man in each. The Sunderland was unable to land due to adverse weather conditions, but Squires circled around and dropped rescue kit. On the 19th S/Ldr Williams was given an unusual opportunity. A FAA crew had recently flown an Italian Cant Z.506B from Malta to Aboukir and Williams was given the chance to fly it on an air test. Unfortunately, after several attempts to take off, the Cant developed engine trouble and had to return to its moorings.

During December the squadron received a new addition to its strength in the shape of a Fairey Fulmar. 852 Sqn FAA had loaned the aircraft to the squadron for drogue towing and P/O Regensburger flew it over to Aboukir from Edku on the

7th. On 13 December Rommel's troops fell back before the assaults of Allied troops at El Agheila and the 8th Army continued its advance into Libya. On 21 December W/Cdr Taylor flew an anti-submarine patrol between Aboukir and Bomba and arriving at Bomba landed to make a survey of the area for possible use as an advanced base. The routine of convoy escort and anti-submarine protection was only broken once during the month when, on the 23rd, F/L Squires, piloting W4023:U, was escorting a westbound convoy from Alexandria. An ASV plot was picked up six mile on the port bow and Squires prepared to attack. The plot disappeared at a range of two miles and Squires dropped flame floats over the position. He circled the position until the convoy was well clear but no further ASV contact was made.

230 Squadron aircrew with Sunderland.

'STUKA JUICE'

SH 'Chalky' White joined the Squadron in late 1942 and remained until 1944 when he was posted back to the UK and Transport Command.

> "I joined the Squadron just before Christmas 1942. We were the first crew to fly through the Mediterranean, as this had been considered too dangerous. Normally crews took the long route via the Cape. One more crew followed us but after that aircraft started to be lost and they went back to using the Cape route.

We did not get to Egypt straight away. After landing at Malta the CO just kept us there to safeguard convoys which were still under heavy attack. Malta was still being heavily bombed and the resident CO was a law unto himself. Another aircraft eventually took over from us and we proceeded on to Aboukir. Daylight operations from Malta could be somewhat dicey and we were glad to move on. Grace said in the Mess on Christmas Day was and is one of the most heartfelt I have ever heard. The chef did wonders with 'bully beef' and we all got very drunk on a home made brew called 'Stuka Juice'.

230 was a mobile squadron and the home base was Singapore. We were the first crew composed entirely of officers and sergeants to ever join the Squadron. 230 still operated using ground staff who were expert in their own particular field. It was quite common to see ground personnel wearing decorations (DFM etc.). At that time a full crew consisted of two pilots, one navigator, two engineers, one wireless operator mechanic, two wireless operators, one rigger and one tail gunner. All of these people were totally qualified and fully capable of completely servicing the aircraft wherever it may be. This was very necessary, particularly with regard to the engines. These were old Pegasus II and had been reconditioned several times. The only new engines that we ever received came with fresh crews from the UK.

Towards the end of 1943 prior to leaving for Ceylon all riggers were posted back to the UK to serve as tail gunners in Bomber Command, where the casualty rate was very high. From then on we flew without riggers."

5. African Adventures
January 1943 – December 1943

The New Year started with tragedy on the day W/Cdr Taylor was mentioned in despatches in the New Years Honours. Sunderland N9029:V set out on an anti-submarine patrol east of Port Said under the command of F/O Holcombe. The aircraft failed to return and the 12 crew were lost. The following day S/Ldr Williams carried out a search for the missing Sunderland in W4021:W after some wreckage had been located by a Wellington. An oil patch and some wreckage were seen and Williams landed to search but no survivors were found.

The squadron's time in the Mediterranean was coming to an end and on 8 January it was notified of an impending move to Dar es Salaam in Tanganyika. On 9 January the first Sunderland, EJ136:Y took off for Wadi Halfa, under the command of F/L Squires, on the first stage of a flight to Dar Es Sallam. W/Cdr Taylor followed in EJ132:X on the 19th and F/L Thornicroft set out in W4022:Z on the 20th, arriving at Dar es Salaam on the 23rd and 24th respectively. Since arriving at Dar es Salaam F/L Squires set out on an Indian Ocean tour in EJ136:Y on 17 January. His passengers included Lt Gen Sir William Platt, GOC in C east African Command, Maj Gen Smallwood, GOC Madagascar and his staff and AVM Wigglesworth, AOC East Africa. Over the next ten days the Sunderland visited Mombasa, Pamanzi, Diego Saurez, Mauritius, Rodriquez, Tromelin Island, Seychelles and returned to Mombasa. The governor of the Seychelles was on board for the return to Mombasa. Rodriquez had been visited to survey for possible anchorages and this was the first time a Sunderland had been to the island.

P/O Lumsden left Aboukir for Mombasa in W4023:U on the 24th followed by F/L Hayne in EJ140:V on the 25th, both arriving on the 27th. The last Sunderland to leave Aboukir was W4021:W, flown by S/Ldr Williams, on 26 January. The squadron left behind a party of 12 maintenance personnel at Fanara to be in a position to service any new Sunderlands arriving from the UK. As no aircraft arrived the handling party joined the Sea party at Kasfareet to await transit to Dar es Salaam. On 27 January the squadron was notified of the award of the George Medal to P/O Richmond for courage, determination and devotion to duty in relation to the crash of W3987:X on 7 September 1942.

With the move to Dar es Salaam came responsibility for patrolling the vast Indian Ocean and the east African coastline. The threat to be countered was now not only the German U-boats and surface raiders, but the Japanese too.

THE ROAD TO EAST AFRICA

"In 1943 we moved to East Africa using the port of Dar es Salaam. We flew to Khartoum the first day, to Uganda the second day and then on to Dar es Salaam. I was highly amused the second day, as we were flying in Dakota's and sitting opposite me was the Squadron cook. I knew he hated flying but I felt hungry and lifted my box of food down and took the lid off. He looked at me eating and shot off down to the rear of the plane and stayed there until we landed, still on the toilet.

At Dar es Salaam the buildings had not been set up. The officers were fixed up but the other ranks were stuffed in an Italian complex that was terrible. Flies were everywhere. Toilets were near the cookhouse. Hygiene was bad and dysentery was rife. Nearly everyone suffered and it was a great relief to move out onto new ground in new sleeping quarters and eating rooms.

Malaria was a big problem in those days. We used nets over our beds. I caught malaria three times and was treated in the local hospital. The joy was a fortnight leave to recover. The first leave I took in Austia, a delightful place in the hilly country. One travelled on trains the first and third days. The second day in estate cars and lorries. I stayed with a PWD man named Rook, a most interesting time. I planned to go back and work as a PWD officer after the war but things didn't work out – Africa changed! I had a very happy time in Dar es Salaam and all to soon the Squadron's role over the Indian Ocean looking for subs was changed and we were ordered to go to Galle in Ceylon."

LN Worth

EAST AFRICA

"When we first arrived in East Africa there were no facilities whatsoever. From scratch we built our own servicing slipways using local native labour. We were able to carry out full major inspections. We also built our own radio station. Eventually a fully equipped and permanent station was built."

'Chalky' White

By February the squadron had settled into a routine of exercises with the navy, convoy escorts, anti-submarine patrols and routine passenger flights to the various islands and anchorages in the Indian Ocean in what was known as 'The Indian Ocean Islands Tour'.

In March the squadron received its first hint of possible action in the early hours of 5 March. W/Cdr Taylor took off from Tulear the previous evening in EJ140:V to escort a convoy. About 1.5 hours after joining the convoy a weak ASV plot was picked up. The plot was considered suspicious but it disappeared before they could investigate. By 10 March the squadron's personnel were beginning to understand the problems of operating close to the equator. An inspection of the squadron camp revealed evidence of yellow fever and malaria. Several aircrew had been struck down with malaria and as a consequence assistance had to be obtained from No 16 Sqn who sent four officers and five NCO's on attachment. Two days later the squadron received another new Sunderland in the shape of EJ141:R, flown in by P/O Watson. This was followed by F/O McNichol in JM659:Q on the 24th. The following day the main party of the squadron arrived by sea on the *SS Takliwa*. The party had embarked at Port Tewfiq in Egypt and the ship had called at Berbera in British Somaliland, picking up 400 Italian civilian internees before sailing to Aden and Zanzibar. The new Sunderlands continued to arrive from the UK and F/L Todd flew in EJ131:T on the 27th. By the end of the month the cases of malaria on the squadron had reached 35. January had seen four and February 13 – poor health was going to be a major problem to overcome.

WIRELESS OPERATOR MECHANIC

Frank Morgan joined the Squadron at Aboukir and served as a Wireless Operator Mechanic, or WOM, until December 1944.

> "I was in the Signals Section of 230 Sqn in Aboukir, Alexandria slipway and Dar es Salaam. In December 1944 I was invalided home with malaria. Three happy years in all. I knocked up quite a number of flying hours in Sunderlands – mainly test flying, not operational. I was a 'WOM' – Wireless Operator Mechanic, working on the well-known T1154 and the companion receiver, the R1155.
>
> The Squadron moved from the Middle East theatre in 1942/43 mainly in the troopship 'Takliwa' and we were based at Dar es Salaam, hunting for Japanese subs in the Indian Ocean. (I can't remember that we found any!)
>
> Apart from my own particular interest in radio, I became fascinated with these beautiful boats. (Note the terminology – 'boats' not 'aircraft' or 'kites'.) The captains were known as 'skippers' but the word was understood to have more to do in connotation with the sea-going variety. For instance, they had to know all about tides and marine navigation. We went 'ashore' in 'dinghies'. Our senior NCO's were 'Chiefies' –

in fact, we were after a couple of months able to talk in their own terms with the Navy with whom we had much in common.

I was delighted to find that in the mainplane was a Douglas two-stroke horizontally- opposed motorcycle engine. This operated the bilge pump! Did anyone outside the Service know that the Sunderland could carry its own spare engine (Bristol Pegasus XVIII, later Twin Wasps)? It was stowed in the galley and could be run out on the depth charge rails under the starboard or port wing, with special ladders to fit to the engine nacelles. Thus the fitter could do an engine change at sea! The galley could yield (in the right hands) a good three-course meal – less wine!

F Morgan

Dar es Salaam seen from the wing of a Squadron Sunderland. (F Morgan)

April saw several convoy escorts and a flight from Dar es Salaam by F/O Slade in W4023:U on the 4th to carry out two operations. 'Operation Pigeon' was to calibrate the H/F D/F station at Diego Saurez and 'Operation Bisoyo' to complete a photographic survey of the area. On arrival at Diego Saurez one engine became unserviceable and the Sunderland returned to base on 20 April. During this period the squadron was also operating a detachment at Tulear.

The first day of May saw the arrival of another new Sunderland for the squadron. F/L Middleton flew JM673 from the UK via Mombasa to reinforce the squadron. JM673 was allocated the code letter 'P' on arrival. A new slipway for the Sunderland's had been under construction at Dar es Salaam since January and it was brought into use for the first time on 3 May when W4023:U was pulled up onto it for a 270 hour inspection. The squadron continued with convoy and naval escorts throughout the month and was able to celebrate the fall of Tunis and Bizerta when it was announced on the radio on 8 May.

The arrival of Sunderland DP180:O from the UK, flown in by P/O Rand on 13 May, saw the squadrons strength standing at 12 Sunderland Mk III. On the 22nd F/L Hayne returned to Dar es Salaam in W4021:W with four defective engines and a damaged hull. He was, however, able to make a safe landing.

OPERATION HUSKY

S/Ldr Bednall, who had left the squadron in 1941 to become Chief Ground Instructor at No 70 OTU in Kenya, returned to the squadron in 1943.

> *"After waiting weeks for another operational posting, two signals arrived at Nakuru at the same time, one from Middle East Command giving me command of 46 Squadron with Beaufighters at Malta and the other to 230 Squadron. Eventually it was sorted out and I went to 230 at Dar es Salaam, Tanganyika as Co designate. Rupert Taylor was then CO and Peter Williams was S/Ldr Flying – they both left the squadron within a short time of one another.*
>
> *The squadron had been sent to East Africa to help deal with a number of Japanese submarines which had sunk many ships off eastern Africa. We had an advance base at Tulear in Madagascar and further moorings at Aldabra Islands, Seychelles, Gan, Diego Garcia and Addu Atoll.*
>
> *Within days of my arrival I was ordered to take a squadron detachment to Tunisia to take part in 'Operation Husky' – the invasion of Sicily – all very hush-hush at the time. Once again the squadron – or a large part of it – was on the move along the whole length of the Nile. The journey was accomplished without incident.*
>
> *When we arrived at Bizerta in Tunisia we discovered somewhat chaotic conditions as the town and harbour had only just fallen to the Americans. Discipline on Bizerta Lake, where we operated from, was somewhat lacking and take off and landings could be interesting! The lake was full of assorted ships and landing craft – some were sunken wrecks.*

We were a bit disappointed to learn that we were merely to form part of an Air Sea Rescue organisation. This seemed a bit of a let down from our usual offensive maritime role, though the rescue role was and continues to be a vital operational requirement. One notable rescue was made – Air Marshal HP Lloyd ordered a Sunderland to go to Naples Bay at night (no moon) to pick up a ditched American P-38 Lightning pilot who was known to be just inside the bay in his dinghy. One of our aircraft, with great skill, located the stricken pilot, but each time a flame float was dropped to give a meagre reference point for landing the Sunderland was attacked by a Ju 88 fighter. The flame float would also give some indication of where the surface of the sea actually was – our altimeters were not that accurate! Some hours were spent in fruitless endeavour and the crew fixed the position of the dinghy and returned to Bizerta with little fuel left. (Only half a load of fuel was taken to facilitate the sea landing).

Air Marshal Lloyd showed his displeasure at breakfast next morning in front of a full Officers Mess tent accusing the pilot of 'failing to accomplish the mission'. I reacted most strongly and said that any other action would have inevitably resulted in useless loss of life, including that of the American pilot. There was obviously a strong political motive behind all this! I said that I was fully confident that later that morning we would indeed bring back the American. The Sunderland had already gone back at dawn with an escort of P-38 fighters from the USAAF.

Shortly after this unpleasant incident the Sunderland arrived back with the American*, little worse for his adventure; the escorting fighters having shot down twelve Ju 52 Luftwaffe transport aircraft as a bonus. No further word was received from the Air Marshal! But 'all's well that ends well' and the squadron was fully vindicated. The pilot concerned, F/L McNichol, an Australian, was awarded the DFC.

On the whole there was not much call on the Sunderlands. I took an aircraft to land in the just captured Augusta Harbour to see if we could fly back an Italian Cant Z506 three-engined floatplane. However, none were found to be serviceable or could be made serviceable within a reasonable time and the quest was abandoned after we failed to find anyone who could clear either of the two Cants on the slipway for booby traps – of which there were said to be plenty about! We were told that a Flight Lieutenant had blown himself up trying to start a Fw 190. Shortly after the detachment returned to Dar es Salaam"

DK Bednall

The survivors were in fact the four crew of a B-25 Mitchell.

On 1 June the squadron began to send a detachment of six Sunderland back to Aboukir in preparation for the invasion of Sicily and Italy. The Sunderland's departed at intervals between the 1st and 14th and routed via Kisumu and

Khartoum. The aircraft and captains were DP180:O, W/Cdr Taylor, JM673:P, F/L Middleton, EJ143:S, F/O Statham, JM659:Q, F/O McNichol, W4021:W, S/Ldr Bednall and W4023:U, F/O Fumerton. W/Cdr Taylor only got as far as Khartoum before DP180:O went u/s and remained so for some time. To replace this aircraft F/O Watson was despatched to Aboukir on the 23rd in EJ141:R, arriving at Aboukir on the 25th. The remaining Sunderland's and crews continued to operate from Dar es Salaam and Tulear and on 24 June F/O Lumsden took EJ140:V on and Indian Islands Tour. The squadron had been living in accommodation at the Pugu Road Refugee Camp but work on the new accommodation was completed at RAF Dar es Salaam on 26 June and they were able to move in. The move did not improve the health of the squadron, however, and for April May and June the cases of malaria were 52, 94 and 73 respectively.

A Sunderland moored at the Advanced Flying Boat Base of Diego Garcia. (J Laydon).

On 11 June the Allies invaded Pantelleria, meeting little resistance after a twenty day bombardment of positions on the island. The Aboukir detachment was ordered to Bizerta in Tunisia on 11 June to work under the control of the advanced HQ of No 216 Gp carrying out transport work between Bizerta and Malta and ASR work as required by No 242 Gp. On 13 June JM673:P, captained by F/L Middleton took off from Kalafrana to carry out an ASR search for the crews of two Liberators, which had been seen to collide by a third Liberator. Two oil patches and some partially submerged wreckage were sighted but after a thorough search no sign was found of any survivors.

The view from the office. The Sunderland cockpit was known as the 'Bridge' to the crew. (F Morgan)

In July the squadron at Dar es Salaam was engaged in Indian Ocean Islands Tours and transport duties. Convoy escorts and anti-submarine sweeps were still being carried out and on one sweep on the night of 12/13 July F/O Ingham in EJ132:X had to make a forced landing at Pamanzi due to engine trouble.

In the Mediterranean the Allies, under Montgomery and Patton, invaded Sicily on 10 July, capturing Syracuse and Licata. By the 16th the Canadians had captured Caltigirone and the Americans had taken Agrigento. On the 17th the Allies set up a military government on Sicily and by the 20th the Italians on Sicily surrendered en masse on the west of the island. The Canadians were pushing towards and around Mt Etna. By the end of the month Mussolini had resigned and a new government under King Victor Emmanuel and Prime Minister Marshall Bagdolio was in place.

While all of this was occurring the squadron detachment was operating from Bizerta, Aboukir and Malta.

On 10 July a Sunderland searched for an aircraft down in the sea off Cap Bon and carried out another search for a ditched DC3 but had no success in finding survivors. The following day F/O McNichol took JM659:Q out on an ASR search between Cap Bon and Maritimo Island escorted by four P-38s. A square search was carried out for the downed Mitchell but no trace was found. F/O Watson was also out on an ASR search in EJ141:R but also had no success. The following day F/O Statham took EJ143:S out to search an area where a SOS signal had been sighted the previous night. Escorted by two P-38s he made a search of the area and found some wreckage but no survivors. Two days later F/O McNichol was airborne from Bizerta on another ASR search between Cap Bon and Pantelleria. Sighting some wreckage he dropped down to 100 feet but no survivors were seen.

The figure on the tailplane gives scale to the huge fin
and rudder of the Sunderland. (F Morgan)

On the 15th F/O Statham, in Sunderland EJ143:S searched for two dinghies which had been reported but after a thorough search of the area nothing was sighted. The following day another search was carried out by F/O Rand in the area east of Pantelleria, escorted by two P-38s. Nothing was seen. On the 16th F/O Watson was out again in EJ141:R, searching in conjunction with a high speed launch, but once again no survivors were found. The following day he carried out another ASR search for a pilot reported to be floating in a 'Mae West'. Working with a HSL he searched for five hours but had no luck. That night he was out again in JM659:Q and after the previous fruitless searches and the disheartening effect these had on the Sunderland crews a little luck came his way. McNichol took off in JM659:Q in the path of a full moon at 2132hrs to search for two dinghies containing survivors. Unfortunately the ASV went u/s almost immediately, depriving the crew of a valuable search asset. The search became more urgent on approaching Maritimo Island as two E-boats were thought to be in the area and may have found the survivors before the Sunderland. After a long search torch flashes were seen and a dinghy was sighted. McNichol dropped a flame float flarepath preparatory to landing but an enemy aircraft appeared. As the Sunderland's mid-upper turret was u/s he decided it would be inadvisable to land and set course for base. Two hours after McNichol landed F/O Watson was airborne in EJ141:R to effect the rescue.

There was much enemy air activity in the area due to the fighting on Sicily and the Sunderland was escorted by 15 P-38s. Watson located the dinghy and landed on alongside. The six crew of the downed Marauder, two of which had minor injuries and a third with a broken arm and leg, were picked up. After take off Watson set course for a position 40 miles south of Naples to try to locate another ditched crew. Due to the limited fuel of the fighter escort he had to restrict the search area and was unable to locate the survivors. Signalling their success in picking up survivors from the first search, the squadron had an ambulance on standby when the Sunderland arrived back at Bizerta. Watson noted that the excellent work of the fighter escort had enabled him to concentrate fully on the rescue work without having to worry about enemy aircraft.

Later the same day F/L Middleton was out on an ASR search in JM659:Q off Naples with an escort of 14 P-38s. A thorough search was made but only an empty dinghy was found. The escort had more luck, though, shooting down fifteen JU 52s on the return to base. On the night of 19/20 July F/O Statham departed from Bizerta on an ASR search in EJ143:S. Off the coast of Sardinia a square search was commenced and on the sixth leg of the search a flare was spotted. Shortly afterward a dinghy was sighted and Statham dropped a flame float, followed by four others to mark a flare path. Statham set the Sunderland down on a heavy swell and a search commenced for the dinghy.

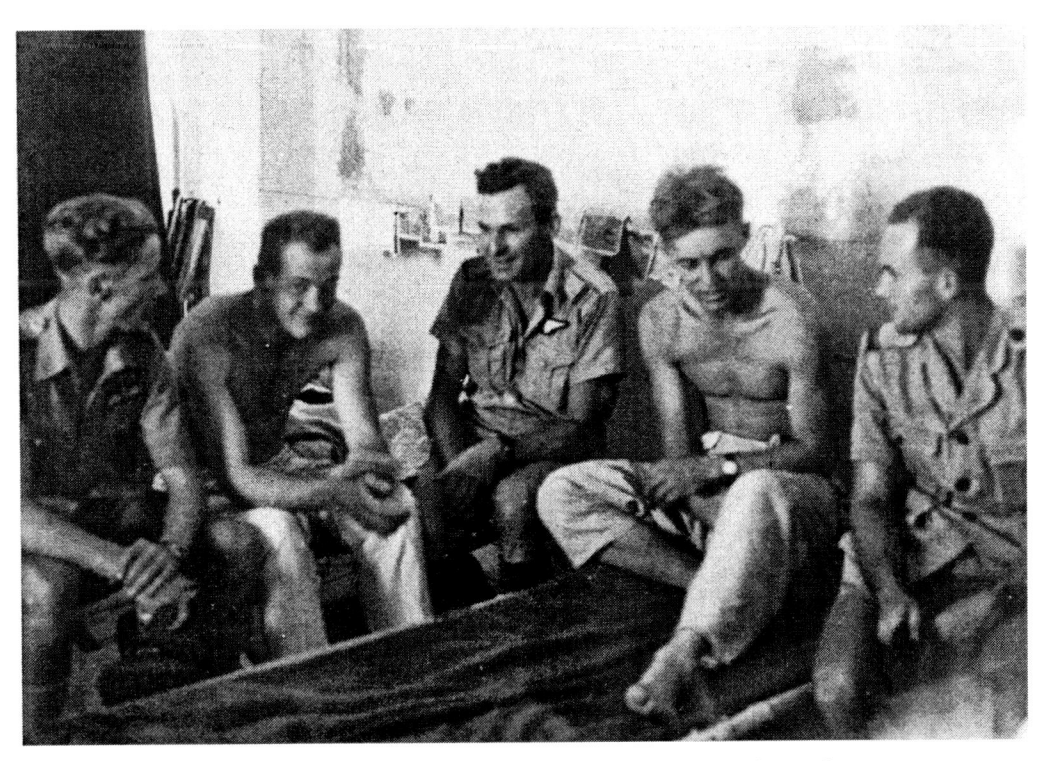

F/Lt Watson (on right) with two American airmen he rescued from the Mediterranean. Their money can be seen hanging on the bed to dry out. (Watson via JA Wilson).

A second dinghy was thought to have been seen but it turned out to be one of the flame floats and Statham's crew resumed the search for the dinghy. Although the Sunderland was being pounded by the heavy swell Statham elected to remain on the water and after three hours, waiting for a visual sighting at dawn, all of the crew were seasick. Throughout the night the crew fired flares, used the Aldis lamp and kept the navigation lights on in the hope of some response from the dinghy. As dawn approached there was no sign of the dinghy and Statham took off in a 10 ft swell, which was breaking over the bow of the Sunderland to return to base. The remainder of the month was filled with fruitless ASR searches and on the 29th the detachment was ordered back to East Africa.

THE INCIDENT IN THE BAY OF NAPLES

"I was listening to the Bob Hope Show at 2051 hrs when a call came for a ASR job off the coast of Italy. After laying a flare path we took off in moonlight at 2327 hrs. On the north coast of Sicily we sighted an enemy aircraft on the ASV and visually and then saw the exhaust of an E-boat. We went to within 40nm of Naples and sighted a dinghy. We were preparing to land after laying a flare path with flame floats when an enemy aircraft intervened. We had to scatter. Fixed position of dinghy and sent message to base."

Diary Entry 17/7/43 – DW McNichol

"After crossing the coastline of Tunisia we tested our guns and found that the dorsal turret was firing only single shots. Standing instructions were that one had to return to base if the guns were defective. However, we continued on our mission. At the end of our pre-plotted track we had not made a sighting. I told the navigator that we would give it another five minutes on the same track.

After a minute or two we sighted a flashing light from a dinghy. I laid a flare path of three flame floats and then climbed above 1,000 ft to send the mandatory signal that we were about to land to pick up survivors.

Our signal had to be relayed through Malta, where an air raid was in progress. As a result of the air raid it was over an hour before our signal got through. During this period 'Jerry' got a fix on us and sent out an aircraft. After our signal was received I returned to our flare path and put the aircraft into wind in order to land. It was then that we sighted an aircraft circling the dinghy at about 250 ft.

I slewed off to port for five minutes or so and then returned to the flare path; the circling aircraft was still there. I slewed off again and again; the aircraft was still circling the dinghy. As I would have been a sitting duck on the water with an unserviceable dorsal turret I decided to scatter in the direction of Sardinia. We then sent a signal reporting the position of the dinghy.

A few hours later another Australian captain with a top and bottom cover of USAAF fighters came out and collected the survivor. The captain of this aircraft (Watson) told me later that I would certainly have 'pranged' in the heavy sea at night. The ditched aircraft was a B-25 Mitchell with a crew of four."

DW McNichol

> For 230 Squadron Detachment, Bizerta
> Headquarters 320th. Bombardment Group (M)
>
> NATOUSA
>
> APO 520
> 21 July 1943.
>
> SUBJECT: Commendation
> To: Commanding officer, Air Sea Rescue Command, c/o Area Controller.
>
> This organisation appreciates the wonderful effort put forth in the rescue of the crew we had down at sea. This rescue has done more for the morale of this organization than one can realise. A service of this type goes a long way in the minds of the men flying on missions.
>
> You are to be congratulated on your victory in shooting down an enemy aircraft while on this mission. The pilots, crews and members of the staff commend you for the rescue of our crew.
>
> KARL E. BAUMEISTER,
> Colonel, Air Corps,
> Commanding.

The above signal referred to the rescue of the Marauder crew by JM659:Q and EJ141:R on 17/18 July 1943.

The squadron detachment at Bizerta returned to Aboukir between 28 July and 1 August except for EJ143:S, flown by F/O Statham, which had run aground on take off on the 31st. The Sunderland offloaded its passengers and freight and flew to Malta for hull repairs the following day. In East Africa the squadron was being kept busy with Island Tours and was informed on 7 August that they would be co-operating with the forces commanded by C in C Eastern Fleet to eradicate the menace of U-boats operating in the Mozambique Channel. Accordingly four Sunderlands were detached to Pamanzi to operate from this base. On 19 August the squadron was informed that F/O CSD Plummer had been awarded the DFC for courage, determination and devotion to duty.

On 20th August the squadron lost a Sunderland. F/L Todd took off in Sunderland EJ131-T to escort naval vessels and on arrival at the position failed to find the ships. At 1838hrs the Sunderland signalled that it was in difficulties and asked for bearings for Dar es Salaam and Diego Saurez. At 2003hrs a signal was received that the Sunderland was making a forced landing, after which nothing further was heard. Over the next days the squadron's Sunderlands and Catalinas searched for the missing aircraft but nothing was found, despite a search covering the whole of the western coast of Madagascar down to Tulear.

On 30th August W/Cdr Taylor became station commander at RAF Eastleton and W/Cdr Bednall took over the squadron.

On 1st September F/O Statham was finally able to leave Malta for Aboukir, having made repairs to the hull of EJ143-S but had to return immediately with engine trouble. On the 4th he made another attempt but had to return after two hours. He eventually made it to Aboukir on the ninth of the month. The rest of September was filled with island tours, convoy escorts and anti-submarine patrols. On one of the latter, F/L Ingham, in EJ132-X, developed engine trouble and was forced to jettison his depth charges and 200 gallons of fuel before landing safely at Mombasa.

Through the summer, as the weather became progressively cooler, the number of malaria cases fell from 36 in July to 12 in August and only 3 in September.

CANNON ARMED SUNDERLANDS

"Whilst at Dar es Salaam I encouraged our engineers and armourers to see if they could fit a fixed 20mm cannon in the bows of a Sunderland. The idea was to give us a bit more 'punch' on an attacking run against submarines, which had begun to stay on the surface instead of crash-diving. They were now equipped with an impressive array of defensive armament and all the Sunderland had was a single gas operated 'K' gun in the front turret.

We had managed to get a satisfactory mounting installed but, unfortunately, a visiting Group officer discovered what was going on and I subsequently received a personal visit from the AOC ordering me to remove the cannon and NOT to make unauthorised modifications to aircraft! As is well known, within a year a battery of four fixed guns became standard armament for all Mk V Sunderlands. We were obviously too far ahead of our time!

Another incident, which did not seem to have much significance at the time, was an experiment with a system of girls make up mirrors to reflect the airspeed indicator reading to a position where the pilot could read it without distraction during the critical attacking approach onto an enemy submarine. It was not really successful as the range of view was too limited – but it must have been a very early excursion into Head Up Displays!"

DK Bednall

The month of October followed a similar pattern to September, with only the move of the squadron's detachment at Pamanzi to Mombasa in exchange with the Catalinas of 265 Squadron. The move was made to provide better escort cover to convoys and assist in maintenance of the Sunderlands. A new Sunderland arrived on 16th November in the form of DP189-L, flown in by F/O Pedley via Mombasa. This brought the squadron strength up to 13 Sunderland Mk.IIIs. The new

Sunderland was soon on patrol when F/O Fumerton took part in a search for a submarine on 17th November. An unidentified aircraft had been flown over Mombasa at about midnight on the 16th and the Royal Navy suspected it had been launched from a Japanese submarine. The Sunderland took off from Dar es Salaam and made a thorough search before landing at Mombasa. The submarine was not found.

During December the squadron was kept busy with the continuation of a regular shuttle service, begun in November, between Kisumu and Khartoum ferrying trainee aircrews. On the operational front, the Sunderlands were deployed to counter a possible U-boat threat in the Mozambique Channel but, although several anti-submarine patrols were carried out, no successes followed.

The month and the end of the year were marred by the loss of EJ140-V and its crew on 29 December. F/O Lumsden and his crew had taken off to carry out an M/F D/F calibration and had flown into the mountains in cloud.

The 'Splendid Hotel' in Dar es Salaam. One of the Squadron's 'watering holes'. (F Morgan)

NEW ARRIVALS

Alan W Deller had joined the RAF after a varied series of escapades, firstly as a secretly commissioned 2nd Lt in the Royal Engineers, working for Shell at the Romanian oil refinery in Ploesti. His task was to sabotage the refinery in the event of a German invasion. Following this he was commissioned into the Royal Navy as a Sub Lt and operated on sabotage missions for SOE from an armed caique in the

Aegean Sea. Entering the RAF he trained as a flying boat pilot and after tours in the Atlantic and training as a Captain he was posted to East Africa for operations on Catalinas.

> *"I went with Ted, another Captain, to Air HQ East Africa where we were told that the Catalina squadron at Mombasa definitely had no need of any crews but that of 230 Sqn, flying Sunderlands at Dar es Salaam, did have a requirement for two experienced crews – would we be interested?...would we?!! It was arranged that the necessary contacts would be made to see whether we could be accepted. Our crews were naturally as excited at the possibility as Ted and I were – and I, of course, was particularly looking forward to seeing my best friend, Duggie Lumsden, again after a whole year.*
>
> *New Years Eve in the Mess at Nairobi's Eastleigh Airport was a dull affair but my miniscule interest instantly evaporated as I was told that Duggie had been killed that very day with all his crew except one who was in the tail turret. He had apparently been flying in cloud and had hit very near the top of a hidden 'kopje', an isolated thousand-foot hill inland from Dar. It was shattering news and rather took the edge off the confirmation next day, January the first 1944, that we were posted to 230 Sqn."* **AW Deller**

15TH DECEMBER 1943

Report on landing of Sunderland MK.111. J.M.659. of 230 Squadron at Malakal on 14.12.1943.

I have the honour to submit the following report.

On the 14th December '43, Sunderland JM659 was in transit between Khartoum and Kisumi, with a normal crew of ten and nine passengers and their kit, and 1,450lbs of freight. At 0915 in the vicinity of Shit, the starboard inner engine lost 600 revs but picked up again. The rev counter showed condensation, within the dial and as the propellers were able to be synchronised a defective instrument was suspected. At 0928 the starboard inner coughed, spluttered and stopped momentarily (there was a noticeable inertia at this time) the mixture was changed to normal and the engine appeared to pick up. At 0930 the Flight Engineer reported that oil was pouring from the starboard inner engine, so the pitch was made fully coarse, the petrol was switched off and the engine switched off. I then decided to return to Malakal, our position being 0738N 3139E. At 0935 – 300 gallons of fuel were jettisoned, but I decided against jettisoning further fuel in view of bush fires beneath and thick smoke haze surrounding the aircraft. Suitable signals were sent to Malakal and received by them. At 09.35 the starboard outer coughed, spluttered and dropped revs and the aircraft yawed violently to starboard. I then ordered freight in the bomb room to be jettisoned. This was done at position 0818N 3140E. Further signals were sent to Malakal and acknowledged. The starboard outer showed a 30-degree drop in cylinder head temperature but picked up with some popping in normal mixture.

Height was maintained at 100-105 knots (I.A.S.) and we landed at Malakal 10.37, where two B.O.A.C. launches were awaiting us and we were towed on to the buoy.

I telephoned the Governor of the Province and informed him of the position and nature of the jettisoned freight and he informed me that a search party would be sent out.

On inspection of the starboard inner engine 5 cylinders were found to be unserviceable and the oil consumption was 9 gallons for 5 hours of which 6 gallons were consumed in 30 mins. The consumption for the previous day for this engine was 4 gallons for 8 hours.

Signed. DW McNichol, Flight Lieutenant Captain.

THE TRUTH

*"What I did **not** report was the failure of my crew to jettison a case of Australian beer (144 large bottles) which had been given to me by officers of the Australian Comforts Fund in Alexandria. As the name implies, the ACF (funded by public subscription) provided 'comforts' to men overseas; such things as tobacco, cigarettes, tinned fruit and tinned meat, cakes and, on this occasion, beer.*

The beer was with other freight in the Bomb Room. When I could see the Nile and that I would be able to make a landing. I called up the Bomb Room.

'Did you throw the beer out?' I asked.

'No, Sir' was the reply.

'Why?' I asked.

'Too heavy, Sir!' was the reply."

DW McNichol

The crew enjoying the rescued beer. Rear L to R: Pete Smith (WOp/AG), Ron Schmidt (2nd Pilot), Murray Storch (Navigator), Dave McNichol (Captain). Front: Stan Gorman (Rigger), K. McLean (Flt Mech), Jock Marshall (Rear Gunner). [T. Hulme]

6. Koggala, Ceylon
January – December 1944

During January 1944 the squadron continued to operate the Indian Islands Tour and the shuttle service between Kisumu and Khartoum but flying was reduced considerably. The squadron was warned of an impending move of base and, initially, the location was kept secret. Their destination was later learned to be Koggala in Ceylon (now Sri Lanka).

The preceding year had been an arduous one for the squadron. When they had arrived at Dar es Salaam there was no camp, workshops or slipway and it was through much hard work that these were completed. In addition the squadron had to contend with 300 cases of malaria during the period. It was with mixed feelings that they left the station that they had had a hand in creating but the opening up of the Mediterranean had forced the U-boats to look further afield for prey and the focus had shifted to Aden and the India shipping lanes. The squadron moved its nine Sunderlands from Dar es Salaam between 7 February and 3 March.

On arrival at Koggala the squadron came under the control of No.222 Group and was based alongside two Catalina squadrons, No.413 (RCAF) and No.205. The squadron groundcrew would not leave Dar es Salaam until 22 March, sailing on the *HMT Manela* and arriving at Koggala in April. The ship routed via Mombasa and the Seychelles picking up a number of FAA officers, WRNS and naval ratings on the way, who participated in the many quizzes, concerts and singsongs organised along the way.

The squadron flew its first operational sortie on 1 March, when F/L Watson took EJ141-R out to search for a U-boat east of the Chagos Archipelago. No sightings were made. On the 3rd the search continued for the U-boat, which had been attacked by Catalina T/205 on the 2nd, F/L Watson worked in conjunction with two destroyers during the search but again no luck was had. F/L Ingham continued the search in EJ132:X and the following day F/L Deller took over in EJ143-S, all to no avail.

CEYLON

"At the end of 1943 we moved to Ceylon and joined two Catalina squadrons. We all made use of an inland lake which avoided the problems that can be encountered when taking off and landing in the open sea. This is particularly difficult during the monsoon season.

Operations here were against long range Japanese submarines. The Japanese operated some of the biggest submarines ever. Some were capable of carrying a spotter plane housed in the conning tower.

'Chalky' White

KOGGALA

"The squadron was then ordered to Koggala Lake, near Galle, in southern Ceylon. Moving a squadron is a complex exercise – we had all our own maintenance crews, the squadron totalling over 600 men.

The move was completed satisfactorily, all the aircraft carrying as much of its personnel and equipment as possible. I think we had ten Sunderlands at the time. Large stores such as flying surfaces, engines etc. were transported with the balance of the men by sea.

Koggala Lake is a narrow dogleg affair nestling in between low hills, with the odd island littering the area! It was not an easy place to operate from, especially at night with a full load. On the whole the prevailing wind was from the west and take off was thus assisted, though the sharpish turn to starboard just as one was about to get airborne, when heavily loaded, was a hazard we could have done without. The night flying facilities were, of course, most primitive comprising a line of small floating flares. Any approach assistance was absent! Nevertheless, no accidents happened at Koggala whilst I was CO of the squadron.

The nearest to disaster occurred to me when taking off. We had just become airborne and at this stage one had to ease the stick slightly forward to pick up speed. On this occasion the stick would not go forward – it was solid. I suspected that something had fouled the holes in which the control locking gear was inserted. These were covered by a hinged plate – not spring loaded for some obscure reason – and it was easy for some tool or other foreign body to foul the controls. I eventually regained control by placing both feet on the control column and pushing furiously! That did the trick and suddenly things returned to normal. The indicated airspeed was just above 60 Knots and falling! Altitude about 100 ft only. It was a very near thing."

DK Bednall

INDIAN ISLANDS TOURS

Having settled into Squadron life at Dar es Salaam Alan Deller began to fly on 'Operation Island' sorties involving round trips of the island in the Indian Ocean delivering passengers, mail and supplies to these isolated and lonely locations.

"After two days preliminary preparation and testing of the aircraft I took off very early in the morning with a big load of passengers on 'Operation Island', a regular commitment of the Squadron which involved visiting a number of flying-boat bases and military and naval outposts in the many islands of the western Indian Ocean, carrying mail and relief personnel and sundry high-ranking officers of the three Services on their important business. For me it was a sudden launching into a completely different operational world, flying into strange and unfamiliar places, entirely responsible – with the crew – for our aircraft and deciding the number of passengers I could safely carry as well as the time of departure – all so different from the precisely regulated operations from one or perhaps two familiar bases back home in the North Atlantic.

That first day we flew to Diego Suarez in Madagascar. Cruising height on these trips was five thousand feet to be in cooler air and heaving 'N' up to that height was quite a job and taught me a lot about that particular boat. We landed on a large lake more or less rectangular in shape and surrounded by picturesque hills covered with every kind of luxuriant green vegetation mixed with the ubiquitous palm trees. With our officer passengers George and I were put up in an Army mess where after dinner we sat out in the balmy evening air, heavy with the scent of bougainvillaea, while a band of the King's African Rifles played jolly music and we drank long John Collinses. To finish the evening we went into town where the warm streets, with an unmistakably French atmosphere, were filled with colourful people and colourful establishments including 'Chez Georges' where we ended up with a somewhat riotous finish to the evening.

Next morning we flew to a small island called Pamanzi in the Comoro Islands between Madagascar and the mainland of Africa. The landing area was a long strip of water between steep hills which were covered with masses of green vegetation and brilliantly coloured flowers which seemed to blaze forth and hang from every tree and primitive shack as we drove from the little landing stage to the rickety but friendly Mess; this was situated high up on one of the hillsides and the experience of sitting out on the small veranda in the warm scented evening with a rather warm drink and looking down on our aeroplane moored far below was one of the most delightful I had ever enjoyed.

The same afternoon we returned to Diego Suarez and refuelled ready for the five-hour flight to the Seychelles the next day with twenty-eight passengers. This was a trip we had looked forward to and it did not disappoint; the first sight of those rich green islands with the surrounding ocean changing from blue to dark green to light green and then crystal clarity approaching the dazzling white beaches was simply stunning. There was a limitless choice of landing area in the sea off Victoria, the capital, on the big island of Mahe'; with the clear water and brilliant light it was easy to miss the prevailing swell and I bounced on landing which annoyed me.

As we approached the shore in the dinghy we were met by the curious sweet-ish smell of copra, the main export of the islands; it pervaded the whole town and we quickly got used to it. Victoria was a typical African town – buildings entirely constructed with local materials, wood and palm frond thatch, with everything wide open to the air, the heat being pretty intense – but with a distinct French accent in addition: the local dialect is a sort of French patois and the cuisine is mainly French colonial or Creole. Our Mess was built entirely of palm trunks and palm frond wattle and was literally on the beach a stone's throw from the water's edge. The whole atmosphere was lush and gorgeous – if this was the Seychelles we could happily stay here forever! The local women were almost uniformly lovely, most exceedingly friendly and, regrettably, in very many cases carrying a particularly virulent form of VD.

Ever since we left Mombasa we had had occasional trouble with ignition on two of the engines and as we arrived at the Seychelles I had to declare the aircraft unserviceable. That meant no trip the next day so it was possible to give way to the enervating atmosphere of heavily scented flowers and humid heat for a little and the day finished with a very pleasant dinner as a guest of the Royal Navy shore base together with the officers of a sloop that was moored out beyond my aircraft. The following day we all worked hard to get 'N' serviceable again but the elusive ignition trouble persisted and the not entirely reluctant decision to stay on was inevitable, leading to another delightful evening, this time an open air cinema show followed by a really superb dinner as guest of a glamorous and amorous half-French, half-Seychelles lady called Eva whose husband Philippe performed a close escort throughout the evening – she was a well known hostess to all the British and French officers who were based in the Seychelles or called there from time to time.

Next day we finally got our mechanical troubles sorted out and I fixed our departure for early the following morning. Meanwhile I had invited a number of officers from the Army and the RAF, together with the RN officers from the shore base and the sloop, to a sundowner party aboard the aircraft; the crew had helped to get everything tidy while George and I collected whisky, sherry and gin and tonic and a pile of attractive snacks from shore. Sundry marine craft ferried the guests out to the aircraft and we all managed to get into the wardroom with an overflow into the galley; the wardroom table looked marvellous with all the bottles and goodies arranged – even some modest flowers! – And the party went down extremely well. I have often wondered whether other Sunderland skippers had done anything of the sort – certainly no other military aircraft could adapt itself so simply to a temporary peaceful social role. The upshot was a trip ashore, maintaining a somewhat strained dignity, and a riotous procession of rickshaws to Eva's for dinner which, it had to be admitted, turned into a bit of a shambles.

Early in the morning of the following day I got my twenty-eight passengers on board and set off for Pamanzi once more, marvelling, as we climbed away, at the sheer beauty of those islands. A seven-hour flight took us to the equally lovely little island: as I taxied up to the buoy the port outer engine started backfiring, the same old ignition trouble again, so instead of going on, as scheduled, to Diego Suarez we stayed the night.

Among the passengers was an Army Film Unit, one of several that travelled around the many isolated bases in the Indian Ocean giving film shows for the lonely servicemen; on this occasion they offered to set up their projector in the town square and the Pamanzians had the first cinema show in their history, with the films projected on to the white wall of the post office.

The crew worked hard the following day and had the offending engine going to my satisfaction by the afternoon, but too late to make Diego Suarez before dusk. So, with few regrets, the whole lot of us sat out on the veranda of the Army Mess, drinks in hand, enjoying the relative cool of the evening and watching the shades of night creeping over the incredible floral beauty of this island whose only alien feature that night was my rather doddery old 'N' swinging peacefully at her buoy.

We left Pamanzi for Diego Suarez at first light with thirty-two passengers and landed after two and a quarter hours with the local passengers ready for a quick disembarkation so that I could take off again at ten o'clock for Mombasa. We picked up one or two new passengers including a fairly elderly RNR Lieutenant Commander whom I invited on to the bridge to watch the take-off. As mentioned earlier, the lake at Diego Suarez was more or less a rectangle; that morning the wind was blowing dead across the longer side that would provide the best take-off run but which would necessitate my throttling back the starboard outer until we reached a speed at which the rudder had enough airflow to enable it to take over the job of countering the weather-cock effect of the cross-wind – but that would mean that poor old 'N's take-off run would be so prolonged, due to the reduced power early in the run, that she would never clear the huge palm trees at the end of the lake. I decided I would start my take-off run dead into wind along the shorter side of the lake with, of course, all four engines at full throttle and then, approaching the far side and well up on the step, turn the aeroplane – at about 70 knots or 85 mph – ninety degrees to starboard and continue the run along the longer side of the lake. This I did and old 'N' lumbered along, coming off the water about half way along the long side and then doing her usual trick of sticking at about six feet altitude while the palm trees came nearer and nearer; the unhappy naval officer was convinced we would hit them and *crouched down between the pilots' seats and in the next five seconds I had a very close look indeed at the tops of the palms as we struggled over them. There followed immediately a smart turn to starboard to avoid a hill just ahead and take to a shallow valley which shortly led off to port into another shallow valley near the end of which we had just sufficient altitude to clear the remaining hills and head out to sea. It had been a very busy but very instructive three or four minutes.*

A nice landing back at Mombasa ended an intensely interesting experience, far removed from winter flying in the North Atlantic. Nevertheless this 'Operation Island' was not just a jolly jaunt; apart from ferrying everything from a Major-General to a humble radio mechanic we kept an eye on shipping in the area so as to spot any unusual traffic; also, earlier on in the war Japanese submarines had operated in these waters and they, together with a number of German U-boats, were still active in the Indian Ocean. The weather was also a hazard, particularly in the Mozambique Channel between Madagascar and the African coast."

AW Deller

Haberaduwa village was on the Galle road just outside Koggala. (J Laydon).

The Silver Slipper was a popular 'watering hole' in Haberaduwa with 230 crews. (J Laydon).

Koggala beach in 1944 was popular for surfing. (J Laydon)

HANDLEBARS AND HOOKWORM

John Laydon was with the Squadron at Koggala and provides an interesting insight into the difficulties of servicing the Sunderland in the primitive conditions encountered in the Far East.

"I joined 230 Squadron whilst it was based at Koggala and my RAF trade was that of Blacksmith/Welder. As such I was attached to the Station Workshops but still very much a member of 230 as per instructions by the Sqn Warrant Officer, Mr Harris I think his name was, (nicknamed 'Handlebars'). Any work for the Sqn did get priority and I can recall only two occasions when I was called upon to do any actual welding on aircraft at their moorings. Both jobs were for welding fractures in the engine exhaust ring on the cowling of a Pegasus engine on a Mk III Sunderland. Not a task one gets trained for at No 8 School of Technical Training. The first time I was scared shitless in case I fell into the water. The stories about 'Hookworm' and crocodiles were not without foundation.

The second occasion was not without incident. Oxy/Acetylene equipment complete with hoses and cylinders is not light and the usual practice was to use a 'bomb scow', a motor driven boat. Well, the NCO i/c that particular aircraft was in a hurry and wanted the 'scow' for some other purpose and had me and a couple of 'erks' put my gear in a large powered dinghy. Dinghies have a single ply Rubber bottom and Oxy/Acetylene cylinders DO NOT FLOAT along with two or three toolboxes. There were some harsh words used that day, I do wish I could remember them. I was on the squadron strength for only about a year. They had converted to Mk Vs by then and when its posting to the Burma coast came through I was in hospital with some tropical malady and someone else took my place, very much to my regret."

J Laydon

On 5 March F/L Rand in DP180:O set out to locate the survivors of the *MV Fort McLeod* which had been torpedoed by a U-boat. After four hours he sighted wreckage and then two lifeboats, containing forty men. Owing to the rough sea Rand was unable to land and dropped emergency rations, signalling that help was on the way. Rand was relieved by F/L Ingham in EJ132:X who kept in touch with the lifeboats. Over the night of 5/6 March he in turn was relieved by F/O Garside in JM659:Q who patrolled over the lifeboats throughout the night. The survivors were picked up by the rescue vessels, which arrived that day.

On 7 March F/O Garside was carrying out a convoy escort when his Sunderland, JM659:Q, developed engine trouble. He decided to return to base and was forced to jettison his depth charges and 600 gallons of fuel prior to making a safe landing. The remainder of the month was taken up with convoy escorts that produced no sightings or attacks.

SPIDERS, SNAKES AND CROCODILES

The Squadron arrived at Koggala on 24 February 1944 and quickly settled in to the station, though there was initially some resentment to the changes brought by the Sunderlands from the two Catalina squadrons based there. Everyone also had to get used to the all pervading dampness and the dangers lurking in the area. Alan Deller recalls a couple of incidents:

"*The station itself was very large with an extensive servicing area and a concrete runway that was used frequently by a small Fleet Air Arm detachment; everywhere there were palm trees and lush undergrowth, away from the occupied areas, and the humid atmosphere and general impression of hot, hot dampness overwhelmed us from the moment we stepped ashore. Many of the offices and stores were in houses, mostly dotted about in among the palm trees and all-pervading greenery; they were very simple, made of plaster covered brick or concrete, with roofs of rather similar tiles to*

those common in Mediterranean countries for example, while the floors were of concrete, the whole looking, smelling and feeling damp. Most other buildings on the station, including our quarters and the Mess were built of palm frond wattle on frames of palm trunks, the haunt of a variety of spiders and the occasional scorpion; cobras often came into the quarters – my first wireless operator went into his room and spotted one asleep on top of his mosquito net from where it leapt down, wriggled out onto the veranda and sat there swaying from side to side with its hood extended and making a rather disagreeable noise – some 'erks' passing by got a big stick and beat it to death. The only quarter on the whole station that was mosquito-proofed was that of the station commander, Group Captain Mills, and those busy pests made the evenings everywhere else nearly unbearable, particularly during the monsoon.

One day some months later, air crews and maintenance people were busy on all the aircraft when suddenly a crocodile appeared, swimming between two rows of moored aircraft, with his body almost submerged and his snout and horrid little eyes looking unbelievably sinister; everybody who happened to be up on the mainplane instinctively checked his foothold. We estimated he was sixteen feet long. A while later he ate half of an unfortunate RAF officer who had fallen into the water and drowned."

AW Deller

THE RESCUE OF THE CREW OF SS FORT MCLEOD

The *SS Fort McLeod* set sail from Colombo bound for Durban on the morning of 2 March 1944. During the passage the Master of the vessel, Captain W Alderton, received several messages warning of submarine activity in the area. Accordingly, he began to follow a zig-zag course. This defensive measure was to no avail however, as at 2135 hrs on 3 March, in a slight sea with a moderate swell and good weather and visibility, under a half moon, the *SS Fort McLeod* was torpedoed The propeller and rudder were blown away and the main engines stopped immediately. The crew was unhurt, and being completely immobilised, the captain decided to lower the lifeboats and get the crew away.

The submarine made its escape as the Senior Radio Officer sent his distress message out. As an acknowledgement was received from Colombo the Captain and officers left the ship in a waiting lifeboat. At 2240 hrs a second torpedo struck the ship on the starboard side with a bright flash and explosion. The ship began to settle immediately by the stern and a midnight a third explosion, presumed to be a third torpedo, was heard. At 0030 hrs the submarine surfaced and began shelling the ship and by 0100 hrs the *SS Fort McLeod* had sunk. The submarine then departed, making no contact with the survivors.

At daylight the four lifeboats closed up and Captain Alderton decided to make for Addu Atoll, two hundred miles away. The following day the crew of the *SS Fort McLeod* had a change of fortune. The Captain takes up the story in his report:

> "At 1430 on the 4th March, an aircraft was sighted in the distance, but she did not see us. We were unable to signal, as our smoke flares and rockets were wet. At 1600 a Liberator aircraft, with the marking 'V', was sighted over the two small boats which we had abandoned. Rockets and smoke flares, which had now dried, were sent up by No 4 lifeboat and the aircraft flew towards us. The pilot signalled that help was on the way, and would probably arrive the following day. He then dropped some stores, which fell out of the container and were lost. The pilot wished us 'Good Luck', then flew away. We lowered our sails and lay to a sea anchor all night to await the arrival of our rescuers."

They did not have long to wait before another aircraft arrived to assist them. This was F/L Rand in DP180:O. Following this F/L Ingham in EJ152 kept in touch with the lifeboats and was in turn relieved by F/O Garside in JM659:Q:

> "At 1400 on 5th March, a Sunderland aircraft arrived, dropped a message stating help was coming, gave us our position, and regretted that the swell was too high for

him to land and pick us up. Medical supplies were also dropped, which fortunately were not required.......

Another aircraft arrived at about 1900 and remained with us until about 0200 the following morning. At 0300 on the 6th March, another aircraft flew over us and at 0430 a further aircraft shone a searchlight onto No 4 lifeboat. At 0830 we sighted smoke on the horizon..."

The smoke was from the rescue vessels, *HM Trawler Sluna* and *HM Tug Integrity*, who took the survivors on board and landed them at Colombo on the morning of 8 March. Captain Alderton was generous in his praise of the aircraft involved in the rescue:

"I should also like to record my appreciation of the efforts made on our behalf by Coastal Command, and by the Officers and men of both rescuing vessels....... The boat's wireless set worked well. I understand that our signals were picked up by a vessel at a distance of about a hundred miles. The set also proved extremely useful in making contact with the aircraft, enabling us to exchange messages."

Extract from a report from the Shipping Casualties Section – Trade Division

C O P
For:- HART. L.E. W/O

GLEN LINE LIMITED,
COLOMBO, CEYLON,
March 9th 1944.

To :   Air Officer Commanding,
            Coastal Command, Ceylon.
Sir,
Will you kindly express to the Officers and Men immediately concerned in the rescue of the entire crew of the steamer "Fort McLeod", the heartfelt appreciation of myself, my Officers and men.
The promptitude of your discovery of us in our plight and the swift and sure manner in which you succoured us in our distress and brought us help will forever remain a wonderful memory in the hearts of all personnel concerned.
I join my Officers and Men in once more thanking you and wishing you and your Command every success in the future and may God speed our Victory.
I remain, Sir,
Yours most gratefully,
Sgd/- W.Alderton, Commander.

During April No 222 Gp assessed that their were only two U-boats operating in the area but this did not stop the squadron from carrying out a large number of convoy escorts. During the month no ships were lost in the whole of the Indian

Ocean but the rate of flying and the lack of groundcrew, still in transit from Dar es Salaam, resulted in an accumulation of aircraft unserviceabilities. With the arrival of the groundcrew on the 9th a concerted effort was made to improve this situation and many engine changes were carried out. The most important escort duty, as far as the squadron was concerned, was the escort of *HMT Manela*, carrying the squadron groundcrew. This important duty was carried out by F/L Deller in EJ145:Y on the 8th.

TRIALS AND TRIBULATIONS

"This period in squadron history was a vexed one. We were then equipped with Sunderland Mk III which had a dorsal turret instead of the two open gun hatches of the Mk I and had a streamlined 'step' which gave better water handling characteristics. We removed the dorsal turrets to give a better performance but the snag was with the engines – Pegasus XVIIIs, which gave constant trouble. The chief cause was sticking valves and no one seemed to be able to cure the disease. Anti-submarine sorties over the Indian Ocean were invariably cut short by engine failures; sometimes two engines on a single patrol! It was a frustrating situation but the real blow to our morale was ultimately having two Catalina squadrons, 205 and 413, posted to Koggala to take over our operational duties!

We had obviously failed but let me hasten to add, NOT through any shortcomings of the squadron personnel who struggled gamefully for long hours to keep the aircraft going. Nevertheless, no one could argue that the Catalina was not a better aircraft for the long patrols, which the Indian Ocean demanded.

The engines of the poor old Sunderland Mk III were simply not up to the job. We needed the Sunderland Mk V with Pratt & Whitney Wasp engines badly! I made many appeals to 222 Group for Mk V Sunderlands and they did all they could on the squadron's behalf, but these aircraft were reserved for the Atlantic battle. As an alternative I even asked for Catalinas or Liberators! Still no joy. Eventually, after I had left the squadron to take over RAF Cochin the long awaited MK Vs arrived and the squadron moved to Burma waters."

DK Bednall

May 1944 was to be an eventful month for the squadron. Convoy escorts and anti-submarine patrols continued, but for the second month in succession no ship was sunk in the Indian Ocean. Equally the squadron had no successes. This is not to say that there was no excitement for the squadron though. On 17 May Admiral Lord Louis Mountbatten visited the squadron giving a spirited talk on future operations in the region from atop a packing case. On 27 May S/Ldr Middleton left Kogalla in DP180:O for Calcutta, en route to a forward base in Assam, North Burma. The Sunderland operated from there for a fortnight evacuating personnel, mainly battle casualties and the sick, of the 3rd Indian Division. The operation was codenamed 'River' and DP180 evacuated over 260 personnel in eight sorties. A second Sunderland joined Middleton in June on this operation.

By 5 June the Japanese rearguard at Kohima was in retreat and by the 18th the British 2nd Division had advanced towards Imphal. The Chindits and the Chinese took Mogaung on 26 June. During June DP180:O and JM659:Q operated from Dibrugarh on the River Brahmaputra and evacuated over 500 casualties from Lake Indawgyi in North Burma. The monsoon was making it impossible for the Dakotas and Sentinels to operate in support of General Lentaigne's columns and the squadrons two Sunderlands undertook sterling work from Lake Indawgyi evacuating casualties on the outbound leg and bringing in much needed supplied on the inbound flights. Unfortunately JM659:Q would be lost in this operation when it was destroyed by a hurricane whilst moored at Dibrugarh.

The remainder of the squadron at Koggala busied itself with convoy escorts and anti-submarine patrols but the U-boats were conspicuous by their absence. This absence was not to last, however, and on 29 June the *SS Hellore* en route from India to Australia was sunk 120 miles from Diego Garcia, followed by the *SS Jean Nicholet*, which was torpedoed and sunk east of Addu Atoll on 2 July. Catalina's operating from Addu Atoll and Diego Garcia carried out extensive searches for the survivors from the *SS Jean Nicholet* and located nearly 250 of them, which were then picked up by a warship. Over 100 of the survivors were landed at Diego Garcia and EJ132:X was sent to return 70 of them, mostly Lascars, to Addu Atoll in a single flight. One of the *Hellore's* lifeboats that had been found, and subsequently lost, by the Catalina's finally reached Diego Suarez after a voyage of two thousand miles and three weeks. This was an epic story of courage and determination to survive. The remainder of the month was filled with routine convoy escorts and anti-submarine patrols.

During August the Chinese captured Myitkyina and the British captured Tamu in Burma. By the 16th Japanese resistance in north east India had been crushed. By the end of the month the British 36th Division had advanced into Burma and taken Pindaw. August saw little activity other than the routine of patrols, escorts and a few ASR sorties. A familiar face arrived at Kogalla when the station commander, G/Capt RL Mills was replaced by Gp Capt G Francis, a former squadron commander, on 3 August. Recognition for the squadron's part in

'Operation River' came in the form of immediate awards of the DFC to S/Ldr Middleton, F/L Rand and F/O Verney and the DFM to F/Sgt Webber during August.

On 2 September the squadron HQ and Section offices moved into the accommodation vacated by the General Reconnaissance & Air Navigation School which had just been disbanded. Two weeks later, on September 15 the squadron provided three flights for a parade to commemorate the victory in the Battle of Britain. During the month F/L Fumerton and F/O Schroder were detached to make an inspection of Minneriya Tank as a possible flying boat base, returning on the 15th. The squadron had now settled into a routine of escorts and the occasional anti-submarine patrol and the months of September and October had little to show for their efforts, though it could be argued that their very presence over the convoys and patrolling the sealanes kept the U-boats and Japanese submarines below the surface and out of attack positions.

There was little change in November and on the 10th W/Cdr Powell arrived to take over the squadron from W/Cdr Bednall. Powell had previously served with the squadron. The month saw many personnel changes with several crews 'tour expired' and others detached to the UK to convert to the Sunderland Mk.V.

Sunderland DP180:O offloading Chindit casualties on the Brahmaputra River. (DK Bednall).

BEER NIGHT

Sergeant Joe Pease (Later Lord Gainford) recalls life at Koggala. Joe had been washed out as aircrew and after retraining as a Compass Adjuster and serving with Bomber Command he volunteered for overseas service:

"My comrades regarded me as mad but I never regretted it. In due course I ended up at Kogalla. My main memories are about how we lived in primitively constructed buildings. With the rations each man had a card entitling him to a bottle of beer per week. Once a week was Beer Night."

Lord Gainford

APPENDIX 'G' TO FORM 540 – 230 SQUADRON – JUNE 1944
"OPERATION 'RIVER'" HISTORY

On the 27th May 1944 Sunderland O/230 left base at Koggala with instructions to proceed to CALCUTTA preparatory to carrying out "Operation 'River'". This operation was to evacuate a number of casualties, estimated at between 900 and 960 belonging to the 3rd Indian Division who were operating in the swampy country to the west of HOPIH. These casualties were seriously hampering the movement of the division and their evacuation was not possible by land plane owing to the terrain. LAKE INDAWGYI situated to the westward of the railway from MYITKYNIA to MANDALAY was considered a suitable alighting area and the 3rd Indian Division had the necessary boats to transfer the wounded from the shore to the aircraft. The crew of the Sunderland were as follows:-

Squadron Leader	JL Middleton	-	Flight Commander
Flight Lieut.	J Rand	-	Captain
Flying Officer	VN Verney	-	Navigator
Flight Sergt.	DM Wright	-	2nd Pilot
do-	RF Webber	-	Flight Engineer
do-	H Neeve-	2nd Engineer	
Warrant Officer	R Guertin	-	1st Wireless Operator
Flight Sergt.	HH Tulloch	-	2nd –do-
do-	DJK Butcher	-	Wireless Operator Mechanic
do-	JB Knox-	Air Gunner	

On the 28th May the Officers and 1st Wireless Operator of the crew flew from CALCUTTA to COMILLA in an American 'Mitchell' to the headquarters of the 3rd Tactical Air Force for briefing by Air Marshal Sir John Baldwin. It was decided not practicable to use CALCUTTA as a base for the operation as the long journey to the lake would have reduced the Sunderlands effective load of casualties. A forward base at DIBRUGARH on the River Brahmaputra, practically in the foothills of the Himalayas, was considered more suitable. On the following day, therefore, the Flight Commander, Captain and Navigator flew to DIBRUGARH in a 'Mitchell' to reconnoitre the proposed alighting area and approaches. On completion of the reconnaissance the 'Mitchell' landed at DINJAN aerodrome and a conference was called by Wing Commander Drake AFC of HQ Eastern Air Command, who had been appointed OC "Operation 'River' ". Arrangements were made for the Sunderland to fly to DIBRUGARH on the 31st May and commence operations on the 1st June. On the 31st May the aircraft flew from CALCUTTA and alighted safely at DIBRUGARH. A final briefing took place at DINJAN with General

Egan of the US Tactical Air Force, where information was supplied regarding enemy air activity, the ground situation and arrangements for Fighter aircraft escort. Major G Beaven RA of PRU Headquarters acted as Liaison Officer between the Army and the RAF, and Lieut Col Knapp was in charge of all military arrangements.

SUMMARY OF EVENTS

June 1st At 0545 (Local time) Aircraft 'O' was airborne from DIBRUGARH and set course for LAKE INDAWGYI. Extremely unfavourable weather conditions prevailed with 10/10ths clod from 500 ft to 20,000 ft and the sortie proved abortive, the aircraft being compelled to return to Base, reaching the alighting area at 1015 hrs.

June 2nd At 1250 hrs aircraft took off in bad weather and without Fighter escort and was successful in reaching the lake. An alighting was made at the north end at 1420hrs and 32 casualties were paddled out in dinghies and taken aboard. Airborne at 1500 hrs and returned to Base without incident. The load carried was experimental in regard to the immediate heavy climb to 10,000 ft from LAKE INDAWGYI and possible enemy action.

June 3rd Airborne at 1235 hrs in similar weather conditions and without fighter escort. Waterborne on lake at 1450 hrs and embarked 56 casualties. Airborne at 1551 hrs and on the return journey sighted two Japanese fighters assumed to be 'Hamps' flying below in the vicinity of TALANG GA. Continued on our course, however, without interference and arrived at Base at 1720 hrs.

June 4th At 1035 hrs with very slightly improved weather conditions took off and picked up an escort of 4 Mustangs – P-51s – over DINJAN. Arrived safely at the lake at 1240 hrs and took on board 29 casualties and left supplies of K rations. Airborne at 1315 hrs and arrived back at Base at 1510 hrs.

June 5th Airborne again at 0600 hrs and picked up an escort of 4 Mustangs over DINJAN. The weather was much the same as on the previous day and on completion of the outward journey, a landing was made on the southern end of the lake, off LONTON. 41 casualties were taken on board. On both the outward and return journeys, 8 enemy fighters possibly 'Zeros' were seen below us but the cloud cover gave us sufficient protection and we were not attacked.

Waterborne at Base at 1110 hrs. A second sortie was then made, taking off at 1245 hrs. Once again we had the same fighter escort and evacuated 40 battle casualties from the southern end of the lake. DIBRUGARH was reached at 1705 hrs.

June 6th The day was spent in maintenance of the aircraft and we welcomed our colleagues F/O EA Garside and crew who arrived in Sunderland Q/230 which had been sent as a reinforcement aircraft. (The activities of this latter aircraft will be the subject of a separate report).

June 7th The afternoon of the 7th was devoted to a photo recce of DIBRUGARH.

June 8th Took off at 1150 hrs carrying 29 passengers a number of Commandos, together with supplies. Fighter escort was not available owing to adverse weather conditions. Alighted safely at LONTON at 1350 hrs and evacuated 41 casualties. All the casualties that were evacuated from the forward area were suffering from battle wounds, malaria, typhus, pneumonia and dysentery and were in an exhausted condition.

June 9th Airborne at 0600 hours and picked up fighter escort over DINJAN but the latter was compelled to return to their base on account of bad weather. The Sunderland continued on through the shocking weather, located the lake and made a safe landing at 0800 hrs. 41 casualties were again picked up and we were airborne at 0841 hrs arriving back at Base at 1030 hrs. This was the final sortie made by Aircraft 'O' although Aircraft 'Q' carried out several after this date.

In all Aircraft 'O' evacuated 369 casualties and although flying conditions were extremely bad during the whole course of the operation, imposing a severe strain on members of the crew, everyone felt gratified that a useful job of work had been successfully accomplished. It should be added that during the operation the crew had the honour of meeting, at various places, the following high-ranking officers: General Egan, General Stratmeyer, Colonel Chandler, Air Vice Marshal Williams

June 11th Aircraft 'O' left Calcutta and proceeded via Madras back to base at Koggala, arriving on 12th.

Signed
Intelligence Officer. 230 Squadron

"OPERATION RIVER"

June 2   Aircraft Q/230 received orders to proceed to DIBRUGARH to reinforce aircraft O/230 engaged there. Airborne Koggala 043 arrived at CALCUTTA 1300.

This crew consists of:-

F/O	EA Garside	Captain
F/S	H Smith	2nd Pilot
F/O	AF Norton	Navigator
F/S	D Turner	1st W/Op
F/S	P Phelan	WOM
F/S	B Meteer	1st Engineer
F/S	T Cronin	2nd "
F/L	FG Marshall	A/G

June 4   Left CALCUTTA at 0700 and arriving at DIBRUGARH at 1230. During the afternoon an American 'Duck', which was being used as Marine Craft collided with port float, damage being sustained. Maintenance considered it possible to make one trip after temporary repairs had been carried out and so it was decided to return to Calcutta where B.O.A.C. were known to have a new float. A take off was made at 1030 on the following morning CALCUTTA being reached at 1530. Work was immediately started but had to be deferred for several hours owing to unfavourable conditions on the Hooghly. Work was started again at midnight and by the united efforts of our own maintenance and help loaned by the B.O.A.C. the replacement was completed by 0600.

June 6 & 7   Took off 0700 and arrived safely at DIBRUGARH at 1230. Made first sortie. The F/Commander S/Ldr LJ Middleton accompanied the Sunderland as he was now well aware of the route and general conditions. A/borne at 0600 without fighter escort; the weather was extremely bad particularly over the mountain passes with 10/10 cloud and rain but a safe landing was made on Lake INDAWGYI at 0800. Embarked 39 casualties, took off at 0840 and arrived back at base at 1040. A second sortie was then made in slightly improved weather conditions. A/borne at 1300 landing on the lake at 1445 and embarked 40 casualties; took off at 1525 and alighted at BASE 1715. On neither trip were enemy aircraft seen.

June 8, 9 & 10   Carried out at 1000 hours inspection of aircraft.

(10th) Conditions on the river were unfavourable owing to drifting mist and any intention of a sortie was ruled out. Airborne at 1230, fighter escort was provided 4 P-51 (Mustangs). Weather was slightly better with 5/10 cloud. Alighted at the lake at 1345 and took on board 40 casualties. A/borne again at 1415 and landed at Base 1700.

June 11 As weather report was favourable it was hoped that two sorties might be carried out but whilst the aircraft was taxiing to take off both starboard engines cut and the trip had to be abandoned. The aircraft was put u/s for 48 hours as water was found in the carburettors and starboard tanks, which necessitated complete defuelling and refuelling and cleaning of carburettors. By dint of much hard work the aircraft was made serviceable by the following day.

June 12 Took off in very bad weather at 0700; conditions grew worse en route and it was decided to return to base which was reached at 1045.

June 13 Weather was so bad that flying was out of the question.

June 14 A second abortive sortie was made; aircraft was compelled to return after being in the air for 25 minutes.

June 15 Bad weather persisted and no sorties were attempted.

June 16 Another attempt was made to get through to Lake INDAWGYI but weather proved too bad and a return was made after an hour and three-quarters.

June 17 More misfortune followed. It was found that a new starter motor was needed; this was immediately demanded and in the meantime the aircraft remained u/s.

June 20 For the second time during the operation an American 'Duck' 'did its worst' colliding with the port float. On examination it was found that although the float was undamaged the float assembly mainspars and all struts were u/s. The float itself was therefore taken off to await arrival of new parts.

July 4 'The most bitter pill of all'. At 1800 hours a very high wind sprang up and without any warning struck the aircraft on the starboard side sending the port mainplane hard into the water. The angle was so steep that water immediately poured through the port galley hatch from which the drogue was streamed to keep the aircraft steady under normal conditions. Water also entered by the front port hatch and the aircraft was lurching at such a precarious angle and the position was so hopeless that the boat guard of F/L Marshall and F/S Turner reluctantly abandoned it. They were picked up by a native craft after their dinghy had been overturned by the storm.

July 7 After all these vicissitudes the crew returned by DC3 transport aircraft to DUM DUM and on the 9th travelling on Sunderland O/230 from CALCUTTA via MADRAS back to the home base at KOGGALA.

  Signed
  Intelligence Officer,
  230 Squadron, RAF

"OPERATION RIVER" - HISTORY

In the 26th June, 1944 Sunderland O/230 received orders to proceed Northwards to DIBRUGARH again to continue the evacuation of casualties from LAKE INDAWGYI. Sunderland Q/230 which had been left there to complete the operation had unfortunately become u/s and as it appeared likely to remain so for some time O/230's assistance was called for. With the same crew as on the previous occasion with the exception of F/Sgt Halfacree for F/Sgt DJK Butcher, aircraft O/230 left Koggala at 2200 hours local time on the 26th June 1944 and arrived at WILLINGDON BEACH, CALCUTTA at 0715 hours on the 27th June. On the following day the journey to DIBRUGARH, ASSAM, was completed, but during the trip the air speed indicator went u/s and so on arrival repairs were effected. An airtest which proved satisfactory was carried out on the 29th June and on the last day of the month the aircraft was ready for service.

SUMMARY OF EVENTS

June 30th   Took off from DIBRUGARH at 1150. The weather was poor with 10/10 low cloud. No fighters accompanied us. Heavy rain was encountered on the way but there was a break over LAKE INDAWGYI and a landing was made in a new area at the extreme Northern end. Supplies delivered included one assault boat with outboard motor. 40 casualties were embarked and a turn round was effected in one hour, aircraft being airborne again at 1510 hrs. A warning was received that Japanese fighters were in the vicinity but none were sighted. The weather deteriorated over the mountains and in the BRAHMAPUTRA VALLEY rain was falling. A safe landing was made at 1720 hours.

July 1st Set off from base in bad weather at 1200 hours without fighter escort. Over the lake found 7/10 cloud with base 400 ft. Alighted without incident at 1420 hours and unloaded supplies and four Army replacement personnel. A turn round was made in 55 minutes and with 40 casualties aboard returned to base in slightly improved weather conditions arriving at 1730.

July 2nd The Met forecast for the day described the whole area over the mountains and lake as obscured 10/10 Cu. Nims. with severe electrical storms. The weather had closed in over DIBRUGARH with heavy rain and as there was no sign of improvement during the morning it was decided to abandon any attempt at a sortie.

July 3rd With considerably better weather it was agreed to bring forward the time of take off by one hour and aircraft was airborne at 1120 hours. An escort of P-51 (Mustangs) was provided from DINJAN. On this occasion special medical supplies were taken and also some coined currency at the request of the Army authorities. A landing was made at 1330 and after embarking casualties and one very disconsolate Japanese prisoner, course was set for base at 1420 hours. On this, the final sortie, the most favourable weather of any of the journeys was experienced. Base was reached at 1640 hours. It was rumoured some time later that at 1500 hours (i.e. twenty minutes after the aircraft had left) Japanese fighters machine gunned the lake and sank one of the large rubber rafts which had been used for ferrying the casualties to the aircraft. On both previous occasions the aircraft had been on the lake at this time. Finally, half an hour after landing and before the refuelling party had gone aboard, the mooring buoy broke and the Sunderland started to drift downstream. However it was recovered by the efforts of the Captain and three of the crew who safely anchored the aircraft until the buoy had been repaired by the Flight Commander and the Navigator.

July 4th On completion of 'O's share in the operation, the aircraft left DIBRUGARH for CALCUTTA carrying as passengers OC Operation 'River' – Wing Commander Drake AFC, and PR personnel. After arrival in CALCUTTA news came through of the loss of aircraft 'Q' and so 'O' awaited the arrival of the Flight Commander, Squadron Leader Middleton and the Captain and crew of 'Q'.

July 8th The personnel mentioned above having arrived, aircraft left CALCUTTA at 0700 hours and arrived RED HILLS LAKE, MADRAS, at 1430 hours.

July 9th The last lap of the journey was completed. Airborne at RED HILLS LAKE at 0900 hours and arrived back at base at KOGGALA at 1325 hours.

230 Squadron Sunderland, Ceylon.

FIRST FLYING BOATS IN THE JUNGLE

Sunderlands Make History

Operating Sunderland flying boats in the middle of the Burma jungle – this is perhaps the most astonishing and daring feat the war in Burma has yet seen. They brought sick and wounded soldiers, most of them 3rd Indian Division men, out of the jungle, and took stores and reinforcements in.

The operation was carried out by two RAF Sunderlands of an Indian Ocean General Reconnaissance Group. For the first time a flying boat has put down on the upper waters of the Brahmaputra. For the first time a flying boat has travelled far over the jungle to put down on a lake deep inland.

From beginning to end the Sunderland crews knew that they were taking the gravest risks – the risk of operating from unknown water, of flying over mountainous country inaccurately mapped, of thunderous monsoon storms, of Japanese fighters. But they did the job magnificently.

Keyed – up

After consultations with Air Marshal Sir John Baldwin – to whose Tactical Air Force, Eastern Air Command, the Sunderlands were lent for the operation – W/Cdr Drake, S/Ldr Middleton, F/Lt Rand, FO Noel Verney, navigator of O for Orange and Warrant Officer Ray Guertin, RCAF, of Rimouski, Quebec, wireless operator, flew in another aircraft to a rendezvous on the Brahmaputra to prospect.

Though the river was far from fit for a flying boat as the current is swift and carries along much heavy rubbish, they decided that here was the best stretch of water available from which to make the jump into Burma.

"I think we were all rather keyed up." Said F.Sgt Knox, gunner, who, like his Captain, comes from Co. Durham. "The river was unsounded; there were tricky currents, floating debris and possibly hidden sandbanks. From the air the river looked muddy and shallow. At the Captains instruction we put on Mae West's and went down. It was all right – we didn't need them – but it was a difficult job negotiating the currents and mooring the Sunderland to a buoy

That was on 31 May. Air Marshal Baldwin had come to see the start of the operation and next morning the Sunderland started out for the Indawgyi Lake. But the weather proved impossible – 10/10 cloud up to 17,000 feet.

Got Through

"Flying blind we made a 'creeping search' for the lake," Said F/Lt Rand "but it was no good. We couldn't see a thing for cloud and had to turn back. We must have passed close to the Japs – we could hear them on our R/T."

Every two hours meteorological reports were received by signal from the Army waiting at the lakeside and the next day 'O' for Orange made her first successful trip.

"The clouds were still thick," said F.O. Verney, the navigator, "and we were still flying blind over wild mountainous country which has never been properly mapped. Our maps showed the highest peaks to be around 6,000 feet so to be on the safe side we went up to 8,000. Suddenly, dead ahead of us, the mist darkened; we were going straight into a mountain. S/Ldr Middleton, who was pilot at the time pulled the aircraft round and in a few moments there was another dark patch ahead – another mountain. We slipped between the two mountains and, regaining our composure, found Indawgyi Lake, and came down without further incident."

No time was wasted at the lake; the great Sunderland would have been too easy a target for enemy aircraft, never far away. Directly she touched down, the stores and reinforcements were unloaded and the casualties were brought out in little boats. The stretcher cases lying across two boats lashed together. The stretchers, made of bamboo, had to be man-handled through the Sunderlands bomb doors. The aircrew did this themselves.

THESE MEN DID IT

Flight Commander: S/Ldr LJ Middleton, Folkestone, Kent.
CREW OF 'O' FOR ORANGE
Captain: F/Lt J Rand, Cockfield, Bishop Auckland, Durham.
2nd Pilot: F/Sgt M Wright, Lindale, Grange-over-Sands, Lancs.
Navigator: F/O VN Verney, Nundah, Brisbane.
1st WOP: W/O R Guertin, Rimouski, Quebec.
2nd WOP: F/Sgt RW Tulloch, Daiston, London.
WOMS: F/Sgt D Butcher, Tunbridge Wells. F/Sgt FGT
Halfacre, Thames Ditton, Surrey.
1st Engineer: F/Sgt RF Webber, Caister-on-Sea, Norfolk.
2nd Engineer: F/Sgt RH Neeve, Leeds 7.
Rear Gunner: F/Sgt JB Knox, Horden, Co. Durham.

CREW OF 'Q' FOR QUEENIE

Captain: F/O EA Garside, Edinburgh 6.
2nd Pilot: F.Sgt HW Smith, Harrogate.
Navigator: F/O AJ Norton, Winnipeg.
Gunnery Officer: F/L FG Marshall, Blackton
1st Wireless Operator: F/Sgt D Turner, Lancs.
WOP/AG: Sgt WH Garlick, Cricklewood, NW.
WOP/AG: Sgt W Phelan, Whitehall, Dublin.
1st Eng: Sgt B Meteer, Distington, Cumberland.
2nd Eng: Sgt TP Cronin, West Hampstead, NW.

Maximum Load

During the next three days, four successful trips were made. Every day the load was increased till the maximum the Sunderland could carry if it was to climb over the mountains at a safe height of 10,000 feet was reached. But had even one of the Sunderlands four engines failed, the aircraft, so fully loaded, could not have maintained height and must have crashed into the mountains.

The operation was planned to last about four days but request for a second Sunderland was made. So on 5 June, 'Q' for Queenie joined 'O' for Orange on the Brahmaputra.

Unfortunately Queenie damaged a float. She flew back to base the same day for a quick repair and joined Orange again on the 6th. On the 7th she made two successful trips to the lake. On the next day Orange was in again.

So the work went on – stores and reinforcements going in, casualties coming out. But now the monsoon had broken and gales and violent thunderstorms meant blank days. Here is the diary continued:

8 June –   *Queenie on inspection. Orange evacuated casualties.*

10 June -   *Queenie evacuated casualties. Orange returned to base.*

11 June -   *Queenie unserviceable.*

12 June -   *Queenie turned back due to weather.*

13 June -   *Weather impossible. No take off.*

14 June -   *Queenie turned back by weather.*

15 June -   *Weather impossible.*

16 June -   *Queenie turned back by weather.*

17-20 June   *Weather impossible and on the 20th Queenie damaged at her mooring became permanently unserviceable.*

The Brahmaputra, in fact, was no longer to be relied on. The monsoon rains had swollen the river five to six feet above its normal level and the current, at 12 knots, was bringing with it whole trees, great chunks of the river bank and the bodies of dead animals. Nevertheless, Orange returned on 29 June and on the 30th flew in after lunch and fetched a load of casualties.

The Japs had got wind of the operation. During the trip on the 30th, when Orange was approaching Indawgyi Lake from the North enemy fighters passed over the area but missed the flying boat.

Machine – Gunned

On 3 July Orange went in once more and took out casualties and one Japanese prisoner, completing the trip during the morning. And at 3 that afternoon the Japs

came over and machine-gunned the lake. There can be no doubt that they had got wise. Orange returned to base but Queenie remained at her mooring on the Brahmaputra to await repairs. On the night of July 4th-5th a whirlwind blew up and she sank; the two members of the crew on boat-guard duties were saved.

In all the Sunderlands made 13 successful flights to the lake, in none of which did their passengers suffer any mishap. Orange made 10 successful trips and one that was abortive due to weather. Queenie made 3 that were successful and 3 that were abortive before she became unserviceable.

That is the story of a RAF operation novel and bold in conception. There are a hundred reasons why it ought to have failed – and two why it succeeded as it did; the two Sunderland aircrews, whose skill and endurance and courage are beyond praise.

(Wartime newspaper article – source unknown)

NEWSPAPER ARTICLE – 4 AUGUST 1944

Flying Boats Took Wounded From Jungle

(From ALAN HUMPHREYS, Reuter's Special Correspondent)

S.E.A.C. H.Q. KANDY (CEYLON)

Friday

One of the most daring operations on the Burma front has been completed with the evacuation, by Sunderland flying-boats, of sick and wounded Chindits from Lake Indawgyi, deep in Japanese-held territory in the heart of Burma.

Over a period of 32 days the flying-boats, borrowed from an Indian Ocean Reconnaissance Group operated from unknown waters

They threaded their way through inaccurately mapped 8,000 feet peaks, blanketed in cloud and monsoon rain, with the constant risk of encountering Japanese fighters to reach the lake ten miles north-west of Hopin, scene of the Chindits famous 'Blackpool' road and rail blocks.

The two Sunderlands, O for Orange and Q for Queenie, were captained by Flight-lieut. John Rand of Bishop Auckland, County Durham, and Flying-officer EA Garside, of Edinburgh.

Monsoon Problem

Directly the flying-boats touched down casualties were brought out in little boats, stretcher cases lying across two boats lashed together.

The deepening monsoon increased the difficulties. A stretch of the Brahmaputra at Dibrugarh for the jump into Burma became unreliable.

The river was five to six feet above its normal level and a 12-knot current brought down whole trees, great chunks of the river bank and the bodies of dead animals.

'Queenie' was damaged at her moorings halfway through the operation and became permanently unserviceable.

On the 32nd day 'Orange' made her final trip in the morning. On the same day the Japanese machine-gunned the lake. That ended a most gallant operation.

CHAP. VI. SECT. 28.

A large eye should be spliced into the free end of the mooring pennant, which should be lashed or shackled to the top of the buoy, so that it may be easily handled by the crew of the seaplane when they make fast (see fig. 8).

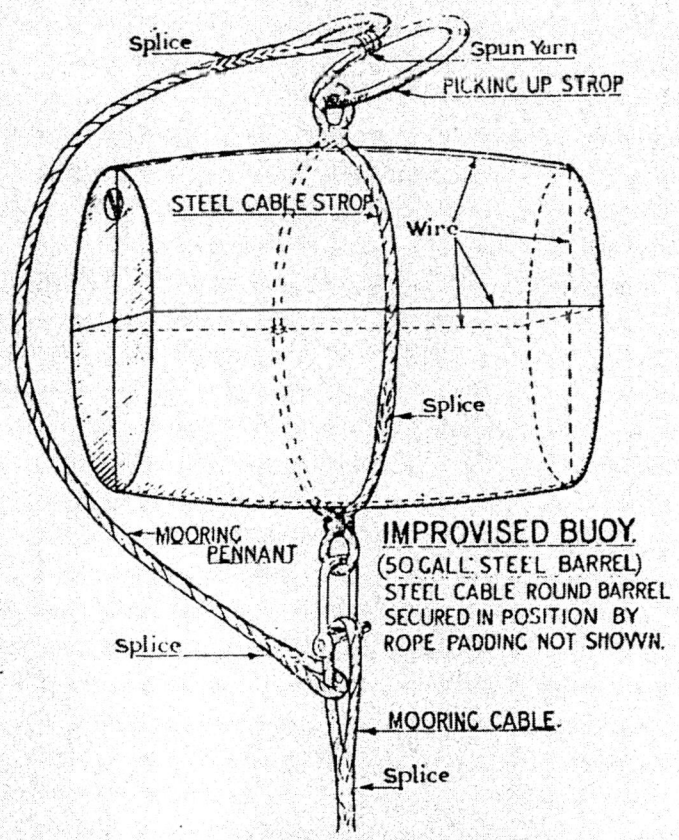

FIG. 8.—Improvised mooring buoy.

291. Buoys.—Each buoy should be able to support its end of the mooring wire or chain and remain afloat in the strongest current likely to be experienced at the moorings, but consistent with this, it should be as small and as light as possible. The buoy should not project more than three feet above the water. If made of metal or hard material it should be padded to avoid damage to the hull or floats. The most suitable buoy generally available is in the form of a drum padded with rope, such as the "Munro" type, a circular steel buoy wrapped with rope fenders.

292. An improvised buoy (see fig. 8) can be made from a 50 gallon steel barrel or a 40 gallon steel drum made water tight, padded with rope and fitted with a strong steel band to grip it firmly round the centre and to hold two shackles upright from opposite sides of the drum. The lower shackle is for the cable rom the sinkers the upper for the mooring wire from the aircraft If there are no facilities for fitting a steel band, a 1¼ in steel cable could be attached as shown in fig. 8

293. The buoy and mooring wire should be arranged so that there is a ring or eye above the water which can be picked up easily by a long boat hook. A small white flag attached to the buoy will help a pilot to find his moorings in a strange harbour. A 60 ft. grass line, with one end attached to the mooring buoy and the other to a small cork buoy, will help a floatplane pilot to pick up moorings.

78

Instructions for the use of an improvised mooring buoy.

W/Cdr Bednall's black painted Sunderland Mk III, JM673:P. (DK Bednall).

BURMESE INTERLUDE

"There was one happy chapter in spite of our troubles. We sent a detachment of two Sunderlands to the Bramaputra River to undertake a series of sorties behind Japanese lines to Lake Indawgyi to rescue wounded Chindits who had been fighting behind Japanese lines under General Wingate. A total of 577 men were rescued – all casualties. S/Ldr LF Middleton was in charge of the detachment and he and Jack Rand were awarded DFCs.

Meanwhile, during my negotiations for better and more suitable aircraft I had been selected for special duties involving flying boat operations. Despite my pleas and protestations from Group, Command would not release me from the Cochin job as they were short of experienced Wing Commanders!

But the Mk Vs were coming – sometime! – with the promise that eventually the squadron would be used for attacks on local shipping off the Burma coast. We therefore tried to keep morale on a high level by training for this promised role.

In spite of the UK experience with night camouflage, I was anxious to see whether a dark paint scheme would help conceal a Sunderland's attacking run in from the west at dawn under tropical conditions. I knew that an application 'through usual channels' would be unlikely to succeed so I decided to have my own aircraft JM673:P painted matt black all over. Tests from a marine craft off the southern coast of

Ceylon showed that the black flying boat was indeed more difficult to pick up than that with conventional light colour scheme.

So my second operational tour on Sunderlands with 230 Squadron came to an end. My regret was that I left when our fortunes were at a low ebb in that we had had, for month, inadequate aircraft and watched each day as Catalina squadrons took over our operational role."

DK Bednall

A 230 Sqn Sunderland in flight over Pamanzi in the Grand Comores. (Watson via JA Wilson).

Two crew members slip the moorings as the captain watches. The flaps have been lowered fully to help the wind to drift the aircraft astern to clear the buoy

Sunderland EJ143:S pulled out of the water at Koggala. (DJ Rees).

Black Sunderland MK III, JM673:P leads Mk IIIs, ML865:J and ML868 H in a flypast to bid farewell to Koggala in October 1944. (DK Bednall).

The month of November saw an increase in ASR activity for the squadron On the 6th F/L Sheardown carried out a search in ML865:J for a twin engined aircraft reported by the Navy to have crashed off the east coast of Ceylon. Nothing was found. On 16 December G/Capt Francis provided ASR cover for a Mitchell carrying Lord Mountbatten on the last 150 mile leg of his journey to Addu Atoll. The Mitchell was only sighted as it was about to land. G/Capt Francis took off later that day to cover the Mitchell's flight to Ratmalana but was recalled to Addu Atoll when the Mitchell force landed on Gan shortly after take off. The Sunderland, ML868:H was then commandeered by Lord Mountbatten, who wished to return to Ceylon as soon as possible. Another new Sunderland, EK595:Q, arrived for the squadron on 22 November from the UK

On 23 November F/L Sheardown was carrying out a search for some fishing vessels which had been blown out to sea in a storm when his Sunderland, ML865:J, developed engine trouble. He attempted to drop his depth charges prior to landing but one of the six hung up. He managed to land safely. On 28 November one of the squadrons Sunderlands failed to return from a patrol. JM673:P, flown by S/Ldr Ingham, with an experienced crew, had set out on an anti-submarine patrol and had failed to return by their ETA. The following day four Catalina's of No 205 Sqn in conjunction with two from No 413 Sqn and another from China Bay searched for the missing Sunderland from dawn to dusk with no success. F/L Nicholson in ML868:H also searched the area with no success. The search continued into December but nothing but pieces of wreckage, flotsam and jetsam were ever found. The search area had covered 36,000 square miles and extended to 90 miles seawards of the track of the missing aircraft. Nothing was left to chance and the coastline was covered twice in the hope that the crew had succeeded in reaching an isolated part of the coast of Ceylon.

Sunderland ML865:J over the Gulf of Siam. (DJ Rees).

In Burma the British had taken Kalewa in the drive to the Chindwin by the 2nd and the last month of 1944 was filled with uneventful anti-submarine patrols and passenger and freight flying. Another new Sunderland arrived from the UK on 13 December under the command of F/L Worsfold (RCAF). ML846 would be coded 'W'.

On 15 December, while the 19th Indian Division was linking up with British 36th Division, JM711:M was searching from Minneriya to Kankesantirai in conjunction with two other Sunderland's from the squadron and Liberators for a Japanese submarine. Naval Force 62 was also involved in the search. Nothing was found during the four-hour search. EK595:Q, piloted by F/O Toller, also took part but had as little luck in his five-hour search. F/L Levy-Haarscher, captained the third Sunderland, W6078:N, involved in the search, but like the others he sighted nothing. On the 18th F/O Moonlight arrived from the UK with a new crew in Sunderland DD866:T.

CYCLONE

Alan Deller recalls the circumstances leading up to the loss of S/Ldr Ingham and his crew:

"Group asked for an anti-submarine patrol to cover the whole east coast of Ceylon about eighty miles out. Met reports spoke of a cyclone situated in the east of the Bay of Bengal several hundred miles away; Group considered that this was not a danger to the patrol, but our station Met Officer, who had spent years before the war as a civilian forecaster in the Malayan Meteorological Service, was deeply perturbed – he knew from great experience how fast and unpredictably these fearsome cyclone could travel and he boldly tackled the Group Met people, urging them to recommend scrubbing the operation, but he was overruled. Ding took off and sent his first two regular position signals (wireless silence was not so vital as in the Atlantic) – then silence. As late morning wore on into afternoon concern grew; if the transmitter had gone u/s his operators would surely have got it going again or, if that had proved impossible, he would have observed the rules and returned to base, abandoning the patrol."

It was decided that a night search was useless and searches commenced the following day and for many days thereafter.

"We worked out that Ding would have been precisely where the cyclone passed on its way to the island. Poor Johns, our Met man, was in tears, wishing he had insisted more strongly but everyone assured him that he could not have done a thing more in view of Group's decision.

Not the smallest trace of either aircraft or Ding and his crew was ever found. So savage had been the impact of that terrible cyclone. We felt that no greater effort could possibly have been made by the exhausted personnel of the squadrons, maintenance, marine craft and ops room staff, for it all to prove in the end to be in vain was a great sadness for everyone."

AW Deller

On Christmas Day the squadron reduced to minimum manning to allow as many personnel as possible to take part in the festivities. The programme included

Bullock racing, the serving of the Airmen's Christmas Dinner, liberty runs to Closenburg for swimming and to Galle. The squadron flew its last patrol of the year on 30 December.

Sunderland Mk III, W6078:N with a full array of ASV aerials flies near Dar es Salaam. (DK Bednall).

Sunderland JM711:M landing at Dar es Salaam

SUNDERLAND Mk V

During December Alan Deller was given leave and on his return to the Squadron he discovered that the first of the new Sunderland Mk Vs had arrived. These were a vast improvement on the old Mk III.

"Back with the Squadron after my two weeks I found that Charles Potter had arrived back from the UK with the first of our new Mk V Sunderlands. This was very exciting as the new aircraft were a great advance on our ageing Mk IIIs; instead of the 1050 horsepower Bristol Pegasus XVIII engines they had American Pratt & Whitney Twin Wasps of 1250 horsepower, thus giving us a total of five thousand horsepower for take off; with the heavier engines the centre of gravity had moved and, to compensate, the setting of the wings was slightly altered as a result of which the handling of the aircraft at take off and landing was very slightly different; we also now at last had fully feathering airscrews which meant that in the event of engine failure the blades could be turned so that the leading edge faced the airflow thus eliminating the 'windmilling' that caused such drag with the older engines and often exacerbated the initial damage inside the engine.

The navigation equipment was also greatly strengthened; the radar now 'painted' a map on the cathode ray tube with the aircraft in the middle, picking up ships, even lifeboats, as well as submarines, islands and coastlines; a new system called LORAN

(LOng Range Air Navigation) produced an automatic plot on the navigators chart that was still maintained for security. We now had a total of twelve machine guns; the customary four 0.303s in the rear turret and two more in the front turret, while the two in the mid-upper turret had been replaced by a bigger 0.5 inch either side amidships – manually trained which seemed surprising since manually trained guns hardly match turret mounted guns when following high speed attacking aircraft. However the greatest advance was the addition of four forward firing 0.303s, two each side, mounted in the bow compartment and fired by the captain. – The first time he moved up from being just a driver while all the others, bar the navigator, did all the banging away; this battery of a total of six guns firing forward was originally developed for Atlantic operations after the Germans decided that the U-boats often had a better chance of survival by remaining on the surface and fighting it out with the attacking aircraft using a new and formidable battery of anti-aircraft guns, mounted on a 'bandstand' that had been added to the after end of the conning tower – the attacking aircraft was thus extremely vulnerable on its necessarily straight run in at the dropping height of fifty feet but the provision of the six machine guns gave the aircraft crews a chance to incapacitate or, at least, discourage the U-boat's gun crews.

The wireless operator now had a greatly improved set of Morse and voice equipment which was badly needed as the earlier gear dated back to pre-war. These substantial changes, together with a number of internal alterations within the hull, necessitated a very large programme of training for the ground crews (not my responsibility) and the roughly one hundred and twenty aircrew which was my task and I embarked on it as soon as I got back from leave, just before Christmas."

AW Deller

Sunderland Mk III, EJ141:R in flight over Dar es Salaam. (Watson via JA Wilson)

A Sunderland Mk V 'on the step' taking off from Koggala Lake, 1945. (J Laydon).

7. Fight to the finish
January 1945 – October 1945

The first month of the last year of the war was a relatively quiet one, from the operational point of view, for the squadron. This was due mainly to the conversion from Sunderland Mk III to Sunderland Mk V aircraft. Many of the operational aircraft had to be made ready for return to make way for the arrival of the new aircraft. The groundcrew in particular found this a very busy period with each aircraft being prepared for the fifty-hour flight back to the UK. Most days saw the groundcrew working up to midnight. While the changeover was in progress the squadron continued its patrols and freight runs as well as instituting a comprehensive training programme to familiarise everyone with the new equipment. On the 3rd British troops took Akyab in Burma and just over a week later the 19th Indian Division had crossed the Irrawaddy. They were followed on 12 February by 20th Indian division, crossing the river south west of Mandalay. By 21 February the Allies were firmly established across the river.

The first new Sunderland Mk V, PP147:U arrived from the UK on 6 January and caused a great deal of interest at Kogalla, with most of the station turning out to greet it. F/L Potter gave the onlookers an opportunity to see for themselves the improvement in performance the Mk V had over the Mk III in a spirited display on his arrival. The next to arrive was PP146:V, flown in later that day by F/L Pedley. On the 28th PP148 and PP145, flown in by F/L White and WO Wykes from the UK. They would be coded 'P' and 'O' respectively.

The first operation of any significance was on 4 January, when F/L Middleton took JM711:M out to search for a submarine in conjunction with four Liberators of No 160 Sqn and a small naval force. Despite searching to the limit of the Sunderland's endurance, nothing was found. The squadron was also kept busy providing escorts to convoys and naval forces throughout the month.

Sunderland Mk V's moored at Koggala, Spring 1945. (J Laydon)

W/Cdr Bednall and S/Ldr Middleton (centre front) with the Sqn HQ staff at Koggala. (DK Bednall).

A graveyard of Mk IIIs at Koggala. (J Laydon).

"CHASING DOWN THE FLAREPATH, THROTTLES OPEN WIDE"

WO CE Wykes, who arrived at Koggala with one of the first Mk Vs, PP145:O, recalls the events of the last months of the war and the early months of peace:

"We left Oban to join 230 at Koggala on 28 December 1944, one of the first Sunderland Mk Vs. We arrived at Koggala on 28 January 1945 after various incidents on the way, which included Gibraltar, Djerbe, Kasfareet, Habbaniya, Bahrain and Karachi.

During February, March and most of April we did various trips to Bombay, Male (where the Prime Minister came out in a rowing boat to greet us), Redhills Lake and Calcutta. During this time we took part in radar homing, bombing and air to sea firing, fighter affiliation and air sea rescue. I had arrived as a Warrant officer and I was sent to Colombo for an interview and received my commission.

Koggala is in the south of the island not terribly far from Galle. We lived in huts and the food was very good. Wherever we were, everybody tried to get back for Sunday lunch, which was fantastic. Koggala is an island lake and the flarepath bent in the middle (to avoid rocks) so that we had to be very careful taking off and landing. I can remember one shaky take off when we just missed the trees at the end of the runway. At this time of the war there was a very popular German song called 'Lili Marlene' and in the Mess in the evenings after a few drinks we sang our own words to this song starting with 'Chasing down the flarepath, throttles open wide' and finishing with 'We're going round the corner, we're going round the bend'.

CE Wykes

Ernest Briggs and crew at Fanara, Egypt, 7 January 1945. (E Briggs).

On 3 February F/L Levy-Haarscher brought Sunderland ML797:Q in from Korangi Creek, where it had been delivered from the UK by a ferry crew. During February four aircraft were detached to Trombay for a special operation, returning on the 27th. Due to the re-equipment with the Mk V very little operational work was carried out during February, the squadron concentrating on training to enable the crews to familiarise themselves with the aircraft. The operators worked hard to become familiar with the new ASV Mk 3 fitted to the Sunderlands. By the end of the month the squadron had five Mk Vs on strength and whilst these were being serviced the Mk IIIs soldiered on. The work on the new aircraft placed a heavy pressure on the groundcrew, who found themselves working very hard, sometimes putting in 13-hour days.

During February an outbreak of smallpox in the local population caused all personnel to be vaccinated against the disease and all of the native employees on the station were treated likewise.

A change of role was notified to the squadron by No 222 Gp in February when notice was given of an impending move to the Burma front and a change to anti-shipping strikes by day and night. The squadron would be based on *HMT Manela*, which would sail from the Middle East where it was engaged on trooping duties, arriving early in March. By the end of March the squadron was to be fully equipped with Sunderland Mk V.

The month of March was relatively quiet from an operational point of view due to the impending change of role for the squadron. The four aircraft detachment under S/Ldr Deller returned to base on the 13th, having operated in Burma transporting essential freight for the 14th Army. ML486:W only got as far as Trombay where F/L Fetter had to remain to have engine repairs made. Also on the 13th, W/Cdr Powell, G/Capt Francis and S/Ldr Sheardown flew to Akyab to inspect the harbour and future alighting area for the Sunderlands, returning on the 15th. On 20 March 19th Indian Division captured Mandalay and by the end of the month the Japanese were in retreat from the Meiktila area.

With the new role thrust upon the squadron shipping exercises were laid on with three aircraft taking part in each sortie. The method of attack was for the three aircraft to make a parallel track search, locate the target and home the other aircraft onto it. The Sunderlands would then circle the target ship at 120-degree intervals outside the range of the ship's flak and then make a concerted attack on the target. One aircraft would be selected to make the bombing run over the target while the others provided flak suppression, breaking away at a range of 400 yards. The navy provided Fairmile motor launches as practice targets and training began with considerable enthusiasm. Another aspect of the change of role required considerable training in bombing and many fighter affiliation exercises were carried out in co-operation with No 81 Sqn to give the gunners air to air firing practice. At a parade of the full squadron the CO announced that the targets would be Japanese coastal shipping and that they would be operating from the depot ship *HMT Manela*. The pleasant life at Koggala would be replaced with a cramped life aboard ship. 50% of the squadron's stores and spares were transported to *HMT Manela* in Colombo harbour and a small complement of personnel boarded under the command of F/L McConnell. The remainder of the squadron would be flown out to the ship when it arrived on station

MALAYA · CEYLON · E. AFRICA · CRETE · DODECANESE

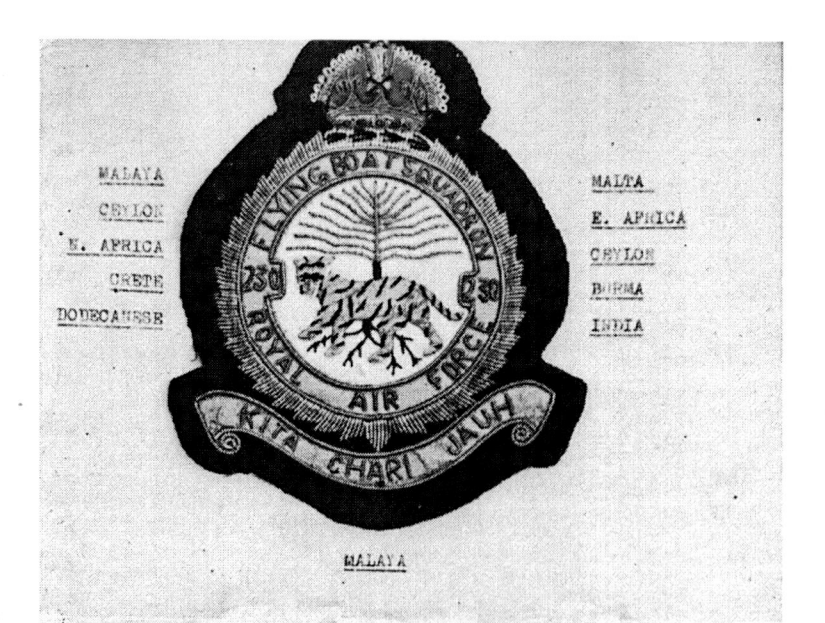

MALTA · E. AFRICA · CEYLON · BURMA · INDIA

MALAYA

    This is a Sunderland Flying Boat of 230, Squadron. This Squadron has been operating Sunderlands in the Eastern Theatres since 1938, and this vast accumulation of experience is your Insurance Policy.

    We are but lately converted from "Operational Flying" and regret that we have not the facilities of Transport Command to make the aircraft more comfortable for passengers.

    The Captain of the aircraft, irrespective of rank, is in sole command at all times, and he will appreciate any suggestions to improve conditions.

    Please read carefully the instructions below - and we hope you enjoy the trip.

****

PASSENGERS.

    Wear your "Mae Wests" for Take Off and Landing.
    Please don't move around the aircraft more than you must.
    Please don't smoke. We sympathise but it is an Air Ministry Order.
    Please don't open bulkheads, but if it is necessary be sure and close them and clamp securely.
    THE BRIDGE IS OUT OF BOUNDS TO ALL EXCEPT THE FLIGHT CREW.

EMERGENCY PROCEDURE.

    Should it become necessary to make a Forced Landing at sea, you will be given warning and assistance from members of the Crew.
    Your "Ditching Stations" are the Ward Room and the large compartment rear of the galley.
    Sit on the bunks - or on the floor - and make yourself as SECURE and comfortable as possible. Use the lilos.
    REMEMBER - WEAR YOUR MAE WESTS.
    Back, to a forward bulkhead, head braced with hands behind head.
    Don't move at the first impact with the sea. Wait until the aircraft has stopped. "Sunderlands" are designed for alighting on the water, and have successfully weathered Atlantic Storms. This aircraft is generously equipped with rations, water, Life Saving Equipment and emergency radio installation. So don't worry - leave that to the Captain!

AFTER DITCHING.

    Remain in position until instructed to move by the Crew. If water is rising rapidly and no instructions are received - move aft and await directions. If the aircraft is obviously sinking - leave by the nearest Escape Hatch - they are painted YELLOW.

KEEP CALM - IT MAY NEVER HAPPEN.

A safety-briefing card provided to passengers flying in 230 Sqn aircraft. (CE Wykes).

From: S/Ldr AW Deller
To: Officer Commanding, No 230 Squadron
Date: 25th March 1945   SECRET
REPORT ON CHINDWIN OPERATION BY 230 SQUADRON DETACHMENT –
2 FEB 45   to   13 MAR 45

Sir,
I have the honour to submit the following report on the above-mentioned operation.

On the morning of 2nd February 1945 I left KOGGALA in command of the detachment, as captain of aircraft K/230 in company with aircraft W/230 (Captain, F/L POTTER). On these two aircraft was carried a maintenance party of a total of seven personnel under SGT CLARKE of the Squadron maintenance section, with spares and tools.

On arrival at Trombay, W.CDR HAWKINS of 222 Group explained the whereabouts of the proposed alighting area on the CHINDWIN River, at KALEWA and gave me details of the load that was to be flown in. After working out the anticipated fuel loads and in discussion with L.CDR KEDGLIE RNVR, the officer responsible for organising the delivery to us of the load, it was decided that each lift should be 5,100 lbs approximately, comprising three marine engines, each in a large case and weighing some 1.100 lbs, together with control mechanisms and underwater gear – the parts necessary to build one entire craft, except for the hull. Owing to an unexpected increase in the weight of some items, it was decided to omit certain batteries in order to keep the load down to 5.100 lbs and enable the entire lift to be accomplished within the original limit of six sorties, thus avoiding minor inspections on any aircraft. In the event some loads contained no engines and weighted about 4,000 lbs, so it was possible to fly in a number of batteries with these. The petrol load we had to carry out of BALLY for the flight to KALEWA and back was only 50 gallons less than for the TROMBAY-BALLY flight so no loss of load was involved by the airlift from TROMBAY.

Loading was carried out on the 3rd of February without undue difficulty, with the aid of the aircraft's port bomb trolley, which incorporates a chain-operated hoist capable of lifting 1,000 lbs., the heavy case thus being lifted direct from the bomb scow into their storage in the bomb room.

At TROMBAY there was a large maintenance staff capable of dealing with SUNDERLANDS and it was understood that spares would be obtainable also, if needed; consequently I decided to alter the original plan and move the whole Squadron maintenance party with the spares to BALLY to make possible a thorough check of each aircraft before the flight to KALEWA. Aircraft K and W transported the party between them, in addition to the load, on their first flight across to BALLY on the 4th and 5th February respectively.

On arrival at BALLY in the evening I saw W/CDR BUTLER of Eastern Air Command, who explained the origins of the operation. Very early the next morning, 5th February, we went by DAKOTA to KALEMYO and thence by road to KALEWA. We met the Officer in Charge of the No 5 Inland Water Transport Group there, the organisation which was to receive and unload the aircraft. A motor boat took us to the alighting area, which is actually at SHWEGYIN, about 4 miles downstream. From the water the area looked reasonable, in spite of hills of about 200-300 feet, rising vertically at each end. A line of yellow painted oil drums had been moored to mark off a strip of water a hundred yards wide between them and a 350 ft high escarpment rising straight from the east bank of the river. I felt this would force aircraft to fly dangerously near the escarpment, especially in even a light crosswind; we carried out some soundings and found the 6 foot line was close to the west shore, so that if the drums were moved to mark the 6 foot line a much greater area of water would be left free, as long as the Burmese villagers could be prevailed upon to remove their fishing stakes from the area. A very satisfactory mooring buoy had been made out of two 40 gallon oil drums painted white and placed at the north end of the area, which owing to the projecting sandy spit, was much narrower than the southern end and left insufficient water for an aircraft to turn safely. I asked for the buoy to be moved to the southern end and Major CORBETT of No 5IWT Group, who accompanied us, agreed to see to this and the other points. I also discussed with him the type of craft which would be most suitable for the unloading and explained the method of receiving and coming alongside the aircraft.

After visiting Air Commodore WASSE, Senior Air Staff officer of 221 Group at KELEMYO, I returned alone to CALCUTTA in the evening of 6th February, expecting to fly K in the following day. In fact K was still unserviceable, having some cylinders changed, and I further discovered that the 212 Squadron detachment's Operations Room at BALLY had had no instructions to control our Operation and could not give us any form of briefing, as they were concerned solely with ASR work, employing an entirely different organisation.

On the following morning, 7th February, I went to 231 Group Headquarters to arrange an organisation for briefing for and control of the flight into KALEWA and out again; the Senior Air Staff Officer sent a message to say that this Group had not been given control of the Sunderlands of the Flight and could not, therefore, give us the required assistance. I travelled immediately to Eastern Air Command and discussed the matter there, the conclusion being that the Photographic Reconnaissance Force, who operate in much the same area, would be able to help. A fruitless afternoon was spent contacting various sections of the Force in different parts of CALCUTTA and by late evening it was obvious to me that only 231 Group could give the necessary information. I went there again and was again told the Group had no orders to look after the Flight; I therefore telephoned Eastern Air Command and asked for a directive on the matter to 231 Group, which was given immediately. Thereupon, without further delay, a full signals briefing was obtained, arrangements were made with the Meteorological Section for a forecast for the following morning, and the Operations Room fixed up warning signals and general control for the flight. The organisation now being complete, I signalled details, with a proposed schedule for the operation, to all formations concerned.

Early the next morning, 8th February, I took off in K/230 from BALLY, the weather forecast for the route to KALEWA being reasonably good; F/Lt POTTER, Captain of W/230, came with me to see the route and alighting area. As the hills were approached, the aircraft was taken, with persuasion, to about 10,700 feet (the highest points on the route are marked on the topographical map as about 8,500-8,700 feet, but it is my conviction that the general level of the higher ridges in the area is over 9000 feet). Contrary to the forecast there was in fact 10/10 Cu and Cb over the hills, with tops then around 12,000 feet and rising; at first it was possible to fly between the tops but when about 100 miles from KALEWA, over the highest hills, there was a solid wall of cloud to over 13000ft. Turbulence was very considerable (at one moment the aircraft dropped 800 feet to under 10,000 ft in about 5 seconds.) and the aircraft was only just making a safe flying speed flying level at full climbing power; I therefore considered it unsafe to attempt to fly blind through turbulent cloud with so little clearance and turned back; 10/10 cloud and heavy rain reached ground level everywhere within 100 miles of CALCUTTA.

On my return I was told that the BURMAH-SHELL, whose refuelling launch was responsible for refuelling the 212 Squadron Catalinas as well as the B.O.A.C. aircraft, now refused to take on the additional work of the Sunderland detachment, in the absence of a promise that the RAF would provide their own refueller within a definite time; meanwhile K/230 could not be refuelled for another attempt. The met forecast for the 9th February was very bad and during that day I was able to persuade the Burmah-Shell manager to refuel the 230 Squadron aircraft during their stay at BALLY. At the same time B.O.A.C. whose marine craft both detachments were using to supplement the one partially-unserviceable RAF dinghy, were complaining of the consequent added strain on their own craft. This also was attended to diplomatically, and K/230 was inspected and refuelled ready to take advantage of the better Met forecast of the 10th February.

On this occasion, cloud was still 10/10 over the hills, but its base was just below 11,000 feet, a height we nearly managed to reach in spite of great turbulence, which made it necessary for all members of the crew on duty to strap themselves in. The alighting area was easily found and proved very suitable for a full glide approach and landing, although any attempt to go around again after a bad landing would have been out of the question. The arrangements made by No. 5 I.W.T. Group were most satisfactory; mooring-up was easy and the I.O.R's who formed the crews of the various marine craft under the supervision of European officers, had obviously been carefully instructed, with the result that throughout the operation no aircraft was in any way damaged or endangered, even though a heavy bulky load had to be handled in a current of about 1 ½ knots. Unloading was easier and quicker than loading, as the same care had not to be taken to avoid damaging the aircraft during stowage. The take-off presented no difficulties and I climbed to 10,000 feet in the less turbulent air over KALEWA before beginning the crossing of the hills; the crossing, flying at up to 12,700 feet, mostly in broken cloud, was exceedingly rough, rates of descent and ascent of up to 1,000 feet per minute being experienced while flying level at cruising power. We never discovered any position on the route over the Chin Hills where a forced landing could have been attempted, apart from one place where a dry land touch-down might have succeeded; parachutes were worn at all times – probably the first time most of us had ever done so on a flying boat.

In expectation of this and subsequent sorties, No. 5 I.W.T. Group were forced to waste much time preparing for an aircraft on days when none came, owing to the fact that 231 group did not appear to be able to pass the E.T.A. signals sent, as they had to be, on the previous evening when a preliminary met. Forecast had been made, even when addressed to KALEWA, arrived there after the aircraft had taken off on its return flight the following afternoon. Later on, arrangements were made to telephone the E.T.A. direct from BALLY to KALEWA, which was very satisfactory until the line broke down just before the final sortie.

On 11th February W/230 (Captain F/L POTTER) made a successful sortie in improved weather conditions, the turbulence having almost disappeared; this aircraft reached 12,000 feet with the full load and flew out again at no less an altitude than 15,200 ft, a rare achievement for a Mk III Sunderland. Unloading at KALEWA was very rapid and the aircraft spent only 50 minutes on the water.

Only two buoys were available for our use at BALLY so, as I had signalled to TROMBAY to send the third aircraft, T/230, across to BALLY on the 12th, W/230 was inspected and refuelled on her return from KALEWA and left for TROMBAY on the morning of the 12th. I could not take K/230 for her second load as Eastern Air Command had information, which necessitated changes in the plan for the operation. I also wanted to brief F/L PEDLEY, captain of T/230, on conditions for the flight to KALEWA.

It was already apparent that a fixed schedule was unworkable in the circumstances and I had signalled all concerned to that effect. Signals of 6th and 11th February concerning an increase in the total lift from 30,000 lbs to 50,000 lbs made it necessary to plan for a further four sorties after the original six. I worked out a plan to do this with only one minor inspection, by trans-shipping one load from one aircraft to another at BALLY; this scheme required cargo-carrying marine craft and buoy accommodation for a third Sunderland at BALLY. The former was provided for by the Chief Engineering Officer at Headquarters R.A.F. Bengal-Burma, and 212 Squadron were already arranging an extra buoy which we could use.

When aircraft T/230 arrived I learned from the captain that separate arrangements had been made between TROMBAY and 222 group for dealing with the extra lift and the question of minor inspections – I had no copies of any of the relevant signals and as the proposed scheme involved aircraft flying all the way back to KOGGALA for minor inspections and them returning and, furthermore, conflicted with the plan I had agreed with Eastern Air Command and for which necessary dispositions had already been made, I took the liberty of signalling all concerned that my plan as detailed on 12th February should stand. I might mention that accurate information on the conditions of the flight to KALEWA, time required, maintenance and inspection capacity of the detachment and loading facilities at BALLY, was available only at BALLY.

It was intended to fly T/230 to KALEWA on the 14th but the weather forecast was bad and as we could not afford the flying time for abortive sorties, I called it off and left myself in K/230 for TROMBAY. On arrival there I found W/230 changing an engine, thus further delaying the operation. W/230's engine (starboard outer) had failed suddenly and completely with a full load on board just past the 5000-foot hills immediately east of TROMBAY: the captain succeeded well in flying her safely back to TROMBAY: a cylinder barrel had cracked, jamming the piston and causing all nine connecting rods to break. On the 15th I had an interview with L/CDR KEDGLIE at Naval Headquarters in BOMBAY and was told that 10,000 lbs of extra lift had been sent off by rail to go through to KALEWA by surface transport, thus reducing the commitment to a total of eight sorties, i.e. a total lift of 40,000 lbs; from the additional information gained at the interview it was evident that it would take the seventh and eighth loads much longer to reach CALCUTTA by rail than to fly them the whole way, and if the aircraft promised as a replacement for W/230 could do two sorties in addition to W/230 completing her second sortie after the engine change, the whole operation could be finished quickly with a further saving of time by eliminating all minor inspections. I signalled all concerned accordingly and returned in K/230 to BALLY with the third load on the 16th.

Arriving at BALLY I found that T/230 had completed her sortie to KALEWA and back on the 15th but that on the return journey at 14,000 ft at the commencement of the crossing of the high hills, both inner engines had become unserviceable; after some experiment it was found possible to take some power out of both and, to avoid the disaster of a double engine change at KALEWA the captain (F/L PEDLEY) decided to continue to BALLY, which he reached safely, losing height only quite slowly the whole way. After examination it was decided that nothing more could be done with the two engines other than to patch them up sufficiently to fly back to KOGGALA; this was put in hand and a signal sent to all interested on 16 February.

Meanwhile at BALLY, no progress had been made with the provision of an extra buoy and the only R.A.F. dinghy, which had been running intermittently for some days, had at last become totally u/s, leaving us with B.O.A.C. craft, every run in which had to be asked for as a favour, and a large diesel-engined river boat, the "Birkie", of 70 tons, which had been taken over by the R.A.F. as a balloon barrage tender and was now used to patrol the alighting area. Maintenance in these circumstances was a problem and K/230 was found to need a difficult cylinder change. On 18th February I telephoned W/Cdr BUTLER and told him that owing to B.O.A.C.s attitude, unless pressure was brought to bear on them, or the R.A.F. provided a suitable marine craft immediately, the operation would be held up by our inability to get from the shore to the aircraft. He suggested trying the Navy and HQ Bengal-Burma. On the 19th I spoke to S.R.N.O. who assured me that the Navy had no serviceable small craft in CALCUTTA and he knew of no place to get any. I should point out that the Hooghly tide is at all times so strong and turbulent that rowing out is impossible and an experimental attempt to float a dumb dinghy downstream to the aircraft from the "Birkie", stationed ahead, proved exceedingly dangerous from the same cause. Eventually the Chief Engineering Officer, RAF Bengal-Burma promised to send a suitable craft the following day.

B.O.A.C. had definitely refused to run any more dinghies for the R.A.F. but I was able to arrange for a single run on the morning of the 20th, to enable us to board K/230 for the fourth KALEWA sortie, which was successful in good weather conditions. We took into KALEWA L/CDR PENMAN R.N.V.R. who was to organise the Chindwin Flotilla, and brought out seven British Officers and men and I.O.R.'s on leave and repatriation. Returning to BALLY, I found that HQ RAF Bengal-Burma had misunderstood my requirements, as their craft, though smaller than "Birkie" had a high wheelhouse which would not pass under a Sunderland mainplane; it also had a very unreliable engine, so I later returned it to its balloon unit. B.O.A.C. were once more persuaded to take us ashore.

On 21st aircraft N/230 (Captain F/Lt Levy-Haarscher) – W/230's replacement – arrived at BALLY and in the complete absence of other craft I decided to take the "Birkie" alongside; wind and tide were in the same direction and the vessel was manoeuvred into position ahead of the aircraft, dropped back slowly until the aircraft mooring buoy was picked up, and then allowed to ride back still further until her substantial jack-staff was just ahead of the port inner airscrew, when it was possible to reach the aircraft's forward door from "Birkie's" stern.

F/L Levy-Haarscher brought me the Squadron's message ordering W/230 to be returned to KOGGALA after the engine change. K/230 at this time was showing signs of engine deterioration, T/230 was about to leave us, N/230 was known by the maintenance party to be in fairly poor shape and W/230, apart from the unusual accident to one engine, had performed better than any. Consequently I asked for the continued use of W/230.

The following morning, the 22nd, T/230 left for KOGGALA. The customary check was made on N/230 and it was judged that she was unlikely to make a second complete trip without risk of breakdown. On 23rd N/230 flew the fifth sortie successfully to KALEWA and back in fine weather, bringing out four British officers and men on leave. An inspection on her return showed that a further round trip would be unwise, while K/230 still appeared fairly sound. Meanwhile I had received the Squadron's signal agreeing to the continued use of W/230. In those circumstances I decided to prepare N/230 to return to KOGGALA direct from BALLY, fly K/230 to TROMBAY the next day, the 24th, and if W/230 was in hopeful condition, signal for N/230 to leave for KOGGALA. On the 24th, when I arrived at TROMBAY, W/230 had just completed a successful air test and all her engines were in very good condition, so N/230 was directed to return to base. My intention was that W/230 should now fly the sixth sortie, K/230 complete the seventh and W/230 make the final one (her third).

The Navy provided only one load on the 25th, which was put on W/230; this delayed K/230 a further day. The Engineering Officer at TROMBAY offered to do the minor inspection on W/230 with his own staff, when she returned there for her last load; this left only K/230's minor to be done at BALLY, so N/230 was instructed to take surplus maintenance personnel and spares from BALLY, while a similar load was put on board a re-inforcement Sunderland passing through TROMBAY to KOGGALA.

W/230 left for BALLY on 26th and K/230 was loaded. I flew K/230 to BALLY on 27th, to find N/230 had left and W/230 was in good condition for the flight to KALEWA. In addition, the R.A.F. dinghy had returned in a serviceable condition to BALLY; this put an end to the difficult feat of taking "Birkie" alongside, which however had been done repeatedly with success (except when the wind was across tide, when no ferrying was possible) the vessel being well handled by her Indian crew under the capable B.O.R. coxswain Lac WADE.

W/230 flew in successfully on 28th, taking also some foodstuffs and so forth, which are in short supply at KALEWA. She returned early in the afternoon, after examining a possible alighting area at MONYWA from the air, with three passengers. The customary check for the flight to TROMBAY was made the same day in order to save time. Her condition appeared very good and she left for TROMBAY on 1st MARCH to pick up the final load.

On 1st MARCH I flew K/230 to KALEWA in good, though somewhat bumpy, weather. On the way in, the wireless operator heard very loud R/T, which was assumed to be Japanese, followed on a neighbouring frequency by American R/T, also very loud, from fighters being vectored on to a target – the last heard was a pilot expecting "to be at the opera in two minutes". We were not present at the performance. Having carried in more food supplies for KALEWA we brought out four more British officers and other ranks on leave and repatriation. The aircraft performed quite well, although she took 25 minutes to climb from 5000 ft to 10,500 ft with the full load, and I was much relieved that she stood up to three round trips.

On the return, the minor inspection on K/230 was started preparatory to returning to KOGGALA when W/230 had completed the final sortie. In the afternoon of the 2nd I had a copy of TROMBAY's signal stating that another of W/230's engines had failed completely (main bearing failure) on the way to TROMBAY; she had flown the last three hours safely on three engines. I considered it would be taking a very big chance to make K/230 do yet another severe trip and therefore signalled the Squadron asking for a replacement aircraft.

On 3rd K/230's minor inspection was completed, and a first air test confirmed that she was in better condition than had been anticipated before the inspection. As a number of cylinders had been changed another short air test was flown on the 4th, successfully. As no signal had arrived concerning a replacement aircraft I concluded there was probably some difficulty and so decided to make the final sortie with K/230. On 4th I signalled my intention to leave for TROMBAY on 6th failing contrary instructions. The Squadron's agreement to this course arrived at midnight of 5th-6th; arrangements for the flight were already made and I had signalled TROMBAY to be ready to load immediately we arrived, thus saving a day –had W/230 not failed; both aircraft could have returned to KOGGALA on the 6th.

K/230 arrived safely at TROMBAY on 6th; W/230 was still waiting an engine. The load was not ready and I immediately telephoned L/Cdr KEDGLIE. Eventually the load arrived at dusk and was on board by 2300 hours. A quick engine check had shown everything to be sound and the following morning I left for BALLY. The aircraft was inspected during the 8th at BALLY and on the 9th, the final sortie to KALEWA, with provisions and two Army passengers and the return with a Burman officer and a B.O.R. on leave, were accomplished in good, though extremely hazy weather.

All concerned were informed of the completion of the operation and the detachment's affairs were cleared up during the three days which were necessary to change three cylinders on K/230, one a very difficult job, and to do an air-test thereafter. K/230 flew to KOGGALA via MADRAS, with the maintenance party and all spares, tools, maintenance stands and personal kit on 13th March.

The fact that, apart from the fortuitous and unforeseeable failures of W/230, K/230 was able to do four complete trips (nearly 100 hours flying) and N/230 and T/230 the complete trips allotted to them, without failure, redounds to the credit of SGT CLARKE and his maintenance party; their hard conscientious work and Sgt CLARKE's advice to me on technical matters made them the mainstay of the operation, particularly in view of the fickle nature of our very old Pegasus XVIII engines – the question of whether or not the engines would continue to turn was one's prime consideration, as the incessant climbing with heavy loads imposed a big strain on them. Night maintenance was not resorted to: I considered it dangerous in view of the lack of marine craft and the rapid turbulent flow of the Hooghly, into which a man, working on the narrow engine stands, might easily fall and be lost.

P/O KEHELY, flight engineer of T/230 was admitted to hospital with a poisoned leg and Cpl RAND, of the maintenance party, with suspected appendicitis, which turned out to be only a strain; otherwise except for minor ailments the health of the detachment was good. I am glad to be able to report also that, throughout, there was no breach of discipline of any kind.

I have felt it necessary to go into considerable detail in this report, as without such detail the many vicissitudes attending the completion of the operation and the courses of action taken to cope with them, would be incomprehensible. Among other obstacles were, for instance, briefing difficulties: originally, half the briefing was obtained from 231 Group, some 15 miles through CALCUTTA from BALLY, although this activity was later transferred wholly to BALLY. Even then, the organisation was a rather makeshift affair as the sub operations room at BALLY, consisting of a small room and a staff (until recently0 of one controller with a typewriter, while apparently making it possible for 212 Squadron detachment to operate, was not really adequate for two detachments doing different work. To a large extent I worked as my own controller and in any case, as important parts of the operation depended on personal arrangement I made with many different people, this proved the most workable system. Another feature of BALLY which had an averse effect was the acute shortage of marine craft; it has to be borne in mind that adequate marine craft are vital to the maintenance, let alone the operation, of flying boats, where even an unexpected need for a spare part necessitates a double journey often across nearly a mile of water, with a careful approach alongside by marine craft at each end. Incidentally, in the event, neither the trans-shipment facilities nor the extra buoy at BALLY were needed.

In conclusion, Sir, to my mind the eminent feasibility of such an operation by Sunderlands has been demonstrated; a sufficiently equipped base near the main scene of operations is, however, desirable – in this case TROMBAY, though a good base, was too far from and out of touch with the most difficult part of the operation. In any case, it is to be hoped that any similar detachment in the future would not have to use old aircraft and engines, as we were compelled to do in this instance by the half completed re-equipment of the Squadron.

The entire operation involved approximately 220 hours flying, allowing for W/230's return to KOGGALA from TROMBAY; of this, about 70 hours are transit time from KOGGALA to TROMBAY and BALLY to KOGGALA. The total weight lifted was approximately 40,000 lbs or 17.9 tons: that is, excluding return flights, 21780 ton/miles flown over the 1210 miles from TROMBAY to KALEWA.

I have the honour to be
Sir,
Your Obedient Servant,
AW Deller
Sq/Ldr.

SUMMARY OF SORTIES ON CHINDWIN OPERATION **excluding transit flights)**

Date	From	To	TIMES	LENGTH OF FLIGHT	LIFT
4 feb	Trombay	Calcutta	0835-1610FG	7 hrs 35 mins	5100 lbs
8 feb	Calcutta	Kalewa	0710-1125	4 hrs 15 mins (abortive)	5100 lbs
10 feb	Calcutta	Kalewa	0840-1125	2 hrs 45 mins	5100 lbs
10 feb	Kalewa	Calcutta	1315-1700	3 hrs 45 mins	Light
16 feb	Trombay	Calcutta	0805-1500	6 hrs 55 mins	4300 lbs
20 feb	Calcutta	Kalewa	0750-1025	2 hrs 35 mins	4800 lbs & 1 passenger
27 feb	Trombay	Calcutta	0820-1515	6 hrs 55 mins	5100 lbs
1 mar	Calcutta	Kalewa	0720-1000	2 hrs 40 mins	5100 lbs
1 mar	Kalewa	Calcutta	1350-1720	3 hrs 30 mins	4 passengers
7 mar	Trombay	Calcutta	0805-1530	7 hrs 25 mins	5100 lbs
9 mar	Calcutta	Kalewa	0705-1000	2 hrs 55 mins	5100 lbs & 2 passengers
9 mar	Kalewa	Calcutta	1225-1530	3 hrs 05 mins	2 passengers
			Total	57 hrs 55 mins	
Other flights during detachment					
2 feb	Koggala	Trombay	0820-1550FG	7 hrs 30 mins	
14 feb	Calcutta	Trombay	0735-1510	7 hrs 35 mins	
24 feb	Calcutta	Trombay	0740-1505	7hrs 25 mins	
3 mar	Air test	Calcutta	1625-1655	30 mins	
4 mar	Ditto		1045-1120	35 mins	
6 mar	Calcutta	Trombay	0750-1440	7 hrs 50 mins	
12 mar	Air test	Calcutta	1040-1125	45 mins	
13 mar	Calcutta	Madras	0745-1350	6hrs 05 mins	
13 mar	Madras	Koggala	1455-1845	3 hrs 50 mins	
			Total	34 hrs 35 mins	

THE SAGA OF T FOR TOMMY

"There was an air of expectancy around the Squadron. Something was coming off. No one seemed to know exactly what, but there was a Panic to get three Mk III Sunderlands ready for detachment. On the 1st February, S/Ldr Deller and F/Lt Potter departed in the early morning amid great mystery in K/230 and W/230. Later the same day, I and my crew took over T/230, which was covered with what appeared to be thousands of bodies engaged in a minor inspection.

Next morning we got some of the 'Griff'. We were briefed by the CO, W/Cdr Powell, to proceed to Trombay, there to take on a load of freight, haul it across India to Calcutta, refuel and fly in, over the Arakan Hills, to a landing area on the River Chindwin south of Kalewa, unload and fly out again "one time".

We arrived at Trombay without incident, to find that we were likely to have to wait there for a few days. This delay was most useful in giving us a chance of a thorough check of the aircraft – one cylinder was changed and numerous small adjustments made. The freight, weight about 5100 lbs, was loaded and all preparations made for the trip. The load consisted of three large cases, weight 1135 lbs, containing a Ford V8 type marine engine each and a large quantity of small items: the whole having been taken from dismantled Landing Craft and being required for boats on the Chindwin.

Eventually word was received at Trombay that we were to proceed on the 12th March. We left Trombay at 8 am and reached Bally (Calcutta) at half past two without incident, after a very quick trip over land with a strong following wind.

The following day was spent checking the aircraft and warning signals of our fly in were dispatched. However, on the morning of the 14th, 'Met' forecast heavy thunderstorms over the Arakan Hills and it was decided not to attempt the sortie.

The following day, February 15th, 'Met' was more hopeful, so we proceeded to the aircraft. The usual Calcutta morning mist was lying over the river, with visibility about 50 yards. The one marine craft was sent ahead, and on his return to report the river clear, we took off on a gyro setting into the gloom. At 200 feet we broke clear of the mist, to find the area carpeted with a layer of soft white down, with the odd chimney sticking up here and there and the morning sun shining brightly – rather beautiful to look at, but not very healthy should a landing have to be made.

We set course east with a strong following wind, and climbed steadily to 10,000 feet. The weather was beautiful - dead calm, not a cloud in the sky, visibility about 100 miles; the view of the razor sharp ridges of the Arakan Hills running north to south in successively higher fingers, with every valley filled with a level layer of white mist was really amazing. At 10,000 feet we were using 2100 revs. In rich mixture and all the boost we could get, at that, we could just maintain a bare 100 knots airspeed. We were thankful that the day was calm – we couldn't have afforded to loose any height in 'bumps'.

As we proceeded east and there was no sign of the mist breaking, we began to wonder whether it would be the same over the Chindwin; however as we crossed the last ridges of 'Hills' with about 800 feet to spare, we heaved a double sigh of relief – there in the valley beneath we could see a few breaks, with the river showing through.

We lost height as quickly as we could, and, nipping through a gap in the mist, we found it was no longer mist – it was now about 500 feet above the ground, and had therefore become 'low cloud'; so we proceeded to do a circuit and land. The landing area was well defined, about 2000 yards long, rather narrow at the north and, widening to the south, a couple of miles south of Kalewa. There was a 300-foot high escarpment along the east bank, and hills about 300 feet at each end. In view of the narrowness of the north and, where it would not have been possible to turn at the end of the landing run, I landed north – south – actually downwind, but the wind was very light.

Immediately we had moored up, at 1030, the Army chappies came along side in three narrow barges fastened together. The load was swung off in about 45 minutes, and we had a short rest for a cup of tea, a sandwich and a chat with the Army types about life in the wilds of Burma. He mentioned, incidentally, that the previous day it had rained solidly all the time, so that had we attempted a sortie, it would have been abortive. And that morning, the mist had restricted visibility to less than a hundred yards until about half an hour before our arrival, when, to quote his own words, ""he mist lifted like a lid on a boiling pan and you bobbed in under one edge!".

The take off, before an audience of all the natives from miles around, was uneventful – the aircraft was very light – and we immediately proceeded to climb. 10,000 feet
was obtained in about 25 minutes and in view of the strong headwinds, increasing rapidly with height, it was decided to skim across the mountains at this altitude and to come lower as soon as we could. Accordingly course was set to the west. By this time the mist had completely disappeared; the only sign of cloud was a solitary whisp of cumulus way to the south.

Just before reaching the first ridge of the hills, everything was proceeding smoothly, when the port inner engine apparently decided it had done sufficient for one day and voiced its protest in no uncertain terms. These took the form of loud bangs, wildly fluctuating Revs. and Boost and puffs of smoke sailing past the tail – much to the surprise of the Rear Gunner, who though they were cannon shells!

The engine was immediately closed down and, as we could not maintain height at that altitude on three engines, we turned round again for the Chindwin. We had *horrible thoughts of weeks on the river waiting for spares, living on hard rations, perhaps even seeing some fighting – not too bad if we'd been prepared for it, but to keep the weight down on the trip in we had left all our kit behind and only possessed what we stood up – or rather, sat down – in. And by this time we were most of us in need of at least a change of pants!*

After ten minutes it was decided to try the port inner engine again – by this time she was dead cold – and on opening up, she cleared with a couple of hefty bangs and settled down reasonably well, giving a fair amount of power. We therefore decided to make an attempt to get out. We circled, persuading the old girl to climb as high as she could, so that should the engine cut again we should have some chance of maintaining sufficient height to clear the hills. At 14,000 feet, just about our absolute ceiling in that condition, we once more turned our nose to the west, with all fingers crossed.

Just as we were passing over the first ragged, inhospitable ridge, the starboard inner decided that it agreed most heartily with the port inner, in that we had done sufficient for one day. Its protests took the form of violent fluctuations of the Revs. every few minutes and vibrations of the whole engine. There didn't seem to be much point in turning back again – it wouldn't have taken any less time to get two spare engines in the jungle than one – so we pushed on towards the west.

After about an hour the lack of oxygen was beginning to make itself felt on one or two members of the crew and it became a question of whether we could increase our rate of descent to get more air and still keep sufficient altitude to reach a possible landing area should the inner engines get any worse. We did come down a little faster, the aircraft (and crew) still shaking more than somewhat.

By two o'clock we were away from most of the hills and within sight of water and sighs of relief were the order of the day. By 1540 we were waterborne once more on the dirty swirling waters of the Hooghly; from where we proceeded to make heavy inroads into the stock of Whiskey in the Officers Mess, Bally.

On examination the next day it was found that the port inner had blown the inside out of a plug; and the starboard inner CSU was u/s. There was no torque loading on the prop and the engine had vibrated so badly that it had broken the gill ring in two

places and broken the exhaust tail fin legs. The port outer prop was also u/s and several cylinder changes were advisable. In view of those requirements and the fact that the engines had done more than 200 hours – quite a lot for 'Peggies' – the NCO i/c Maintenance, Sgt Clarke, considered the aircraft unfit for further operations over land and advised its return to base.

Such repairs as were possible were carried out; meanwhile assistance was rendered to S/Ldr Deller in the general organisation of Bally as a base – the facilities being scarce in the extreme. On the arrival of aircraft N/230, it was decided that *there was no further need to hold the aircraft and crew at Bally and on the 22nd February the return trip direct to base was made. The aircraft still vibrated quite a bit and the starboard inner CSU was still rather erratic, but the journey was over the sea and a landing could have been made at any time, so we were not unduly disturbed.*

Thus ended what was (I hope) my final long flight on a Sunderland Mk III.
Alans S Pedley F/Lt
<u>**Captain**</u>

The SS Manela at Singapore in 1945. (DJ Rees)

In April the Allies had been racing towards Rangoon and by the 14th Yamethin fell. Two days later Taungup in south west Burma was taken. The beginning of April saw several flights between Koggala and Male when Sunderland EJ141:R force landed there due to engine trouble. On the 1st F/L Pedley flew in PP146:V to pick up the downed Sunderland's passengers and return them to Koggala. Two days later WO Wykes delivered spares for the aircraft in PP157:S. On 6 April ML846:W finally returned from Trombay having had an engine change

F/L Nicholson was airborne on 13 April in PP157:S to search for a Mosquito, which had been seen to ditch the previous day. The search was carried out in conjunction with two launches, two Liberators of No 200 Sqn and a Catalina of No 205 Sqn. After a search aircraft wreckage and a dinghy was found but there were no survivors. A launch was homed to the wreckage and one body was found. On the 16th W/Cdr Powell and S/Ldr Sheardown flew to Akyab in PP158:T and PP145:O. These were the first aircraft to leave for the squadron's new base. They were followed by F/O Toller and F/O Holstein in ML799:W and ML800:X on the 17th. PP154:Y and PP148:P followed on the 18th flown by F/O Moonlight and F/L Seward (RCAF). WO Wykes flew the last of the advance party out in PP157:S on the 19th. F/L Potter flew two crew to Akyab in PP155:X via Coconada on the 30th and on the same day the squadron carried out its first operation in the new theatre when F/O Toller carried out a cross over patrol in Sunderland ML799:W. The patrol was carried out south east of the Andamans as part of a combined operation covering the landings in Rangoon. Toller was relieved by F/O Holstein in ML800:X who, in turn, was relieved by F/O Moonlight flying PP154:Y.

230 Sqn Sunderland near Mombasa in March 1945. (Watson via JA Wilson)

AKYAB

"On 20 April we flew to Akyab in Burma. There were no facilities on the land so we were based on the 'SS Manela', a troopship, some distance from the land. The buoys were around the ship. At this stage of the war the 14th Army were advancing towards Rangoon.
CE Wykes

The same Sunderland over Mombasa. (Watson via JA Wilson).

At this stage the reader may have become somewhat confused by the number of aircraft apparently carrying the same code letter. This was not uncommon as aircraft arrived to replace existing equipment and the original aircraft did not always leave immediately. During this period the code letter/serial number arrangement appears to have been as follows:

M	JM711, PP145
P	PP148
Q	ML797
R	EJ141
S	PP157
T	PP158
U	PP147
V	PP146
W	ML799 and ML846
X	ML800 and PP155
Y	PP154

Sunderland 259:M from which the photo above was taken. (Watson via JA Wilson).

The *HMT Manela* was delayed in its departure from Colombo, needing to go into dry dock, and eventually sailed via Trincomalee and Madras to collect provisions. On arrival at Akyab moorings had not been provided for the ship and alternatives had to be found. This in turn delayed the laying of the aircraft moorings causing the first aircraft to wait at Koggala till the 16th. During the move the squadron was hampered by the need to bring forward the remaining stores and the poor condition of the marine craft allocated, which were cast offs from other squadrons. Many of them were fit only for the scrap heap. At Akyab this shortage of marine craft was exacerbated by the arrival of a detachment of Catalinas of No 212 Sqn, which also made demands on the craft. Communications caused other problems as frequent runs by marine craft from the *Manela* to Akyab had to be made until a telephone was provided on the last day of the month.

A certain amount of amusement was provided by the Navy when they requested one of the squadron refuelling lighters to refuel an aircraft carried with 5,000 gallons of fuel! The Marine Craft section was able to oblige and the Navy departed contented.

During the month the squadron received several briefings on its new role and its part in the Rangoon operation and several awards were announced, F/O

Garside and F/L Watson receiving the DFC, while WO Smith received a Mention in Despatches.

F/L Toller's patrol covering the Rangoon operation on 1 May provided some excitement when two aircraft were sighted by the crew. The two Japanese Sonia's made a curving attack on the Sunderland but Toller was able to escape into cloud before they got within firing range. S/Ldr Sheardown carried out a somewhat unusual sortie for a Sunderland on the same day when, in PP145:O, he escorted 38 Dakota paratroop aircraft to Calventurias Island where they dropped their troops before returning to base. Rangoon was liberated by the 3rd.

Warrant Officer CE Wykes and his crew on passing out of OTU. (CE Wykes).

On 5 May W/Cdr Powell carried a group of high-ranking officers on a reconnaissance of Rangoon in ML799:W. They flew down the coast via Pagoda Point, Diamond Island and Elephant Point before flying up the river to Rangoon. After searching for a suitable landing point and photographing the city Powell made a landing in the north west channel and the Sunderland was moored to an old river buoy. A Royal Marines landing craft arrived and took the party, including W/Cdr Powell, to the city for a conference.

Artwork by a squadron artist on the Intelligence Officers office wall. (Watson via JA Wilson).

The Sunderland was refuelled and as there were no suitable facilities ashore due to the disorganised nature of Rangoon which was troubled with warring factions, looting and sniping from pockets of Japanese, the crew remained on board the Sunderland for the night. With enemy patrols still operating on the west bank of the river an armed watch was maintained throughout the night. In the early hours of the morning a Japanese landing craft, which had been in hiding, made an attempt to make its way upriver to join other enemy forces there. This resulted in a sharp action in the vicinity of the Sunderland and the crew manned the gun turrets in case the fight moved within range. The next morning the CO and passengers returned to the Sunderland, having spent an uncomfortable night sleeping on a floor. The crew's trial were not over, however, as on departure it was found the aircraft anchor chain had become tangled up in the chains and ropes on the buoy and the aircraft was only freed after a long period of work with a hammer and chisel.

With the recapture of Rangoon it was decided to move the squadron HQ there and during the move the aircraft were detached back to Kogalla and Redhills. Those returned to Kogalla were pulled up onto the slipway for inspection and much training of co-pilots was carried out to bring them up to 1st pilot standard.

June saw the squadron become more active in the anti-shipping role and on the 9th F/L Holstein, flying PP157:S, carried out an armed recce in the Gulf of Siam during which he sighted numerous ships in Jumbhorn harbour. Attacking two of them, he dropped DCs, which straddled the ships but failed to sink them. The following day F/L Seward sighted several schooners and attacked one of them. Unfortunately the DCs failed to explode. A second attack run was made but the DCs undershot and caused no damage. On the 11th F/L Levy-Haarscher carried out another Gulf of Siam patrol in PP157:S attacking two sampans with machine gun fire before sighting two twin masted schooners that he attacked with DCs. One of the schooners blew up. Later two trawlers were sighted and the Sunderland drew some light AA fire from them. On the 13th F/L Holstein was tasked with searching for an enemy convoy. Flying PP157:S he sighted several ships in Satchib harbour. On further investigation he sighted an aircraft directly above the ships and took evasive action by climbing into cloud. The ships were identified as six warships but the type was not confirmed due to the evasive action. On the 15th Holstein had more success on an armed recce when he sighted and attacked two landing barges loaded with oil drums. After three attempts to drop DCs they fell away on the fourth and destroyed one of the barges, the other running aground. At Khai Island another vessel was sighted and attacked with depth charges, which blew it up. Holstein then sighted a 10,000-ton oil tanker but did not attack it as a Japanese fighter escorted it. Instead he sought cloud cover and Liberators sank the tanker the next day.

SERVICING AND SURFING

Ernest Briggs joined the Squadron, as a Flight Engineer, at Koggala in June 1945 after having been previously engaged in ferrying flying boats out to the Middle and Far East.

I did not join 230 Squadron until June 1945 at Koggala, Ceylon. From Koggala we moved to Redhills Lake near Madras. Here we had been training for 'operation Zipper', the attack on Singapore, when the war out east ended.

Whilst at Koggala during off duty spells we enjoyed surfing from a nearby beach. Not the fancy surfboards of today, any old piece of board would do. Sometimes hired from the locals for a few Anna's.

Flying 'Boats' was entirely different from other sections of the RAF. Who these days would believe that we cooked in the galley on two Primus stoves whilst in flight. Cooking bacon and eggs etc. And of course numerous cups of tea. After all we could be airborne for up to twelve hours or even longer. We even had a toilet and wash basin on board.

As Flight Engineer and with my Flt Mech/AG, we often had to do our own DI's and see to refuelling when on detachment. Another of our chores was to check the bilge's for water and if necessary we could use a small petrol engine, which was stored just inboard of the starboard wing.

Another difference to other sections of the RAF was that all Sunderland crewmembers had to have an Air Gunners course, irrespective of their other duties. Back at Redhills Lake a few days after the Japanese surrender we had a flypast over Madras. Three Sunderlands in formation, a sight hardly seen. Our aircraft 'Q' of 230 was on the starboard side of the leader. Very soon after this we were very busy taking supplies and Red Cross personnel to Singapore, returning each time with ex-POW's on the first stage of their journey home. In December 1945 230 returned to its old base at Seletar. From there we did various detachments to places such as Borneo and Batavia."

E Briggs

On the 16th F/O moonlight in PP154:Y found the tanker still blazing from the Liberator attack that morning. Turning his attention to other targets he found two oil barges and attacked one with DCs and the other with bombs leaving one on fire and the other smoking. F/O Toller had a successful sortie the following day. Flying PP152:W he came across one motor craft and two barges, which he attacked with bombs and MG fire. The target was straddled but failed to sink. He then sighted a further barge camouflaged with foliage and a motor craft laden with rubber tyres, which were attacked by the Sunderlands gunners. He followed this by attacking another vessel with a barge alongside with DCs, sinking them both.

F/O Moonlight had an exciting sortie on 18 June when he went on an armed recce in PP154:Y. At 0352 hrs he attacked a vessel and a barge with DCs and the enemy vessel returned fire. The Sunderland was hit several times in the hull, port wing root cockpit and tailplane. Moonlight broke away and flew out of range. The wireless operator and the port beam gunner had been slightly wounded in the attack and Moonlight turned for base. An hour and a half later it was feared that the Sunderland might have to ditch and a distress signal was sent. On reaching Rangoon the area was cloud covered and *HMT Manela* despatched a Catalina to assist Moonlight in finding the landing site. Having found the Sunderland the Catalina informed Moonlight it would return to Rangoon to check the weather condition before leading the Sunderland in. Unfortunately, in the intervening period another Sunderland from Koggala arrived and the Catalina mistakenly escorted it to Rangoon. On realising the mistake the Catalina took off again but failed to find the Sunderland, which had flown off to the east in the hope of getting around the storm. Moonlight eventually broke through the weather and landed at 1040 hrs having plugged the holes in the hull with Plasticene. The MO, F/L McLachlan attended to the casualties immediately on their arrival.

During the month the Japanese had become wise to the methods of the Sunderland and tried to circumvent the attacks by sailing in shallow water to defeat the depth charges and lying up until nightfall to escape. They also began to return fire during the attacks but this did not deter the squadron's crews who, during the month, sank six ships amounting to 750 tons and several other vessels were destroyed. In addition three other shipping forces were sighted which were sunk later by Liberators. The squadron was in high spirits and keen to continue these attacks. Also during June it was decided to return the squadron to Koggala, but to maintain a detachment in the operational area. The squadron would now be based alongside No 209 Sqn, which was bringing its Sunderlands in from East Africa.

It was assessed that the Japanese might try to break out of south west Burma, with a possible line of march through Rangoon and to that end the Sunderlands were kept fully fuelled at all times in case of a rapid exodus. This was hampered by a naval slip up, which caused the squadron to become short of fuel, with only 3,00 gallons (30 hour flying time0 left at one period. The situation was further exacerbated by the difficult conditions on the Pegu River at Rangoon, which caused six different aircraft to be damaged and require repair. This coupled with the lack of fuel severely curtailed the squadrons operations during the month.

LOW LEVEL SHIPPING ATTACK

Although there were now few targets to be found the Japanese occasionally presented the Squadron's Sunderlands with one and Alan Deller accompanied F/L Nick Nicholson on one such attack:

"I did feel a little uncomfortable that the others were all flying busily down across the Kra Ithsmus and roaming the far side of Siam and the Malay Peninsula while I was sitting, not comfortably but at least securely, trotting out the equivalent of "Take off I say", the mythical staff officers' mythical invocation to yet more endeavour by tired aircrew. I was determined to get a look at what was going on and with the CO's permission I joined Nick and my old crew on an armed reconnaissance of the Kra Ithsmus, the Bay of Bandon and south to Singora, returning by the same route.

We took off soon after daylight, the marine craft having carefully checked the river for any of the huge teak logs that were floated down the river to the sawmills – an aircraft hitting one of those, waterlogged and almost submerged, at speed would have been instantly wrecked. We flew low, at about four or five hundred feet down the west coast of Burma and I took over the controls from Nick to cross over into Siam at somewhere near Chumpon and continue on down the east coast.

Flying between the mainland and Ko Samui, one of two small islands just off-shore we found a ship of the type used to supply the Japanese and decided to attack it with bombs of which we had four plus depth charges. I dropped to fifty feet and without opposition let go the four bombs to straddle the target; the second bomb of the stick made a direct hit on the wooden vessel but did not explode – obviously, as we reasoned later, because the fuse fitted was of a type to be detonated by hitting the target vertically whereas, dropped at only fifty feet, the bomb was still travelling horizontally when it hit. We left the ship stopped in the water and went on, Nick taking over; we alternated in that way and each had a share in making machine gun attacks using the two guns in the front turret as well as – for the first time in our careers – the very effective four fixed guns fired by the pilot.

There was undoubtedly a certain thrill in swooping down and opening fire with six guns simultaneously, each firing at twelve hundred rounds a minute, and seeing sails, masts and chunks of ship flying through the air as a result. By that time the ships' crews had become crafty and rigged lines over both sides so that they could jump over the side opposite to that from which the attack was coming, shelter behind the hull while holding on to a line and then clamber back on board when the attack was over!

After having a go at several ships in and around Singora we started on the return trip, dropping altogether forty thousand leaflets on the way. When we got to Ko Samui we found our ship still just afloat but clearly heavily damaged and completely waterlogged, with no sign of life. Nick was flying at the time so he did a low level run and dropped the four depth charges, also right of the line, and they all exploded, one of them very close to the ship which disintegrated into matchwood. When we arrived back at Syriam in the evening I realised that that was almost certainly my very last operational trip of the war and that indeed was the case."

<u>AW Deller</u>

During July several aircraft had to return to Koggala for repairs after being damaged at their moorings and PP146:V required repairs to the rear fuselage, a four inch hole in the leading edge of the port tailplane and both pipelines to the rear turret after they were shot away by MG fire on operations. PP146:V was the only aircraft available for operations from Rangoon for most of the month and flew five sorties despite the fact it had been damaged. Luckily the damage was above the waterline. PP145:O and PP155:T arrived at Rangoon from Koggala on the 13th and remained till the 22nd.

During the month eight aircraft, four of which had been damaged at their moorings were under repair at Koggala and added to this the *HMT Manela* had had to move away from its mooring for naval purposes and this caused an added strain on the groundcrew trying to keep the aircraft at Rangoon serviceable.

There was a lack of suitable target for the Sunderlands during July and they had to make do with attacks on smaller vessels and barges. Even these, though, seemed to be hard to find, taking shelter in the many inlets around the coast. The disappearance of most of this coastal traffic was due mainly to a lack of fuel. On 26 July the squadron left Rangoon for Redhills Lake where it would commence a month of intensive training for its new task. A small detachment was left behind at Koggala to return those aircraft still under repair to service.

The mouth of Singora harbour photographed by a Squadron Sunderland on an armed recce (left).
A Japanese ship found in Singora harbour (right).

Operations of note in July included an armed recce by F/L Comrie in PP149:R to obtain photographs of Pattani harbour. A number of sightings of small craft were made and Comrie attacked a large sampan with bombs and MG fire. No hits were observed but a number of the crew was seen to jump overboard into a towed dinghy. The bombs undershot by about 50ft. Comrie then attacked two camouflaged barges in two runs and observed hits on both. On the second run his bombs hung up and return fire from the barges caused some damage to the aft hull above the water line. The photographs of the harbour revealed some 20 small craft to be anchored there. On 5 July Comrie was in action again and sighted and attacked an enemy vessel. He made three attacks with DCs and MG fire but after several near misses, which caused the vessel to come to a stop he had to break off due to having expended all of his ammunition.

Taken from Sunderland 230-O these Sunderlands are over the southern section of Lake Koggala, July 1945. (E Briggs).

F/L Comrie was airborne again on the night of 7/8 July in PP149:R. This time he sighted and attacked an enemy vessel known as a 'Sugar Dog' with DCs and MG fire. The 'Sugar Dog' was a small Japanese tanker of under 500 tons with its smokestacks at the aft end of the vessel. The Squadron would encounter many of these over the coming months. He followed this up with an attack on a sampan with MG fire and then attacked two wooden barges on the beach. He dropped bombs, which narrowly missed the barges, but the gunners scored hits on them. Another 'Sugar Dog' was found and attacked with bombs and MG fire before Comrie moved on to Bandon airfield where he photographed two tin engined and one single engined aircraft. The twin-engined aircraft appeared to have crashed but the other appeared to be serviceable. Throughout the sortie Comrie drop 'Nickels' – leaflets urging the Japanese to surrender – at several positions.

On the night of 12/13 July F/L Comrie was out on patrol again. This time it was an armed recce of the west coast of the Kra Ithsmus. At 0347 hrs he found and attacked a 'Sugar Dog' with DC,s and MG fire. The DC,s slightly undershot and, due to the shallow depth of the water, failed to explode. The gunners had more success though, scoring several hits. Forty-five minutes later Comrie attacked another 'Sugar Dog'. This time the bombs overshot and again failed to explode. The gunners once again scored hits on the target.

A Sunderland flies over Koggala against a spectacular cloudscape. July 1945. (E Briggs).

On the night of 14/15 July it was F/L Levy-Haarscher's turn for some action. He got airborne in Sunderland DP200:Z to carry out an armed recce of the Kra Ithsmus. At 0315 hrs he sighted a sampan, which his gunners attacked with MG fire, observing several hits. Later, flying at 300ft, he sighted two stationary, heavily camouflaged 'Sugar Dogs'. Once again the gunners scored hits on the vessels but the 'Sugar Dogs' chose to fight back and scored several hits on the Sunderland. Accurate fire from the 'Sugar Dogs' holed the hull in eight places as Levy-Haarscher attacked from 50ft. An hour later an unidentified four-engined aircraft was sighted at a range of ten miles and the Sunderland sought cloud cover. Levy-Haarscher was not finished with his attacks though and found another

'Sugar Dog', which he attacked with four 250lb DCs and MG fire. The DCs scored a near miss off the stern of the 'Sugar Dog' but failed to explode. Levy-Haarscher brought the Sunderland round for a second attack and attempted to drop bombs. Unfortunately the bombs failed to release. The gunners had more success scoring several hits.

F/L Comrie, who was having a busy and successful month, was out again on the night of 20/21 July. Flying PP149:R he was patrolling off the Kra Ithsmus when he found a sampan. The gunners opened up on it and scored several hits. At 0715 hrs three large unidentified aircraft were sighted and Comrie turned south to evade them. Following this two stationary powered barges were located and Comrie dropped four 250lb GP bombs on them while his gunners sprayed them with MG fire. The bombs overshot but the explosion caused the leading barge to be thrown back onto the stern of the rear barge. About 30 troops were seen to be thrown overboard by the blast. Looking for fresh targets, Comrie came across a sampan, which was attacked and hit by the gunners.

He then found a 'Sugar Dog' lying stationary in the water, which the gunners successfully attacked. Comrie decided not to drop DCs as the water was too shallow. A second 'Sugar Dog', also in shallow water, was attacked by the gunners and Comrie dropped four 250lb DCs. The targets continued to appear thick and fast and Comrie next attacked two sampans and a camouflaged barge, his gunners scoring hits on all targets. At the mouth of the Yai River he found a tempting target. Two stationary 'Sugar Dogs', ten small sampans, five large sampans and one powered barge loaded with large packing cases or vehicles. A small train of twelve camouflaged carriages was also spotted. Unable to attack such a large target alone he left it for another day.

The night of 21/22 July gave F/L Nicholson, in PP158:T, the opportunity to increase the squadron's shipping score. On an armed recce of the squadron's hunting ground off the Kra Ithsmus he found a 'Sugar Dog' which was attacked by the gunners as Nicholson swept in at 75ft. Flying on the Sunderland found an abandoned 'Sugar Dog', which was fired upon by the gunners. Shortly afterwards three large sampans were sighted. One appeared to be flying the Chinese flag and the others were attacked with MG fire. The next target was more inviting to Nicholson. A two masted schooner was sighted and he attacked it with four 250lb GP bombs and MG fire. The bombs fell on the vessels stern causing damage and the after mast to collapse.

On the left we see one of the sampans attacked by F/Lt Nicholson on 22 July 1945).
On the right he overflies the schooner prior to the attack on 22 July.

On the bomb run at 150 feet (left). After the attack the schooner is low in the water (right).

Nicholson continued to patrol and soon found two passenger ferries, a 'Sugar Dog' lying close inshore and, near Singara, two sampans that were being attacked with MG fire. He then found another 'Sugar Dog' lying on a sandbank and four others lying in shallow water. Nicholson successfully attacked two of them. Later he sighted two sampans flying the flag of Thailand and two others, which he attacked. Returning to the schooner he had attacked previously, it was found to be sinking. Nicholson dropped four 250lb DCs to finish it off and the schooner disappeared. It had been a very successful nights work for Nicholson and his crew.

The following night, newly promoted F/O Wykes was airborne in PP145:O on another recce of the Kra Ithsmus. At the mouth of the Yai River several small craft were seen and an empty powered barge was attacked by the gunners, scoring several hits. At 0420hrs Wykes circled the airfield at Prachjao Khirikhan at 150ft taking photographs before moving back out to sea and finding two large sampans, which were successfully attacked with MG fire. At Samoi Island he found twenty moored sampans and then attacked four others with MG fire. Coming across a 'Sugar Dog' he attacked it with four 250lb GP bombs. Only two of the bombs exploded but the 'Sugar Dog' began to list to starboard after the attack.

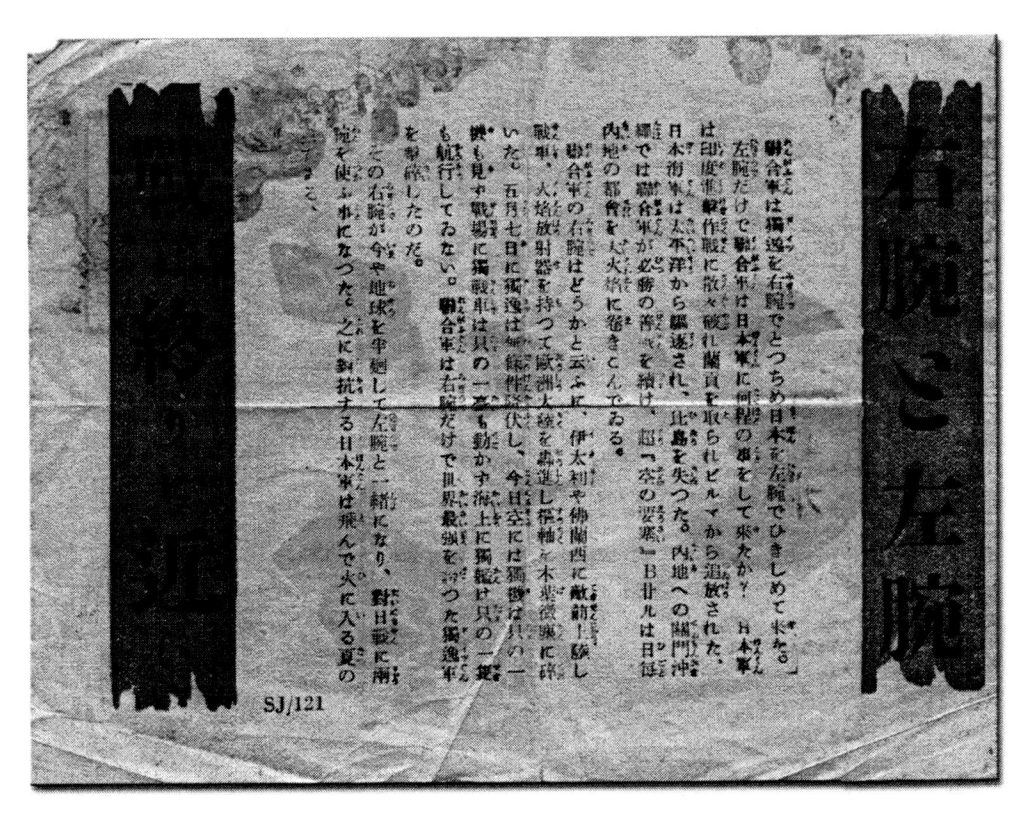

Leaflets dropped by Squadron Sunderland's to encourage the Japanese to surrender. (CE Wykes).

By the end of July the squadron was finding targets hard to come by and in August no operational flying was carried out. In its place the squadron moved the Sunderlands detached at Koggala to Redhills Lake and instituted a programme of flying training and ground lectures. With the dropping of the atomic bombs on Hiroshima and Nagasaki and the sudden and unexpected surrender of the Japanese, which was officially announced in the early hours of 15 August, the excitement on the squadron was intense. Two days' holiday were granted on the 16th and 17th and the squadron celebrated what they had been waiting for during the last six years. With the end of hostilities, the squadron ceased operational training and the aircraft were made ready for a new role: the Sunderlands would be used for transport of freight, passengers and VIPs to and from the areas to be occupied by British forces following the surrender.

The squadron was keen to return to its pre-war base at Singapore and hoped it would soon be able to do so. In order to fit the Sunderlands out for the new role all non-essential equipment was stripped out to increase the aircraft's payload. All of the combat armament was removed and plans were made to remove the gun turrets as soon as the necessary equipment to do so arrived. Studies were carried out to determine the seating capacity of the Sunderland and ditching drills for passengers were made up. The Japanese in Burma announced that they were ready to surrender on 23 August and the surrender was signed in Rangoon on the 28th. By the end of August the detachment at Koggala had been completely closed down and all of the squadron was at Redhills Lake.

An autographed menu from the Victory Dinner at Redhills Lake in 1945.

Ernest Briggs and crew in Madras, 30 August 1945. (E Briggs).

Sunderland PP145:D photographed during the VJ Day flypast at Madras. (E Briggs).

World War 2 ended on 2 September with the formal surrender of the Japanese aboard the *USS Missouri* in Tokyo bay and on 12 September Mountbatten accepted the surrender of all Japanese troops in south east Asia at Singapore. On 12 September 1945 F/L Mallisey flew Sunderland PP149:R in the Singapore Surrender ceremony Flypast, representing the squadron. Singapore town appeared to have been hardly touched by the Allied bombing and when the first 230 Squadron Sunderland, PP147:U touched down at RAF Seletar it was a great moment for the squadron which had last seen its pre-war home in February 1942.

Apart from the destruction of two hangars the station appeared to be relatively undamaged, although three years of neglect was evident. Initially only Japanese moorings were available and they were of dubious serviceability. Throughout the month the squadron was kept busy carrying freight and passengers and was also engaged in the repatriation of prisoners of war from the Japanese POW camps. The prisoners were found to be suffering from a variety of diseases including leprosy, beriberi and malnutrition. Observing these poor wretches disembarking from the Sunderlands, the groundcrew realised that all of their efforts had been worthwhile. The freight and supplies transported by the Sunderlands was moved to shore on the only vessel available, a Bomb Scow. The only refueller had to be filled from 60-gallon drums and then in turn the fuel had to be lifted onto the aircraft. This was a long and tedious job, done in good spirits by the groundcrew.

With the disorganised situation ashore, the crews and groundcrews lived on board cooking for themselves. Later two pulling dinghies were found and these helped to alleviate the shortage of marine craft. As the days passed the weather deteriorated and several of the Sunderlands came close to running out of fuel battling against the strong headwinds encountered. F/L Brown in PP157:S had a near thing when half way across the Bay of Bengal he was forced down to 800ft and his starboard outer engine cut out. This was quickly followed by the failure of the starboard inner and with a violent swing to starboard the Sunderland began to lose height. With the height down to 150ft and an airspeed of only 95 knots things looked bad but with skilful piloting brown managed to keep the Sunderland in the air, restarting the starboard engines and regaining control of the aircraft. The failure had been caused by debris collecting in the fuel tanks due to the filthy condition of the fuel picked up at Rangoon and Singapore. The passengers – nine Red Cross sisters, one army officer and a civilian, were totally unaware of the incident and later remarked to Brown "What a grand thing it was to fly with safety in modern aircraft"!

During the early part of the month the squadron had been busy removing the Sunderland's turrets and replacing them with hatches. The Sunderlands also began to be equipped with VHF radios and Loran navigation equipment. From 13 September the squadron began a regular ferry service between Singapore and Redhills Lake basing three aircraft at Seletar for this purpose. Three new Sunderlands were received during the month brining the squadron strength to twelve. The month ended with the impending move of the squadron to Singapore on everyone's mind.

SELETAR

"We returned to Seletar in Singapore and the first job was flying the ex-POWs (the more badly injured) back to India. Then we evacuated many Dutch women and children from Japanese POW camps in Batavia to Singapore.

It was at this time that I had my only accident. We landed at Penang (without any passengers) and it appeared to be a perfect landing, when suddenly the float on one side was hurled off. Panic! The crew had to dash out and stand on the opposite side until we were able to taxi to the buoys near the shore. There were various objects in the water and it was eventually classed as an unavoidable accident.

CE Wykes

During October the squadron continued to carry out its courier work and flew out POWs from Singapore until all had been repatriated. The work was not achieved without loss to the squadron however. On the morning of 15 October F/L Levy-Haarscher took of from Seletar with a crew of six, in PP155:X, carrying fifteen ex-POWs. The Sunderland went missing and extensive searches were carried out by Sunderland's and Mosquitoes. No news was received until 17 October when an army unit reported the wreckage of a burnt out aircraft, with several unrecognisable bodies, on a hillside west of Johore. S/Ldr Nicholson, together with a rescue party made their way to the scene of the crash, with the aid of Chinese Guerrillas. Travelling through dense jungle they reached the site only to find the charred remains on eight bodies among the wreckage. A brave crew and the unfortunate POWs, who had already suffered so much, had been killed. The impending move to Singapore was confirmed by signal on 21 October giving a target date of 15 November for the move of the advance party and the move to be completed by the 30th. The squadron suffered another aircraft damaged earlier in the month. On 3 October F/L Moonlight was landing, in PP158:T, on the Kuantan River when he struck a submerged object. A large hole was torn in the hull just below the bomb bay and water began to pour in. Moonlight reacted quickly and beached the Sunderland, thus saving it from sinking. A salvage party was flown in and the aircraft was repaired sufficiently to allow it to be flown back to Seletar.

During November the squadron continued to fly ex-POWs out of Malaya and freight and stores into Singapore for the squadron move. On 26 November the Sea Party embarked on the *SS Derbyshire* and arrived at Singapore on 1 December. Two new Sunderlands arrived for the squadron during the month and in addition to transport work several ASR searches were carried out. In December the squadron was busy flying women and children from internment camps in Batavia to Singapore. These were mostly Dutch and the crews and groundcrews set about the task with great enthusiasm. The squadron began to settle in at Seletar and in addition to brining the accommodation up to a liveable standard, the groundcrew were kept extremely busy servicing not only the squadrons Sunderlands but also those of Nos 209 and 240 Sqns. This placed a heavy drain on both spares and manpower, but the groundcrew accepted this cheerfully. On Christmas Day the officers served the Airman's Christmas Dinner and an extra ration of beer was issued. Football matches between England, Scotland and Wales were played with teams being selected from various units on the station. The squadron celebrated its first Christmas of peace since 1938 - the tiger had come home.

CE Wykes and crew at Redhills Lake (CE Wykes).

Sunderland Mk V, DP200:B at Seletar (DJ Rees).

The Squadron at Seletar in 1945. (E Briggs).

Sunderlands moored at Seletar in 1945. (DJ Rees).

Japanese seaplanes abandoned at Seletar in 1945. (DJ Rees).

A Japanese 'Ohka' Kamikaze aircraft abandoned at Seletar in 1945. (DJ Rees)

David Rees and Frank Murphy, groundcrew with the Squadron, model the latest in hats! (DJ Rees)

Dutch internees being loaded on board Sunderland Mk V. (CE Wykes).

POW'S AND REFUGEES

The war was over but for No 230 Sqn there were still many task to complete. The whole of the area was covered with POW camps, internment camps and refugees all in dire need of food medical supplies and repatriation or relocation. Bill Elliott, a pilot on the Squadron during this period recalls the time:

"After we had left Redhills Lake and were stationed at Seletar one of our jobs was ferrying ex-POW's and Dutch internees from Batavia back to Singapore and Madras. I was detached to Labuan in Borneo with a small unit of three aircraft and we were engaged in transport of troops police and supplies from Kuching round the coast to Lahad Datu on the east coast, since the airstrips were only of PSP and unsuitable for transport aircraft. One day in January 1946 we had a visit from the Ghurka Brigade Travel Officer, who asked if we could help out by delivering some food to starving natives, thinking this would be somewhere along the coastline. This however was up in the mountains and the Sunderland was not the most obvious choice for airdrop overland! We said however that we would give it a go.

We made our first attempt on January 21st and took off fairly early in the morning but by the time we got to the estimated position (by DR) it was completely obscured by cloud. We tried again the next day by getting into the aircraft during the night and waiting for the approach of first light to take off. This we did successfully and arrived at Marudi and navigated from there to the given position."

W Elliott

Sunderland ML797:Q in North Borneo, 21 January 1946. (E Briggs).

Ernest Briggs and crew at Killadeas, whilst training at No 131 OTU. (E Briggs).

Sunderland PP157:S on the VP slip at Seletar, January 1946. (E Briggs).

Sqn personnel of No 2 Inspection Party with PP157:S in the background. (K Burton).

Servicing a Sunderland in the hangar at Seletar. (K Burton).

Sunderland PP154:Y at its mooring, Seletar 1945.

Refuelling a Sunderland at Seletar.

The Squadron barracks at Seletar.

The cockpit of a Sunderland Mk V. Note the flare racks on right

Squadron groundcrew make their way out to an aircraft by motor launch.

Another offering from the Squadron Intelligence Officer's wall.

Report on the supply drop in the Bereo area

The text of the brief supplied by H.Q.B.M.A. (B.B.) accompanies this report, together with a copy of the consignment note, issued by the B.T.O. of the Gurkha Regiment.

0/230 was airborne soon after first light on 22nd January with 741 packages of food, weighing 7000lbs and including rice, salt, mutton, sugar, tea and milk. This was the second attempt to make this drop as the sortie on 21st January had been abandoned since the area was covered in low cloud when reached.

The position for the drop was given as 03.49N 115.01E, but this was very approximate (see brief) and in addition to this the maps of the area were decidedly inaccurate and no two were the same. It was decided to make for Marudi, a town on the river Batang Baram, which was known to be accurately mapped, and from there to set course for the position given. On E.T.A. after leaving Marudi nothing was seen; the aircraft was by this time at 9000ft and flying in broken cloud. A square search was commenced, watches being kept from all positions as with cloud conditions prevalent at the time, little if any of the ground could be seen.

The area under search bore little resemblance to the maps in use, and there were several six and seven thousand foot tops not shown at all. On the eleventh leg of the search, the Skipper sighted a white mark in the bend of a river eight miles to the north. Positions were checked and though this was twenty miles N.E. of the position given, it was decided to investigate. A long descent through broken cloud into the valley was necessary and the aircraft was finally levelled out at 1200ft just above the village. It was identified by the white square of bamboo, set inside the dropping area, the latter being approximately 100yds. square.

Upon inspection of the area, it was decided that the only way in which a drop could be made was to approach along the river valley from the south, crossing the dropping area on a northerly course and turning sharply starboard to avoid trees on a hilltop 300ft above the general level of the terrain. This meant flying up the valley with the 7798ft Mulu to port and ground on the starboard rising to the 7200ft Mt. Lengoetan. The northern end of the valley was by this time covered in cloud and the base of the cloud over the village had fallen to 500ft.

A dummy run was made over the area and it was obvious that individual dropping of supplies from all hatches was out of the question, as owing to the small area, the period of "dropping time" over the area amounted to only a few seconds. It was then decided to overcome this by piling about seventy packages at the rear door entrance on the starboard side and on the signal the whole lot would be dropped at once.

The first run was then commenced flying at 200ft on a northerly course. Nearing the target, height was lowered to 100ft after passing a tall clump of trees to the south of the village. Though a lower height than 100ft would have been desirable (since the food was only packed in double sandbags), it was impossible under the circumstances as after the drop the aircraft had to be turned sharply to starboard and climbed steeply to avoid a tree topped hill. On the first run in, 50% of the supplies undershot and some were observed to fall in the river.

The second, third, fourth and fifth drops completely obliterated the white area. In all ten runs were made, and the observer in the tall turret estimated that 85% of the supplies were retrievable.

Up to this point, no sign of life had been seen, but about five minutes after the last run, a native was seen paddling downstream in a canoe. He was seen to stop opposite the village and run around the dropping area, and then from nowhere several more natives appeared, waved to the aircraft, and commenced to retrieve the supplies from the river bed.

The aircraft was then climbed to 9000ft through thick cumulus which had been building up throughout the sortie, and course was set for Labuan; the position was checked before leaving and was verified as being 115.01E 03.57N a few miles only from the position given, but on the other side of the 7000ft range of hills.

Reports reaching Labuan a week later confirmed the success of the drop as the D.O. informed H.Q.B.M.A. (B.B.) that 98% of the supplies had been retrieved. He also stated that immediately the aircraft left the area, the cloud base lowered to the ground and the sortie was finished just in time. He further stated that the day chosen was the only one in several that it was sufficiently clear for the drop to be carried out.

0/230 sqdn. was airborne for three hours thirty five minutes.

The crew consisted of   Captain   F/Lt. W. Elliott
                                    F/Lt. K. J. Evans
                                    F/Lt. F. E. Davies
                                    F/Sgt. Tomlinson
                                    F/Sgt. Gordon
                                    F/Sgt. Clare
                                    F/Sgt. Kendrick
                                    Sgt. Vincent

Report on the supply drop requested by the Ghurka's. (W Elliott)

```
IT IS IMPOSSIBLE TO PORTER RICE TO THE AREA, IT IS SO ISOLATED
FROM OTHER CENTRES OF POPULATION BY WILD MOUNTAIN COUNTRY.
AIR DROPPING IS THE ONLY WAY TO HELP THESE SUFFERRING PEOPLE.
HQ LABUAN SIGNALLED (NOV 7 ) ITS READINESS TO HELP IN THIS WAY.
I THEREFORE INSTRUCTED THE CHIEFS TO PREPARE A DROPPING ZONE ON
THE ONLY SUITABLE LAND AT LONG SERIDAN.
MESSENGERS HAVE NOW ARRIVED TO SAY THAT THE WHOLE POPULATION SET
TO, AND in 5 DAYS CLEARED A SUITABLE AREA, AND PLACED IN THE
CENTRE A LARGE SQUARE (HOLLOW SQUARE) OF WHITE BAMBOO.
THE PROMISED DROP IS EAGERLY AWAITED.
I REPEAT POSITION:
            ONLY FLAT LAND IN DENSE MOUNTAINS AREA, MARKED AS
ABOVE, AND NEAR ONE OF ONLY TWO GILLAGES (LONG HOUSES) IN AREA.
MAPS VERY UNRELIABLE.
ON THE OFFICIAL SARAWAK 4 MILE SERIES, No 1531 SHEET 6 LONG LAMA
THE RELEVANT AREA IS NOT EVEN INDICATEDAS EXISTING.
I MAKE IT, AS NEAR AS POSSIBLE, 115.1 EAST, 3.49 NORTH
THE POINT IS AT THE JUNCTION OF THE ROCKY RAPID SERIDAN AND MAGOH
RIVERS.  APPROX 8 MILES NORTH EAST OF THE POINT WHERE THE MERGER
OF THESE TWO RIVERS JOINS THE LARGER TUTOH, ABOUT SIX MILES ABOVE
(SOUTH OF) THE LAYUN, WHICH COMES IN FROM THE OTHER BANK AND IS
SHOWN ON ALL MAPS.
TWO LANDMARKS: THE VILLAGE IS ABOUT 13 MILES SOUTH EAST OF THE
GREAT MULU MOUNTAIN MASSIF, HIGHEST IN AREA (TRIPLE PEAKS, CENTRAL
MUCH HIGHEST; GREAT LIMESTONE CLIFFS.  AND ABOUT 20 MILES SOUTH
WEST FROM THE UNMISTAKEABLE TOWERING WHITE LIMESTONE PINNACLE OF
BATU LAWI.
POPULATION 360 SOME ALREADY COMPLETELY WITHOUT FOOD, AND ALL FACE
WITH STARVATION.
REQUIRED:  FOOD FOR ABOVE FOR NEXT FOUR MONTHS, MAINLY RICE, SALT
MEAT AND VEG. IF POSSIBLE SUGAR TEA MILK.
```

The request for a supply drop received from the Ghurka Brigade. (W Elliott)

Description and No. of Conveyance	Description of Supplies or Stores, and Number of Packages, and Net and Gross Weight of Each	Details of Pack	Total Net Weight	Total Gross Weight
To be dropped by AIR	RICE U.P.	122x45	5490	lbs.
	SALT	4x56	224	"
	MUTTON PRES.	12x36	432	"
	SUGAR	10x42	420	"
	TEA	7x30	210	"
	MILK	5x42	210	"
	COMPLETE ORDER IV No. I/520		6976	

Station: LABUAN
Waybill from MAIN SUPPLY DEPOT   Date 15.1.46.
to CIVIL AFFAIRS OFFICER at BEREO

S.439

Handwritten:
Rice 549 Bags
Sugar 42 "
Salt 23 "
M.Pres 58 "
Milk 48 "
Tea 21 "

Skipper's Copy

Signature of Consigning Officer: Albar for OC
Received the above — Elliott F/Lt Carrier
230 Sqdn.

The captain's copy of the waybill listing supplies to be flown in at the request of the Ghurka Brigade. (W Elliott).

230 Flying Boat Squadron.

"Kita Chari Jauh"

January 10th 1946.

1st Squadron Reunion
on Return To Seletar.

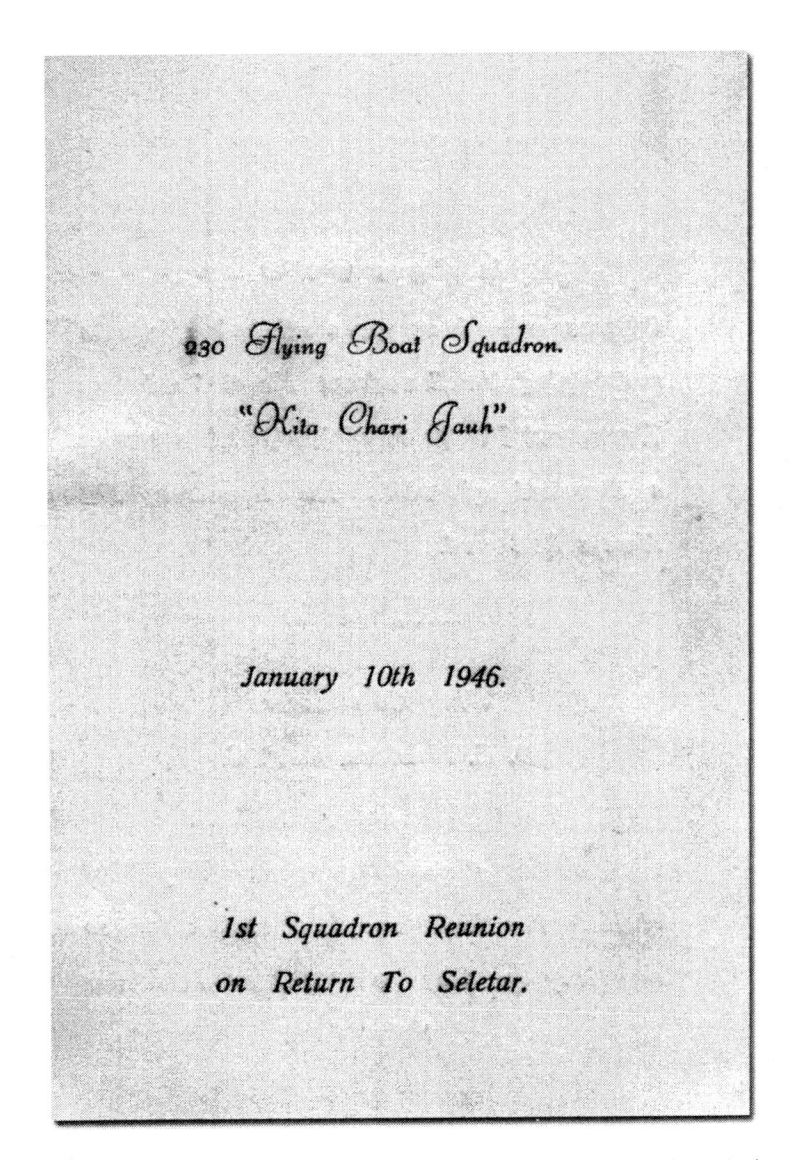

A booklet from the first Squadron reunion on returning to Seletar. (J Laydon).

It had been a long war for No 230 Squadron. The periods of action in the front line in the Mediterranean and along the Burma coast had brought much success to the squadron, interspersed with the long and tedious patrols off East Africa, which on the surface showed little in the way of successes against shipping and submarines. Those patrols though, kept the submarines submerged an out of attacking positions, thereby ensuring the safe passage of many a convoy. Several submarines had been sunk in the Mediterranean and the successes against coastal shipping off Burma had shown that No 230 squadron could truly 'hunt like a tiger'.

8. Post war postscript

The squadron remained at Seletar until April 1946, when it returned to the UK for the first time in many years. Based alongside No 210 Sqn it formed the only flying boat wing in Coastal Commands post was establishment. In July 1948 the squadron became involved in the Berlin Airlift, during which it flew 1,000 sorties without incident.

In 1952 the squadrons Sunderlands supported the British North Greenland Expedition from Young Sound and in 1953 the Sunderlands flew many mercy flights to assist the survivors of earthquakes in the Ionian Sea area, one of the squadrons old stamping grounds. The squadron was disbanded at Pembroke Dock on 28 February 1957, bringing its long association with the Sunderland to an end.

Nineteen months later the squadron reformed when No 215 Sqn at Dishforth was re-numbered on 1 September 1958. The squadron was now flying Scottish Aviation Pioneer CC.Mk.1s in the army light support role. This role took the squadron to Cyprus during the EOKA troubles and on returning to the UK the squadron re-equipped with Twin Pioneers. The squadron took its new aircraft to the Cameroon's to carry out similar work.

In August 1962 the squadron gave up its aircraft for helicopters and was re-equipped with Whirlwind HAR. Mk.10s. In January 1963 it moved to Gutersloh in Germany in support of BAOR. A detachment was maintained at Nicosia in Cyprus until 1971. In 1964 the squadron returned to the UK and was based at Odiham, Hampshire. In December 1971 the Whirlwinds were replaced and the detachment in Cyprus became part of No 84 Sqn. The squadron now had Aerospatiale Puma helicopters. The squadron moved from Odiham to Gutersloh and then in 1993 to Aldergrove, Northern Ireland where it is based today.

Appendix A: Squadron Commanders 1939-1945

Dec 1938 – May 1940	W/Cdr GM Bryer OBE AFC
Jun 1940 – Aug 1941	W/Cdr G Francis AFC
Sep 1941 – Oct 1941	W/Cdr TWG Eady
Nov 1942 – Nov 1942	W/Cdr MC Collins
Dec 1942 – Aug 1943	W/Cdr CR Taylor
Sep 1943 – Sep 1944	W/Cdr DK Bednall
Oct 1944 – Jul 1945	W/Cdr CEL Powell
Aug 1945 – Sep 1946	W/Cdr DE Hawkins DFC

Appendix B: Squadron Awards & Honours 1939–45

Date	Name	Award
Aug 1940	RS Diss	MID
14 Sep 1940	F/L WW Campbell	DFC
3 Dec 1940	W/Cdr G Francis	DFC
7 Jun 1941	F/L AMG Lywood	DFC
17 Jun 1941	Sgt GW Baxter	DFM
9 Jul 1941	S/Ldr PH Alington	DFC
19 Jul 1941	W/Cdr G Francis DFC	DSO
23 Jul 1941	S/Ldr PR Woodward	DFC
23 Jul 1941	Sgt J Smith	DFM
19 Aug 1941	Sgt V Cordery	MM
19 Aug 1941	Sgt C Starkey	MM
22 Aug 41	F/L R Martin DFC	Bar to DFC
22 Aug 41	LAC JW Waterland	DFM
Nov 1941	LAC WH Yates	DFM
3 Nov 1941	Sgt WG Scarth	DFM
3 Mar 1942	Sgt J Dupont	DFM
1 Jun 1942	W/Cdr KV Garside	DFC
1 Jun 1942	F/L DW Milligan	DFC
7 Jul 1942	F/Sgt BG Kemp	DFM
28 Jul 1942	Sgt SE Gould	DFM
18 Sep 1942	F/Sgt D Barnett	DFM
18 Sep 1942	F/Sgt E Lewis	DFM
18 Sep 1942	Sgt WG McGhee	DFM
18 Sep 1942	Sgt KJ Cole	DFM
26 Feb 1943	P/O AGG Richmond	GM
4 Aug 1943	F/O SD Plummer	DFC
1943	F/L McNichol	DFC
25 Sep 1944	S/Ldr LF Middleton	DFC
25 Sep 1944	F/L J Rand	DFC
25 Sep 1944	F/O VN Verney	DFC
25 Sep 1944	F/Sgt RF Webber	DFM
2 Jan 1945	S/Ldr KV Ingham	DFC
3 Apr 1945	F/O EA Garside	DFC
3 Apr 1945	F/L COP Watson	DFC
3 Apr 1945	F/O LEO List	DFC
Apr 1945	WO Smith	MID
1945	S/Ldr AW Deller	DFC
1945	F/L AS Pedley	DFC
1945	F/L CF Potter	DFC

Appendix C:
Aircraft Allocated to No 230 Squadron 1939–45

Serial	Code letters	Mark	Fate
Sunderland			
L2159	NM-W	I	Damaged beyond repair in Air raid, Greenock, 7.5.41.
L2160	X	I	To 4 OTU.
L2161	NM-Y	I	Sunk by air attack by Ju 87s Scaramanga, Greece, 23.4.41.
L2162	G	I	
L2164	NM-U, Z	I	Set on fire in air raid and sank, St Pauls's Bay, Malta, 10.3.41
L2166	NM-U	I	Shot down by U-boat in Mediterranean, 1.8.41.
L5803	NM-T	I	To 228 Sqn.
L5804	NM-S	I	Sank in gale, Scaramanga, Greece, 25.2.41.
L5806	NM-Q, DX-?	I	Missing 25.7.42.
N9029	NM-V	I	Crashed in Mediterranean, 1.1.43
T9050	NM-P, Y	I	Crashed on landing, Aboukir, 30.9.41
T9071	NM-N, M	I	Crash landed at Ras Amr, Egypt after being attacked by enemy aircraft, 22.12.41. Damaged beyond repair.
W 3987	W, NM-X, DX-?	II	Crashed on take off, Aboukir, 7.9.42.
W4021	NM-W	III	Hit reef on take off at Castellorosso and sank, 7.11.43.
W4022	NM-Z	III	Struck off charge, 3.1.45.
W4023	NM-U	III	Struck off charge, 29.8.46.
W6078	N	III	Struck off charge, 16.8.45.
DD866	T	III	
DP180	O	III	Struck off charge, 31.1.46.
DP189	L	III	Struck off charge, 16.8.45.
DP200	B, Z	V	Scrapped and sunk 10.57.
DW112		III	To Iraq Comm Flt.
DW131		III	Missing from patrol, 27.3.43. Later found crashed in Mozambique.
EJ131	T	III	Missing after forced landing.
EJ132	X	III	Struck off charge, 29.5.45.
EJ135		III	To 302 FTU.
EJ136	Y	III	Struck off charge, 15.4.45.
EJ140	V	III	Flew into Sangalla Hill, near Voi, Kenya, 29.12.43. All crew killed.
EJ141	R	III	To 205 Sqn.
EJ143	S	III	Struck off charge, 12.3.45.
EJ145	Y	III	
EJ152		III	
EK595	O, Q	III	
JM659	Q	III	Sank in hurricane, Dibrugarh, India, 4.7.44.
JM673	P, J, H	III	Missing in bad weather on Patrol, 28.11.44

JM711	M	III	
ML797	Q	III	*To 205 Sqn.*
ML799	W	III	
ML800	X	III	*To Aeronavale, 28.7.57.*
ML846	W	III	*Struck off charge, 18.9.45.*
ML861		III	*Struck off charge 28.6.45.*
ML865	J	III	*To Station Flt, Koggala.*
ML868	H	III	*Struck off charge, 31.1.46.*
PP145	O	V	*Hit by PP117 at Pembroke Dock, 29.4.46. To 6103M.*
PP146	V	V	*Struck off charge, 6.11.47.*
PP147	U,V	V	*Struck off charge, 16.10.57.*
PP148	P	V	
PP149	R	V	*Struck off charge, 21.5.54.*
PP152		V	*Struck off charge, 26.9.46*
PP154	Y	V	
PP155	X	V	*To 88 Sqn.*
PP157	R, S	V	
PP158	T	V	*Hit underwater obstruction and beached, Kuantan, 3.10.45.*

<u>Dornier Do 22</u>
307
308
309
311
312
313

<u>Latecoere 298B</u>
HB2-5

<u>Rogozarski Sim XIV</u>
157   *RAF Serials allocated to Yugoslav aircraft were AX708 – AX715.*

Appendix D: The Short Sunderland

	Mk I	**MkII**	**MkIII**	**Mk V**
CREW	10	10	10	13
ENGINES	Pegasus Mk XXII	Pegasus Mk XVIII	Pegasus Mk XVIII	Pratt & Whitney R-1830
ARMAMENT				
Guns	6 x Browning 0.303 in MGs, 2 x Vickers K 0.303 in MGs	As Mk I (Mk II/III had power operated turret in place of beam mounted Vickers Ks)	As Mk II	2 x 0.50 Browning MGs, 12 x 0.303 MGs
Bombload	2,000lb			
RADAR	Nil	ASV Mk II	ASV Mk II/ Mk VIC	ASV Mk VIC
MAX SPEED	210 mph	210 mph	205 mph	213 mph
RANGE	2,880 miles	2,880 miles	2,880 miles	2,980
WING SPAN	112' 9"	112' 9"	112' 9"	112' 4"
LENGTH	85'4"	85' 4"	85' 4"	85' 4"
ALL UP WEIGHT	50,100 lb	50,100 lb	58,000 lb	65,000 lb
WING AREA	1487 sq ft	1487 sq ft	1487 sq ft	1487 sq ft
FIRST FLOWN	16.10.37	11.41	28.6.41	3.44

REFERENCES

No 230 Sqn Operational Record Book Form 540. (PRO).

Going to War with a Sunderland – L5804 NM-S. With 230 Squadron RAF: unpublished account by Roy S Diss. (via 230 Sqn).

A short history of 230 Squadron: Squadron history leaflet. (230 Sqn).

230 Squadron Royal Air Force 1940-41 and 1943-44. Personal reminiscences of DK Bednall: unpublished account. (via 230 Sqn).

"Operation River" Intelligence Report – June/July 1944.

"Operation River" newspaper article – source unknown. (via 230 Sqn).

Chindwin Operation report. (230 Sqn).

'Flying boats took wounded from jungle'. – newspaper article – source unknown. (via 230 Sqn).

Sinking of MV Fort McLeod – Shipping Casualties Section – Trade Division report, 3 May 1944. TD/139/2046.

Sinking of MV Fort McLeod – Letter from Glen Line Ltd 9 March 1944.

Sun On My Wings by Dundas Bednall. Paterchurch Publications 1989.

A War In Four Movements by AW Deller. Unpublished manuscript.